MODERN MOTHERHOOD

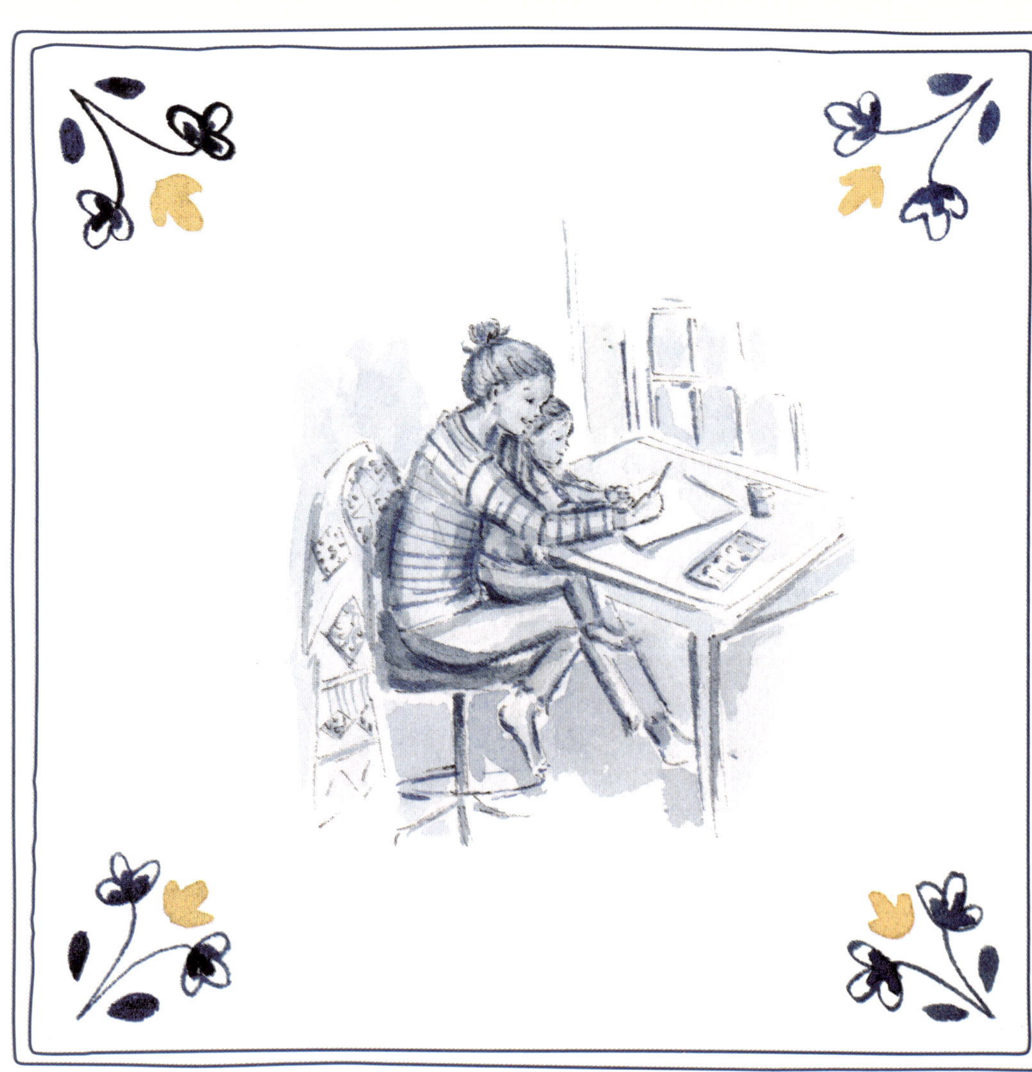

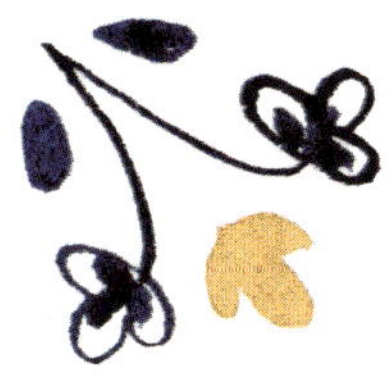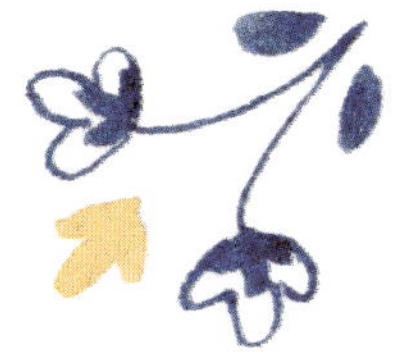

MODERN MOTHERHOOD

Celebrating Quiet Moments of Love and Care

Riley Sheehey

Abrams Image, New York

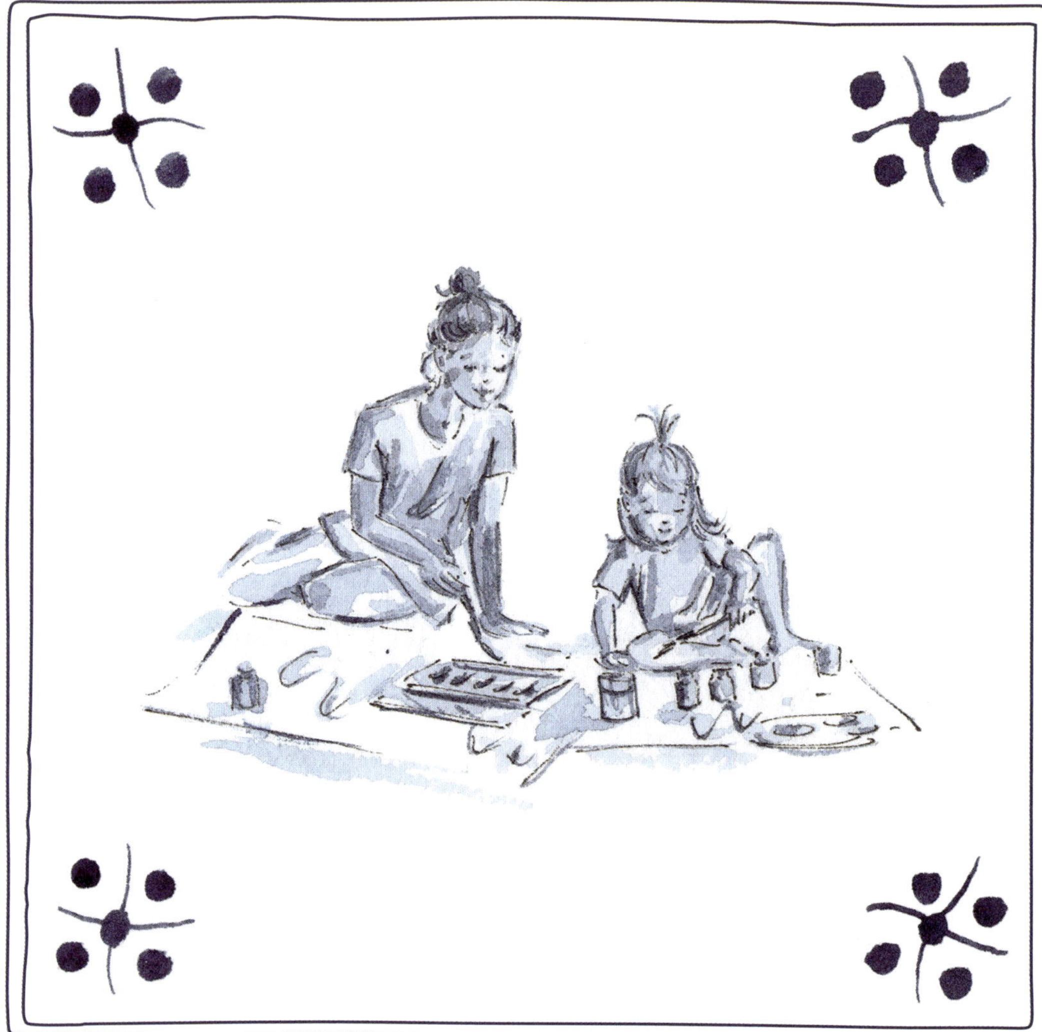

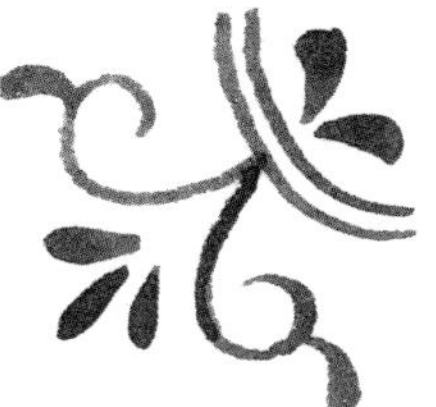

For Bryn

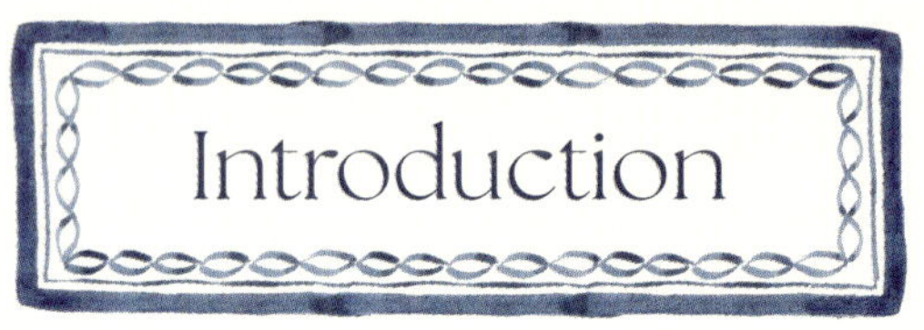

Introduction

Like many good ideas, the idea for my Modern Motherhood painting series first came to me in the shower. I was at home with my then one-year-old daughter, Bryn, and in an effort to keep her entertained while washing my hair, I was playing peekaboo with her using the shower curtain. She giggled hysterically as I tried to keep shampoo out of my eyes, and I thought to myself, This is the sort of thing I want to remember years from now, the little moments of pure joy within the multitasking and juggling of everyday life caring for my daughter.

If I had to choose one word to describe my now three-year-old daughter, Bryn, it would be joyful. "Bryn," her preschool teacher told me at a recent pickup, "is a very happy girl." And it's true; as a former teacher, I know that it's impossible to predict a child's disposition from their parents, and as an anxious worrier myself, I feel incredibly lucky. Bryn is always smiling and giggling and is excited by small things that I would have missed if not for her. When I'm making dinner (almost exclusively mac and cheese when I am cooking; my husband is the cook in our family), she requests that I play music—usually something from a Disney movie, so that we can take a break to dance. When I'm doing the laundry, I'll turn my head away for a moment, only to look back around and find her hiding in the laundry basket. She insists on dressing herself, wearing tutus and patent leather Mary Janes to the grocery store, a baby doll always in tow.

When I started the series, I wanted to create something tangible to memorialize the things I was experiencing every day as a new mother. Sure, there are monthly milestone cards and birthday crowns and baby books with blank spaces for entering heights and weights and dates, but I felt the need to make something to capture the day-to-day experiences—the singing and dancing in the kitchen, the stroller jogs with snack cups strewing Goldfish in our wake, or even playing peekaboo with the shower curtain—the, as the subtitle of this book says, "quiet moments of love and care."

I jotted ideas down in my sketchbook over the course of almost a year and tried to sketch and paint them in a few different mediums, but nothing seemed quite right until I read an article about four-hundred-year-old delft tiles, and something clicked. I loved learning about the tiny functional pieces of artwork that told stories and thought that the format and color scheme might work well for what I was hoping to portray. I started by painting four 4-by-4-inch blue-and-white watercolor scenes, including the game of shower peekaboo that had initially inspired me.

As I work, I will often share "behind-the-scenes" process photos on my Instagram Stories—little glimpses of different projects mixed in with everyday life. I shared a photo of the painting process for the first four illustrations and realized pretty quickly that I had struck a nerve, as messages started coming in right away. As it turns out, I wasn't the only caretaker who was playing shower peekaboo with their energetic toddler, giving a baby a "sink bath," or playfully placing a pair of pants on their child's head while folding laundry.

I have always felt the most drawn to artwork that tells a story and will often use my artwork as a means to tell my own story. So when I hear that something I've made has resonated with someone else, not only do I feel an instant connection to that person, but I also feel like I'm weaving our collective experiences into the world. As I continued to hear from other women who saw themselves and their children and grandchildren in these little paintings, I felt so connected with them and inspired to keep going with the series.

As I've further developed the series into the book you hold in your hands, I have continued to hear from these women—women who are reminded of the pillow forts they built with their now grown children, women who got back from their first beach vacations with their babies, women who have shared the names of their children's favorite bedtime stories with me. The stories are mainly happy ones (one woman told me that her mother used to sing to her and her sisters using a spatula as a microphone, like the mother in one of my paintings), but some are very bittersweet as well. I have heard from women who have experienced unimaginable losses who were reminded of their babies and from women who are yearning to be mothers but told me that they look forward to the day they will experience these moments for the first time with their children.

I have also heard from caretakers of other kinds—teachers, nannies, aunts, grandparents—who have seen themselves and the children they care for in the little paintings. I know that the first times I experienced a lot of the moments from this series were actually as a former camp counselor and teacher, and I see my daughter's teachers in so many of them as well.

Motherhood, I have found, can mean many different things to many different people, but at the heart of it, it's taking care of small humans, and it takes more than one person to do that essential work.

These little paintings act as snapshots of the moments that feel so unique to each of us in our own caretaking journeys but are universal too, in the sense that we're all experiencing them—together but also on our own. Working on this book has made me pause and notice these moments, and I hope that looking through these illustrations allows you to do the same.

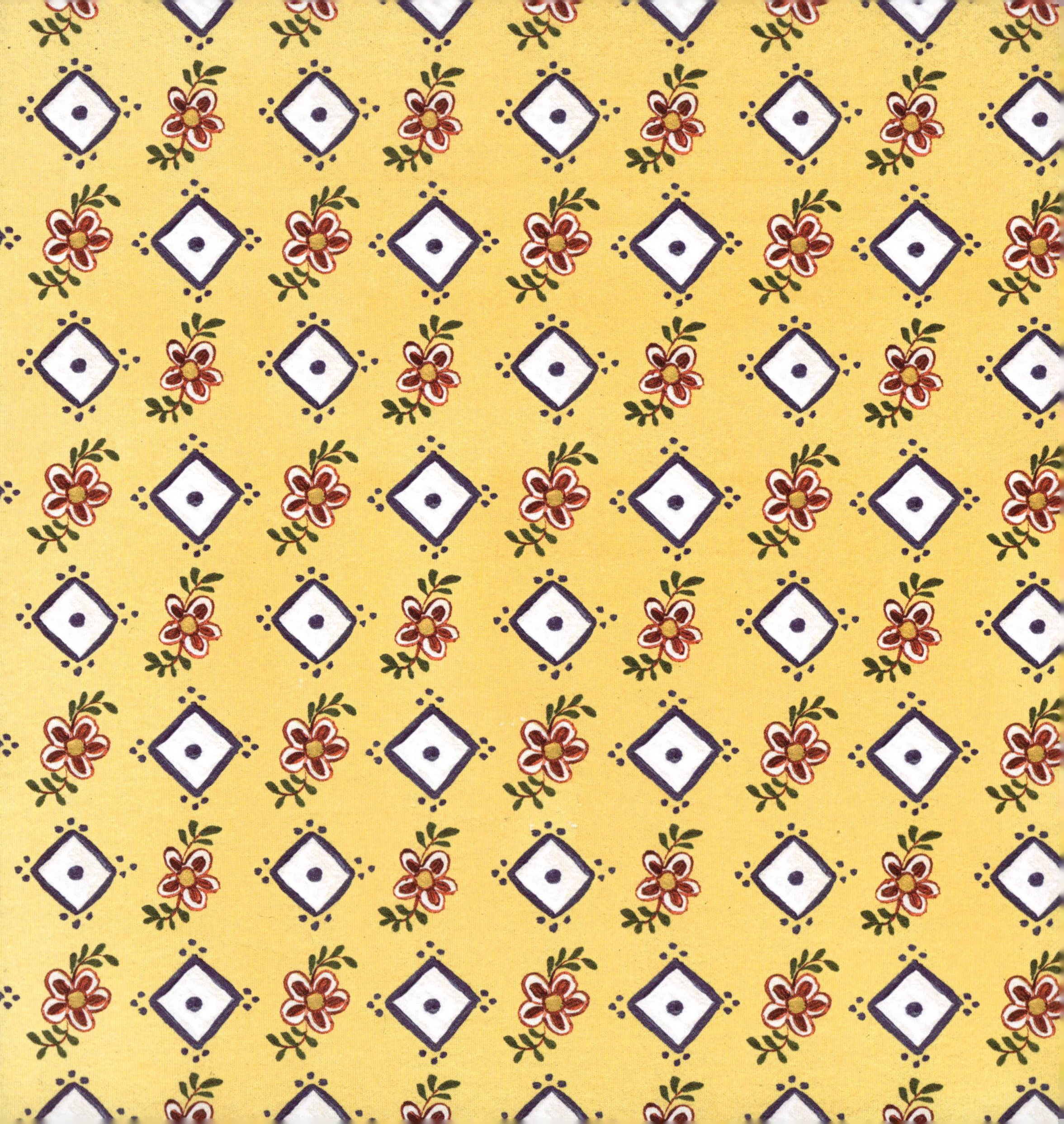

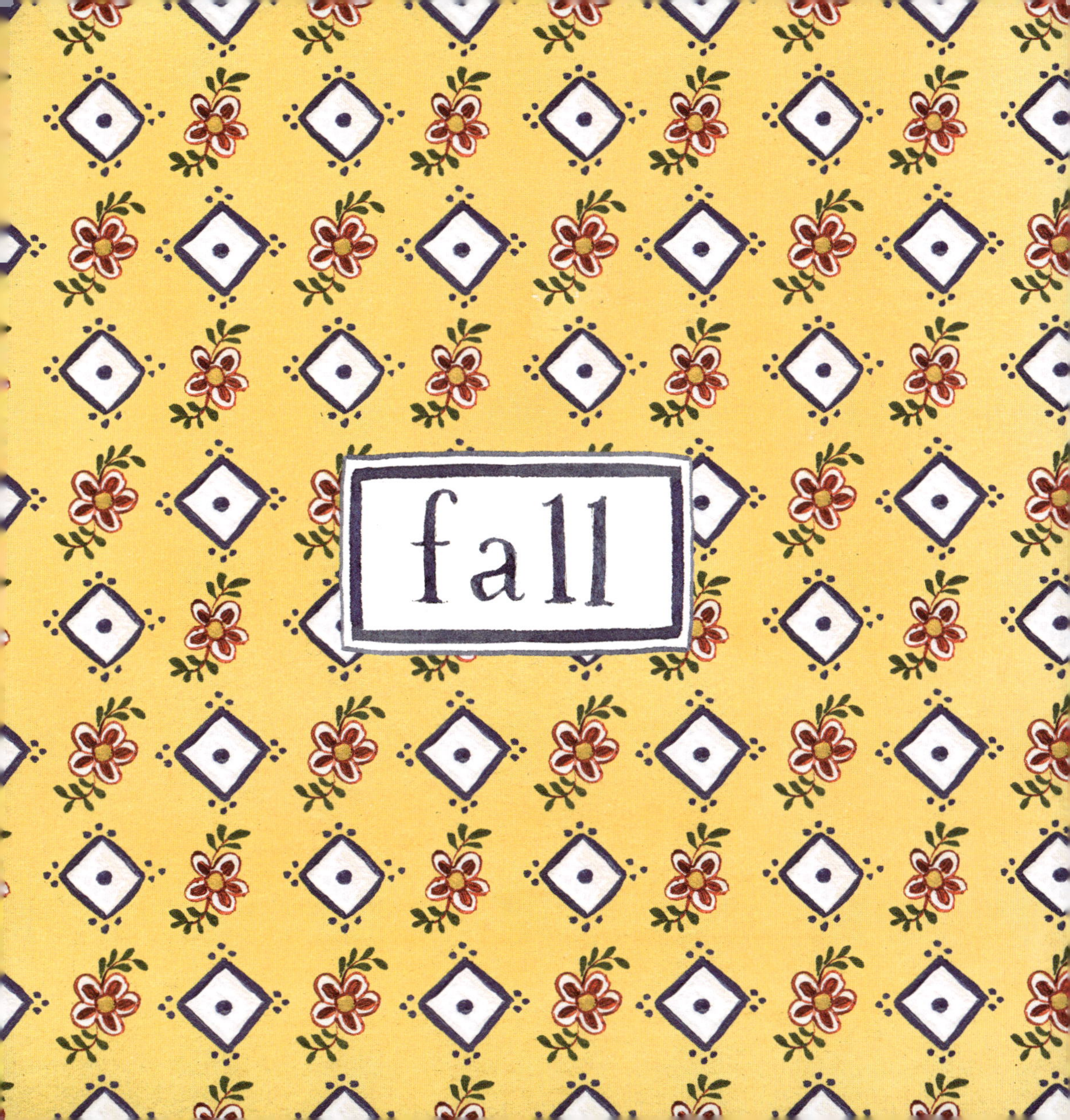
fall

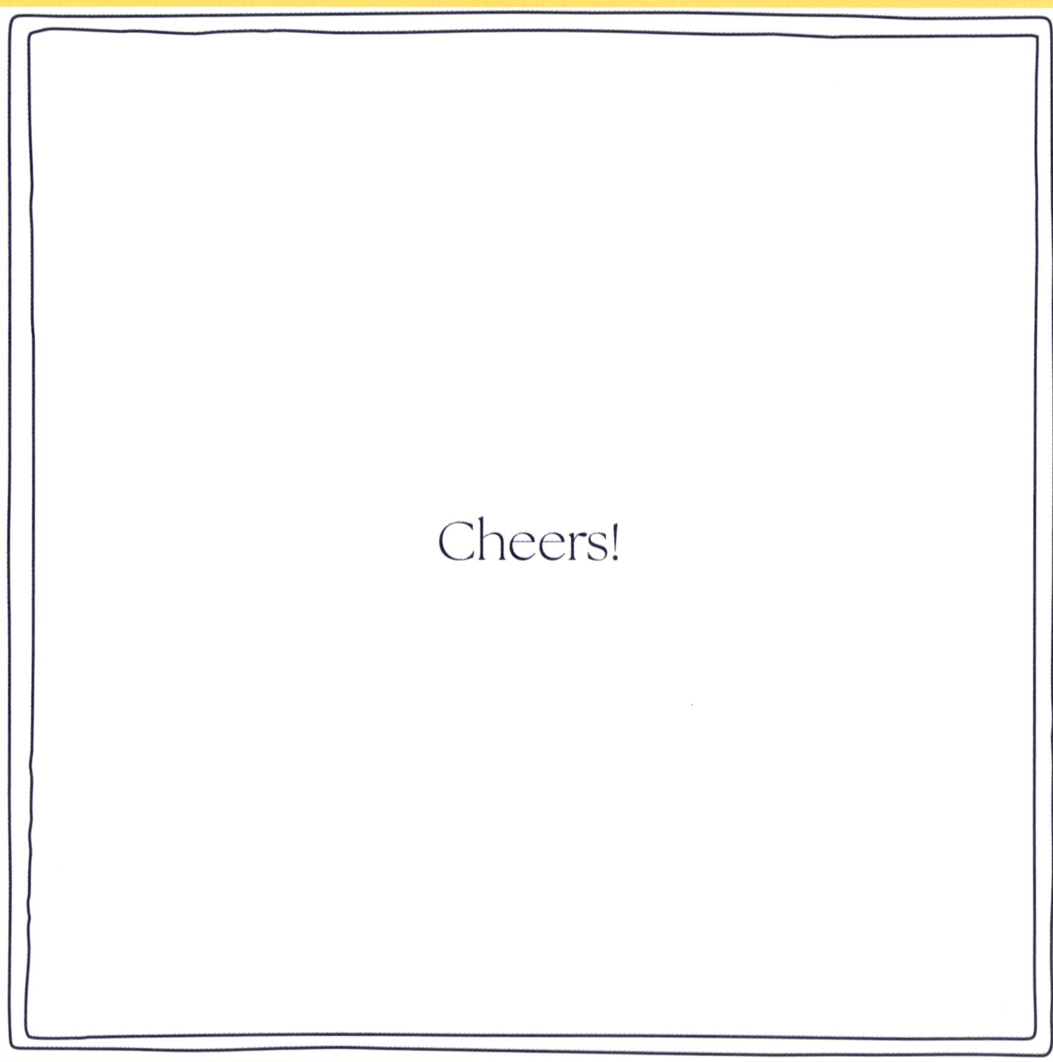

Cheers!

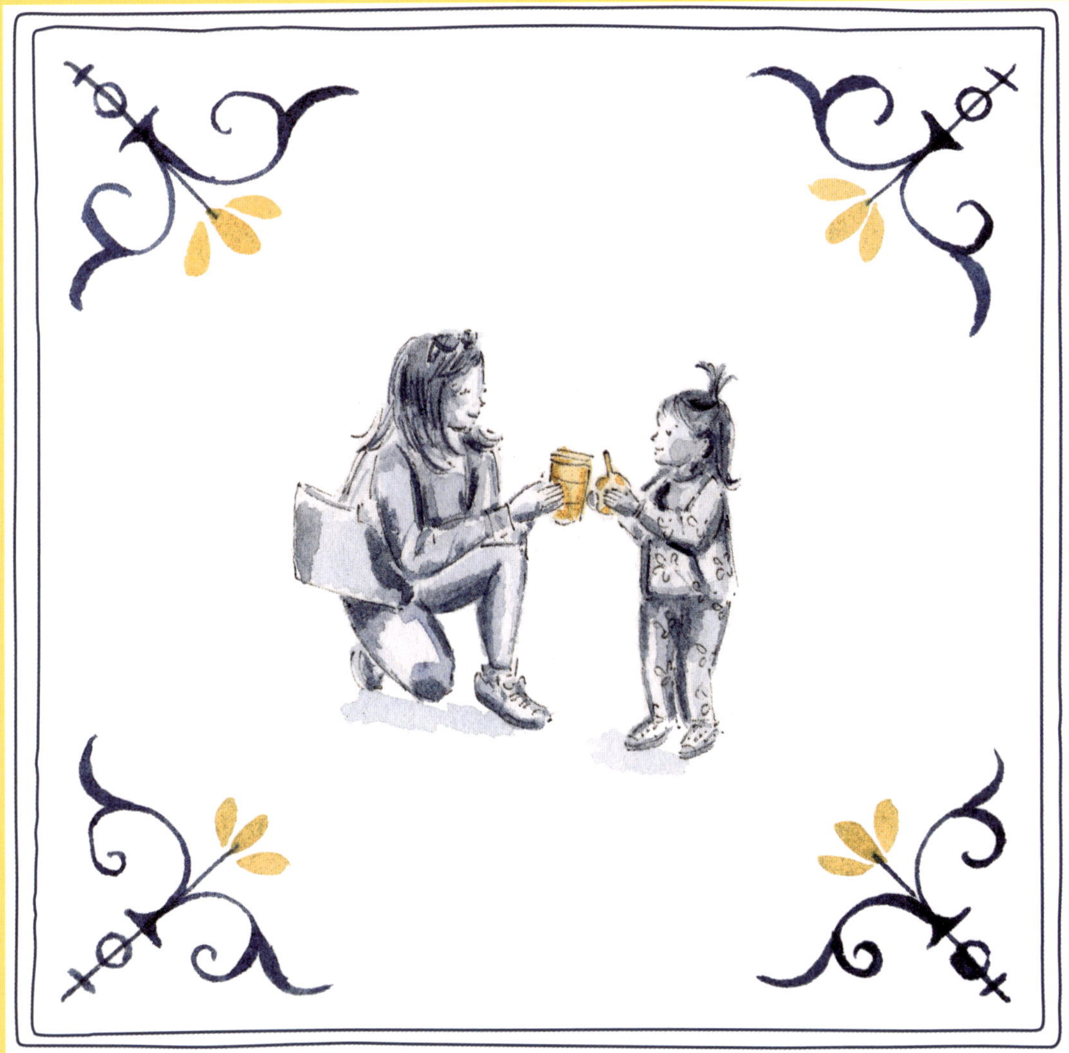

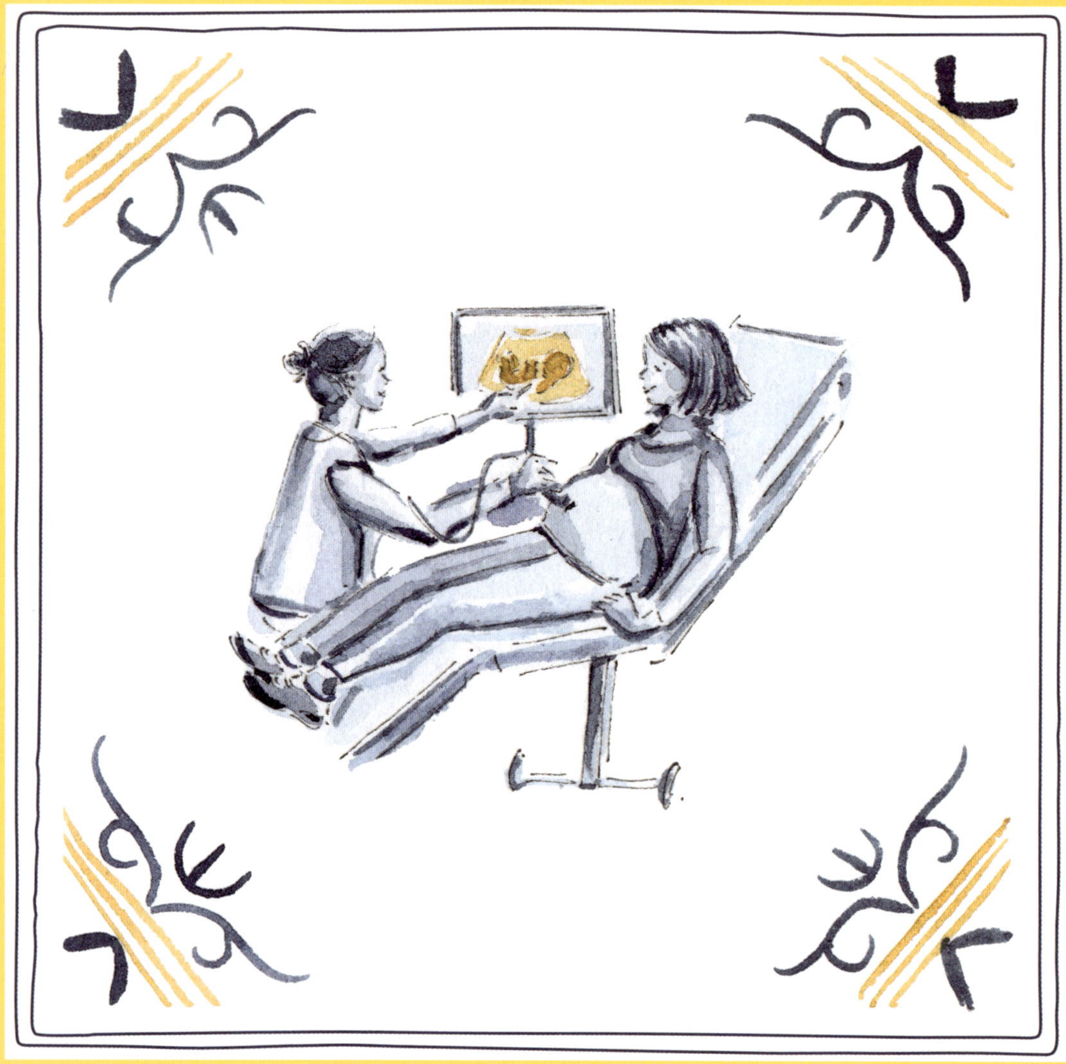

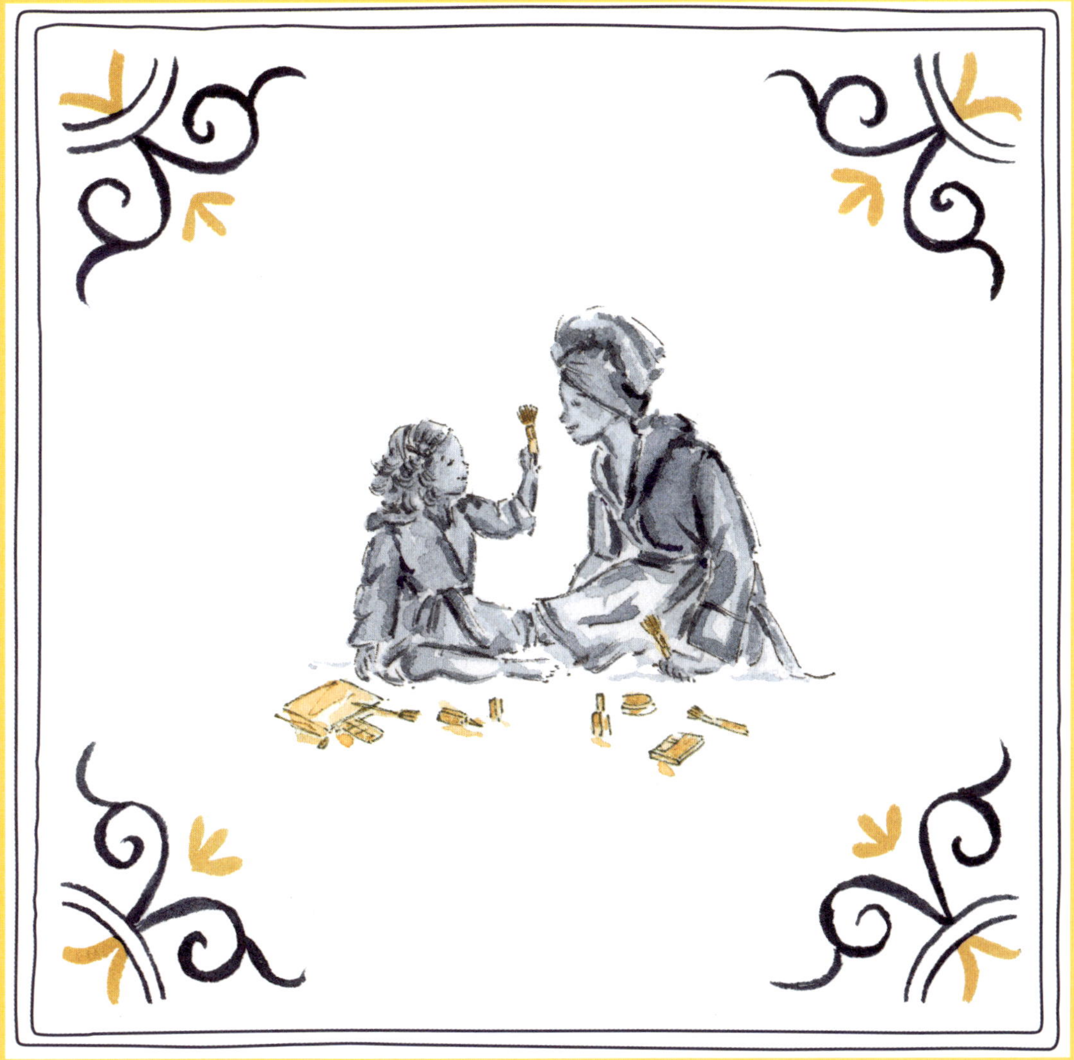

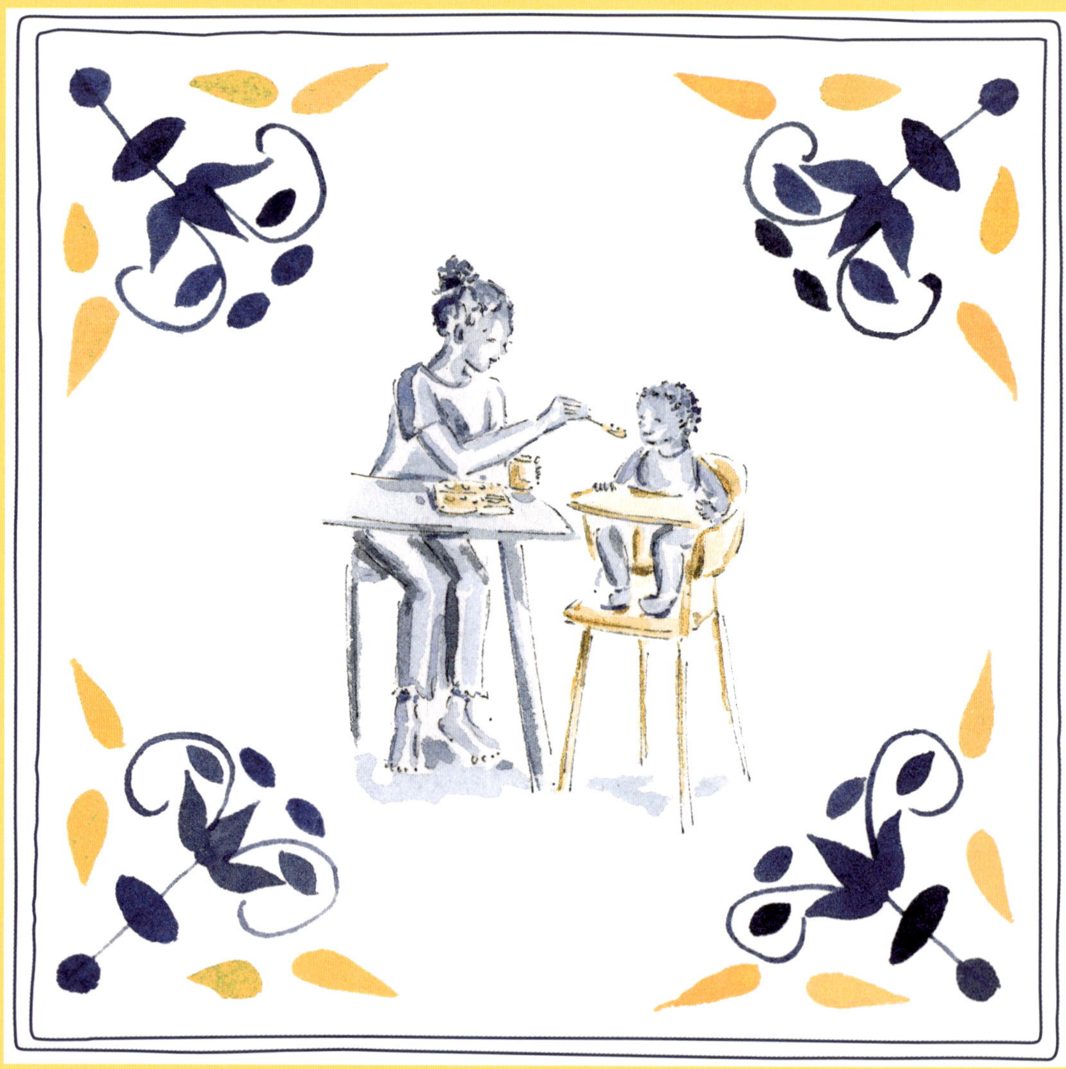

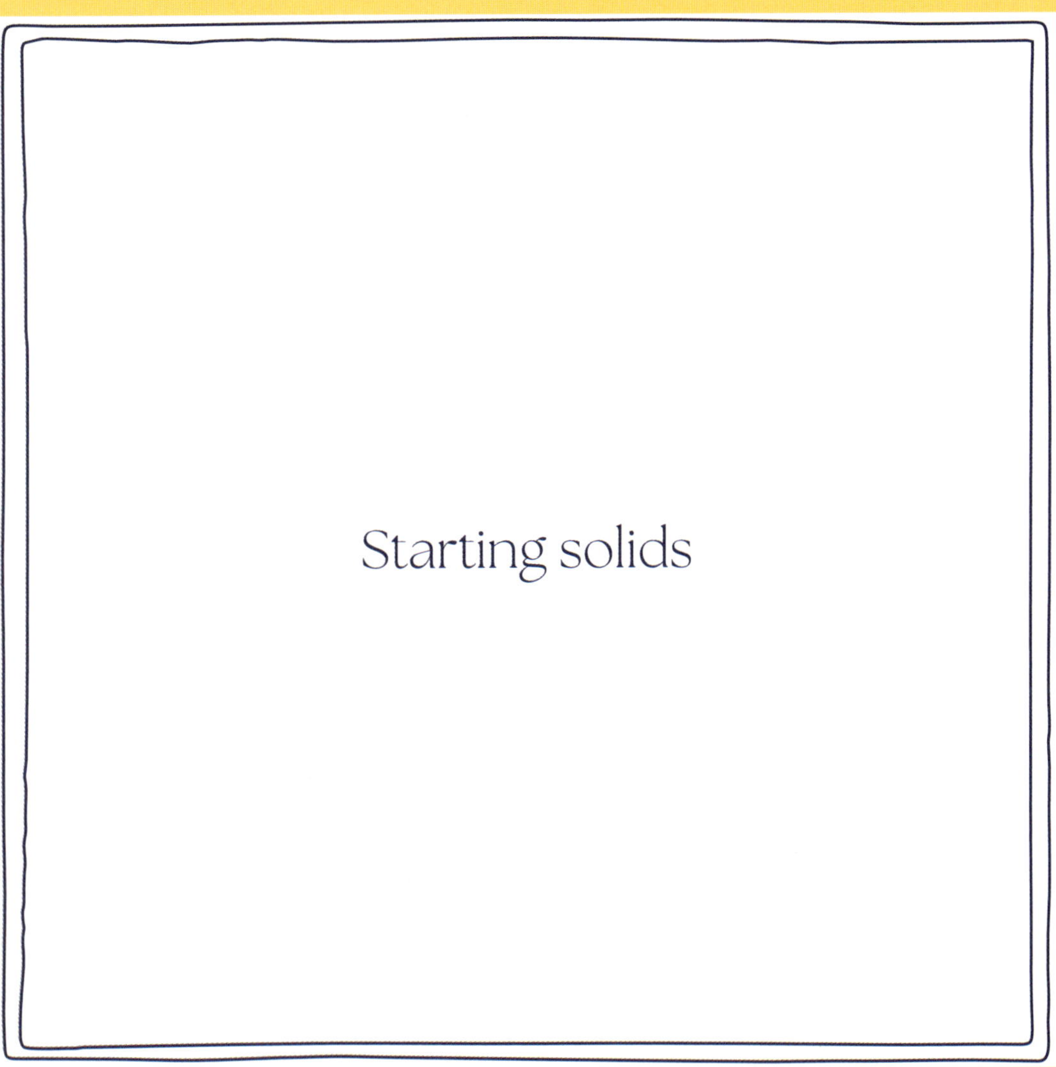

Starting solids

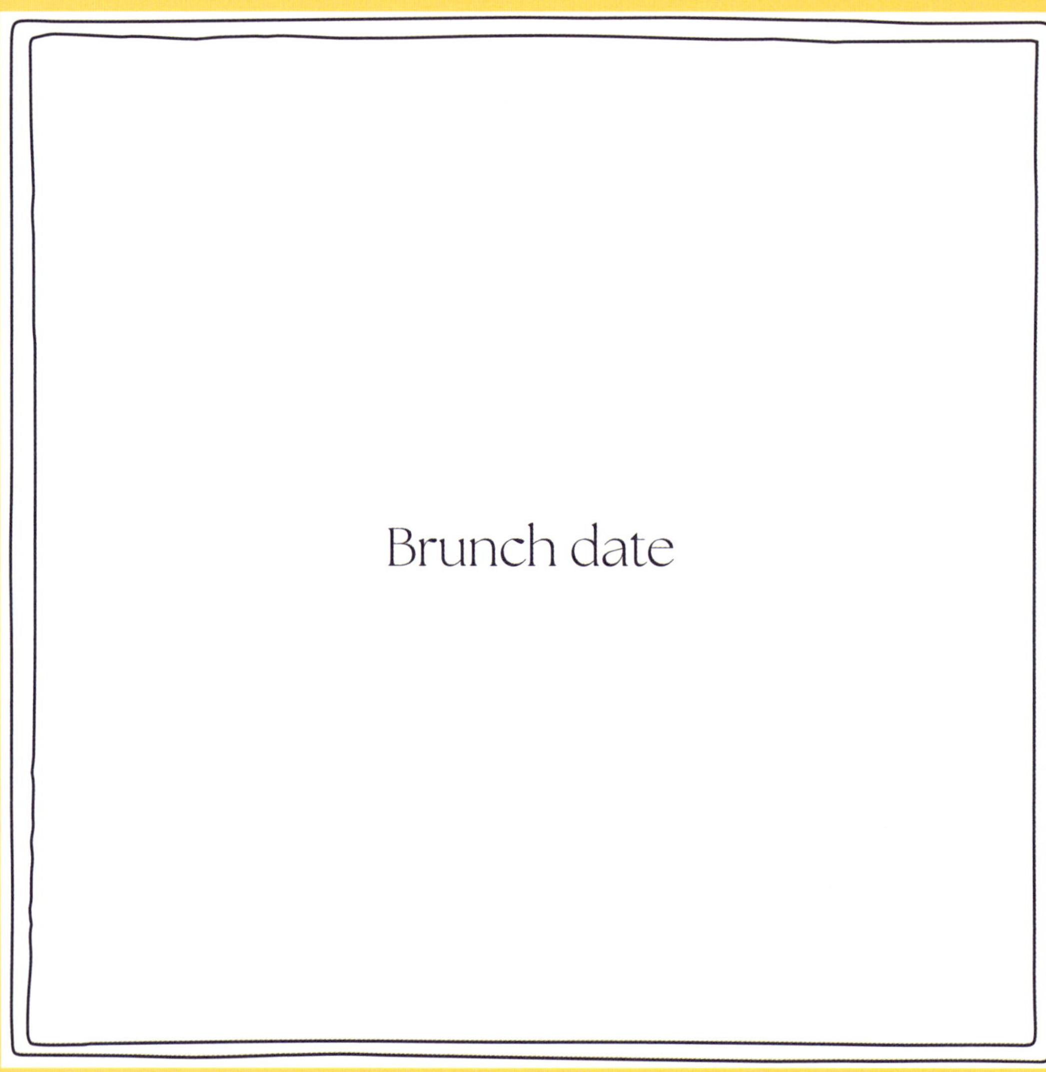
Brunch date

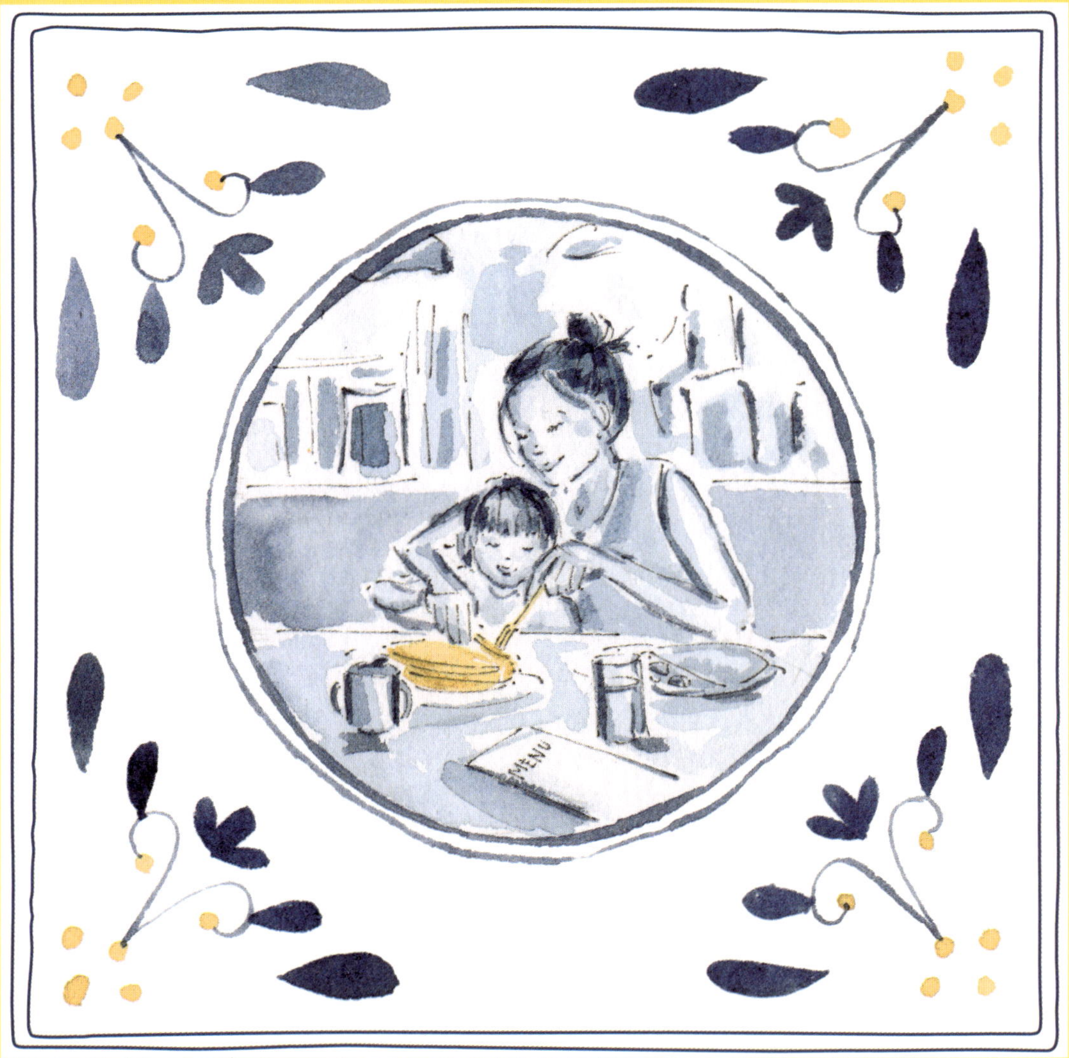

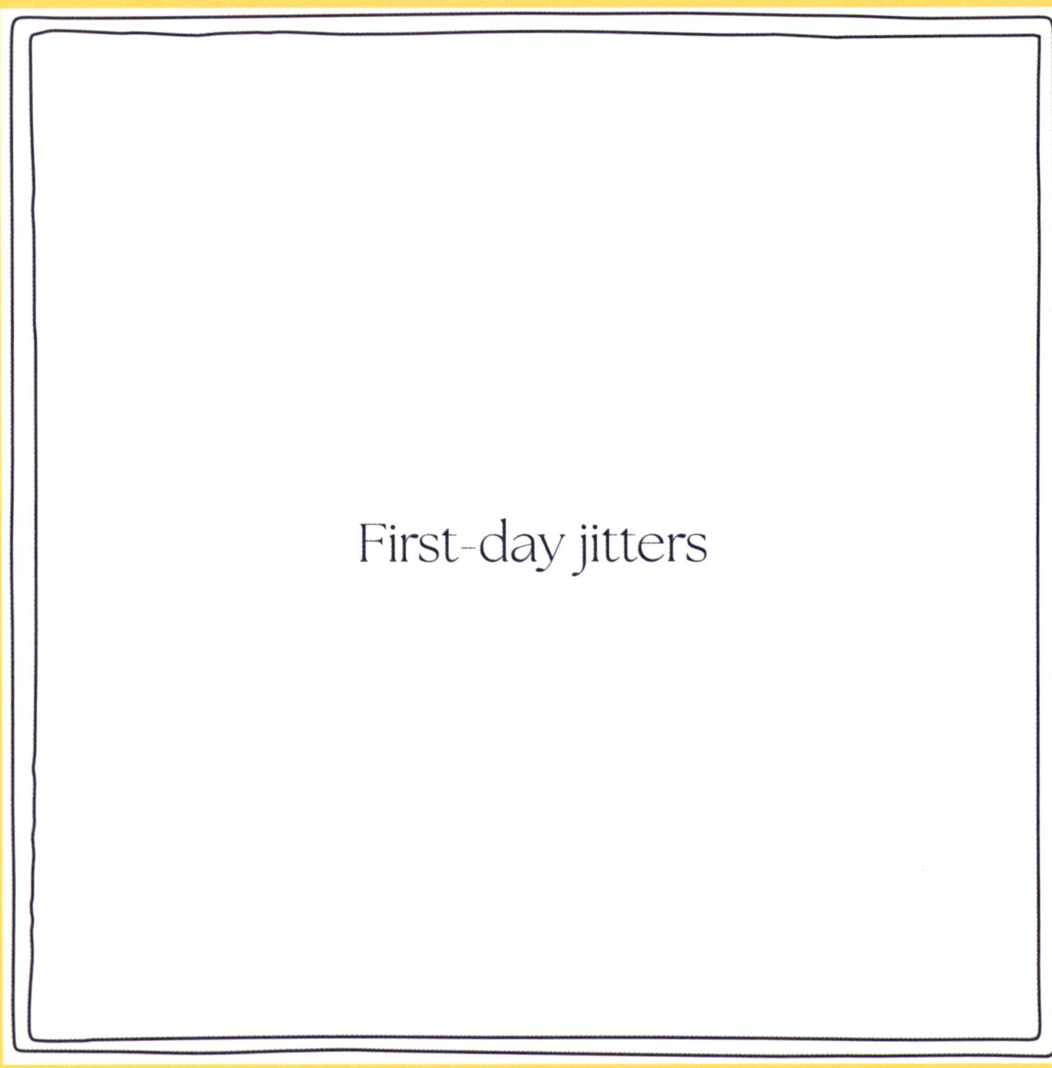

First-day jitters

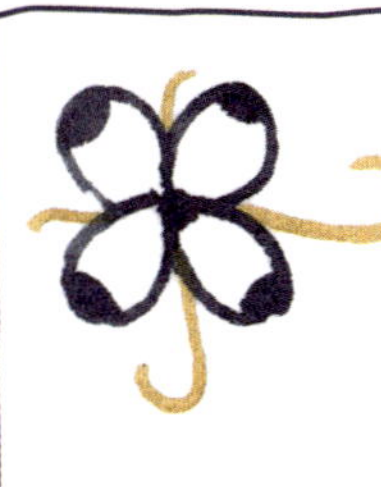

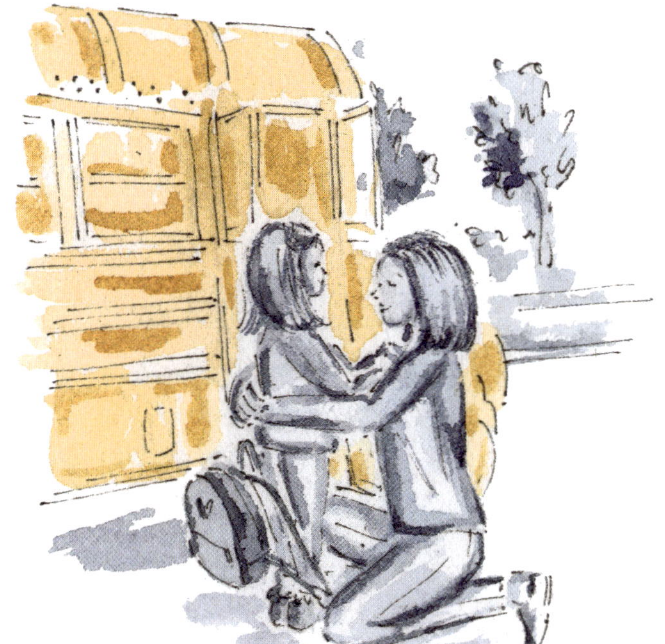

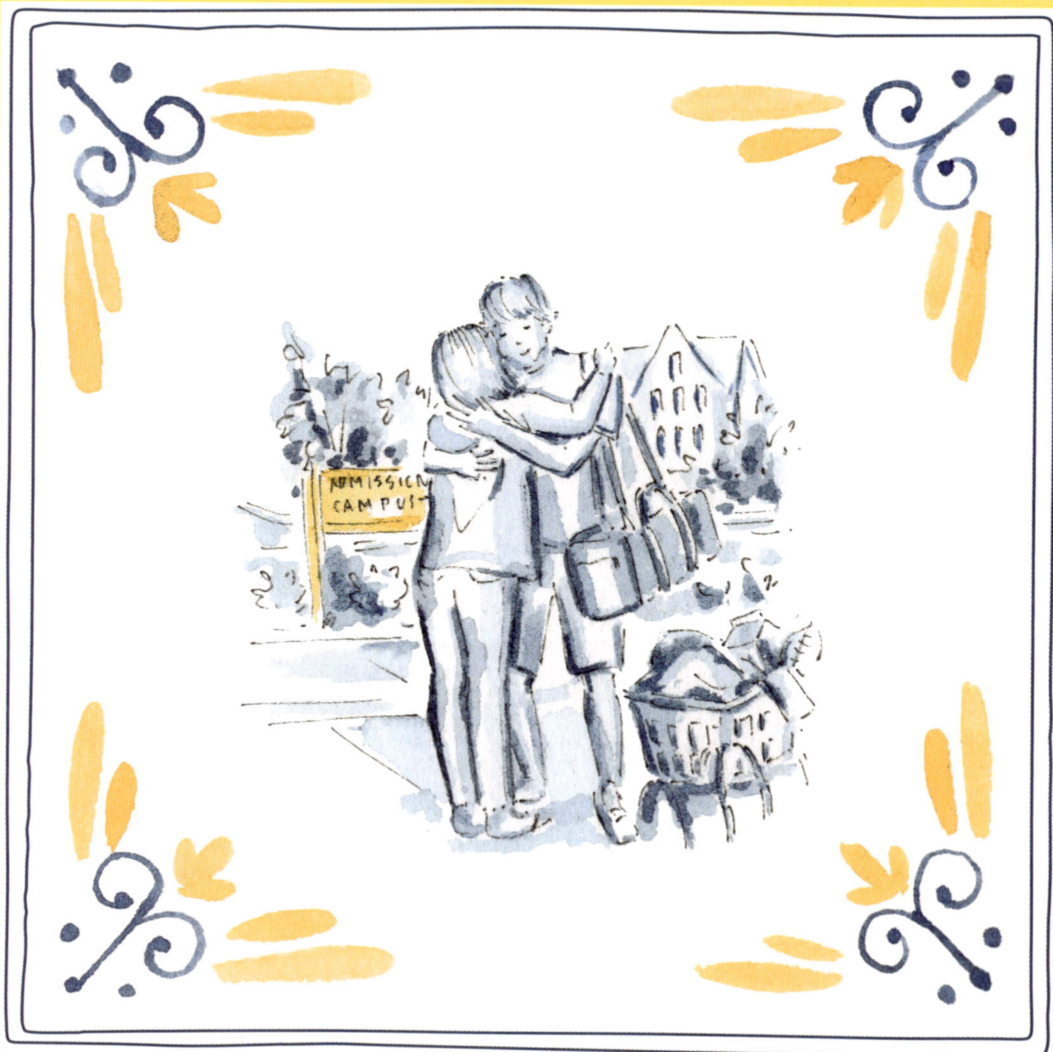
ADMISSION
CAMPUS→

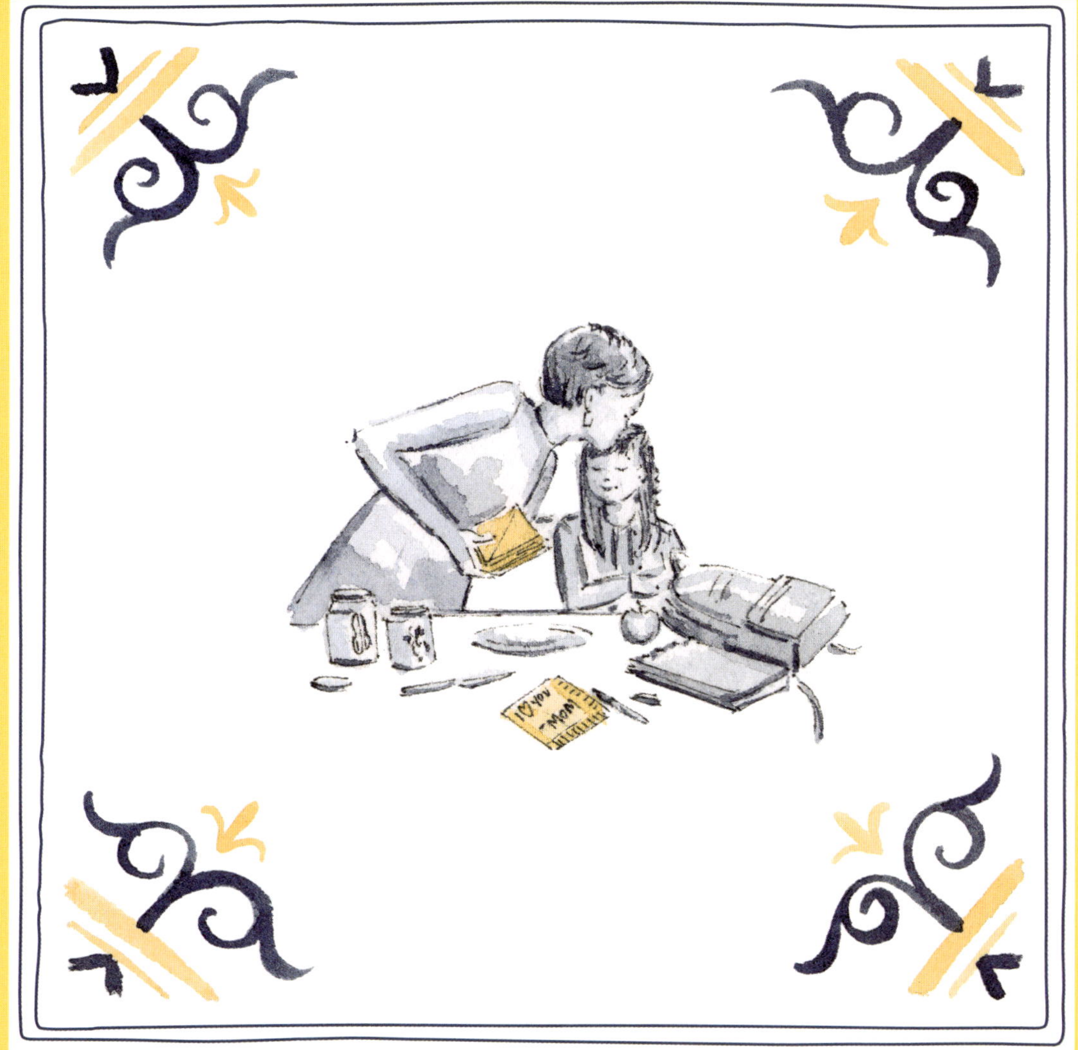

I ♥ you
Mom

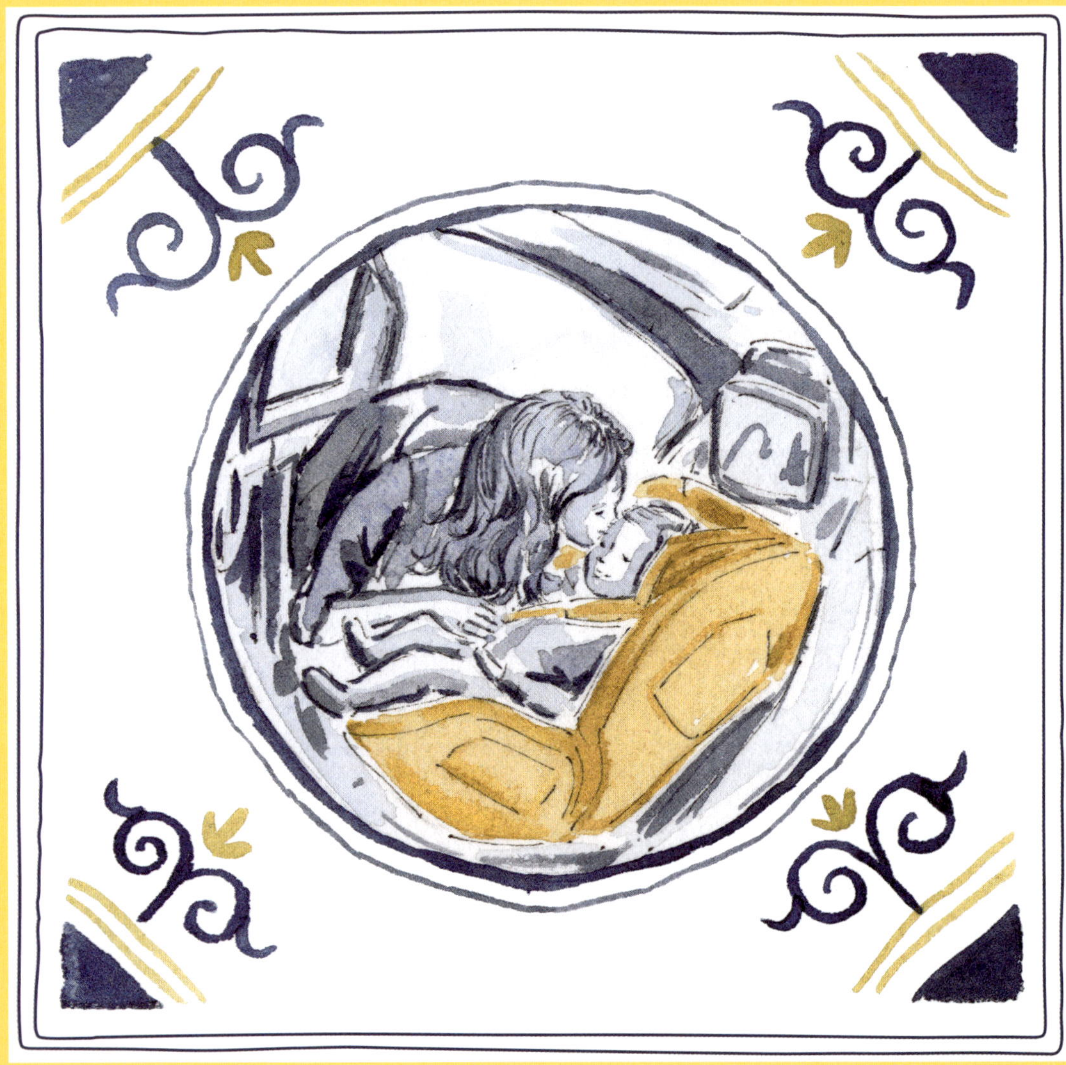

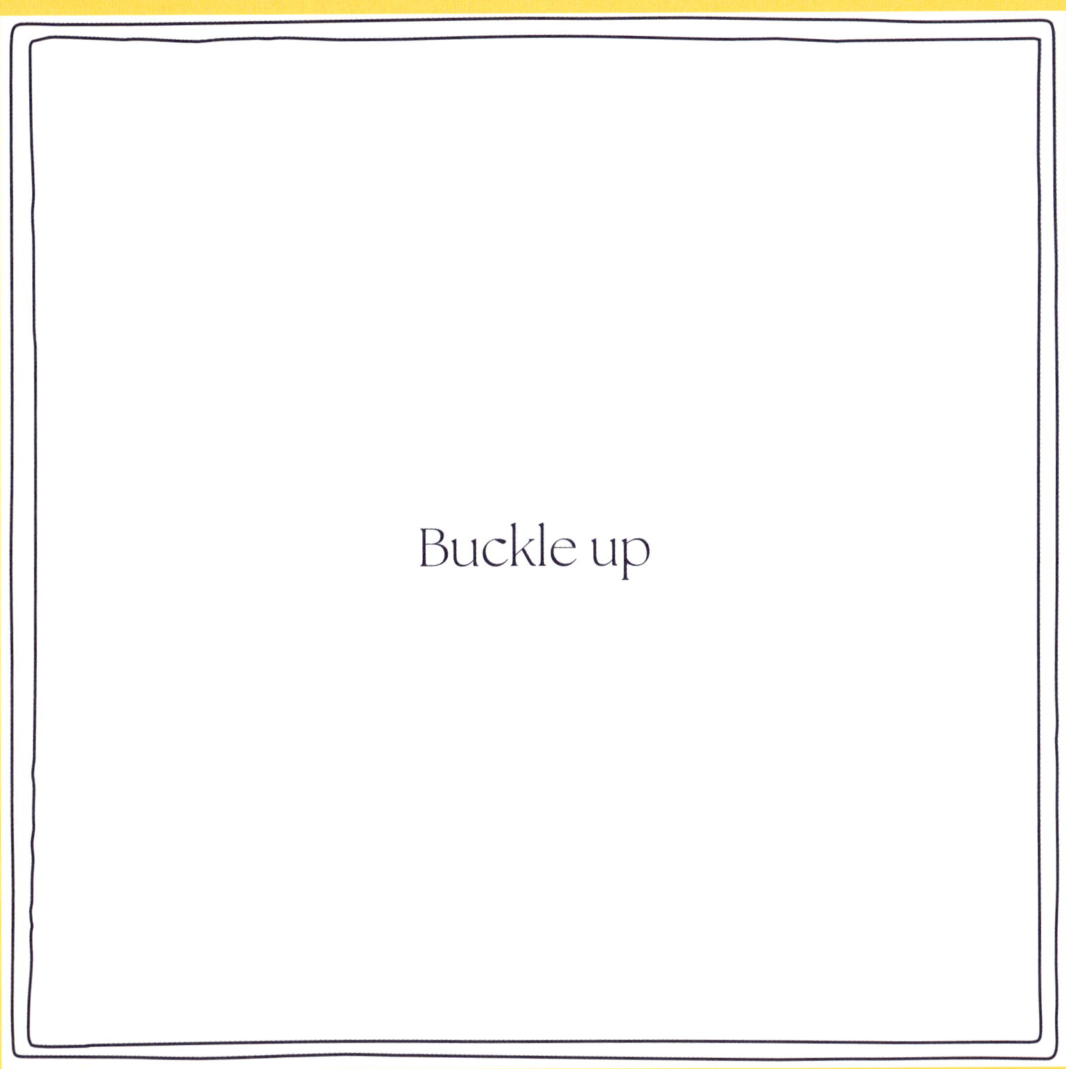Buckle up

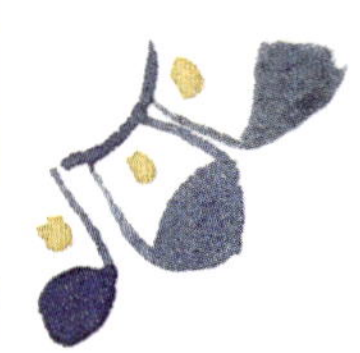
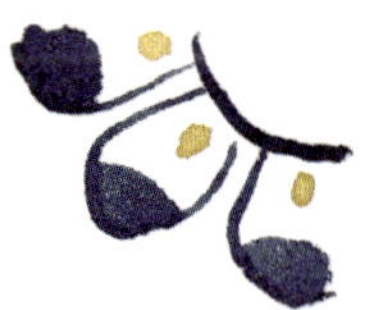
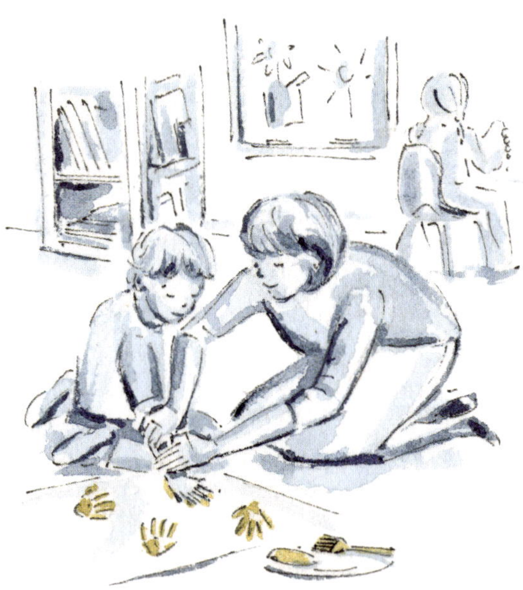
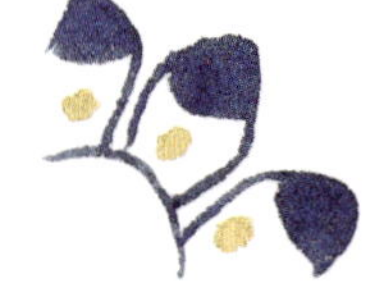
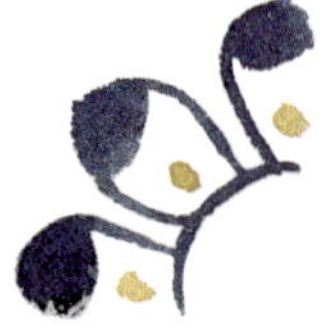

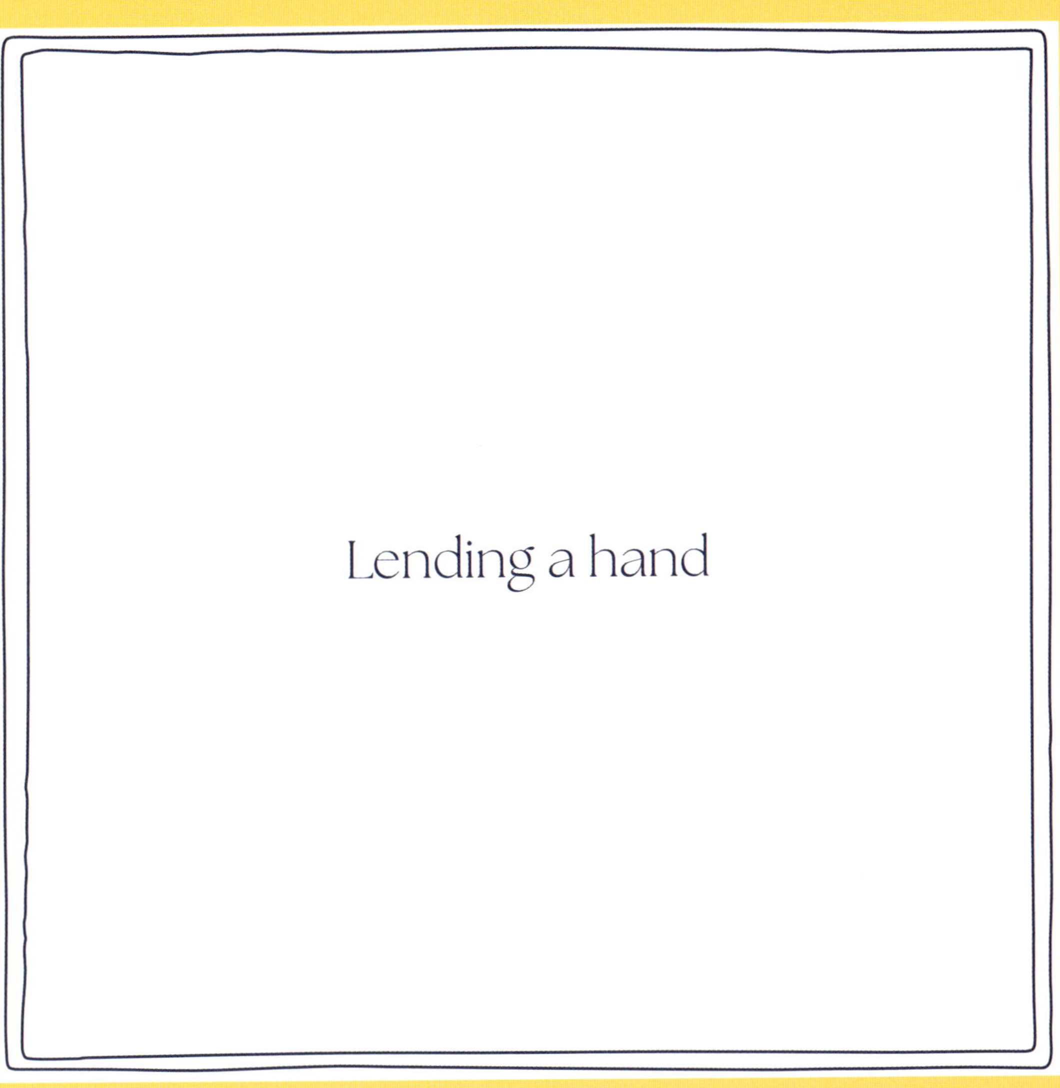

Lending a hand

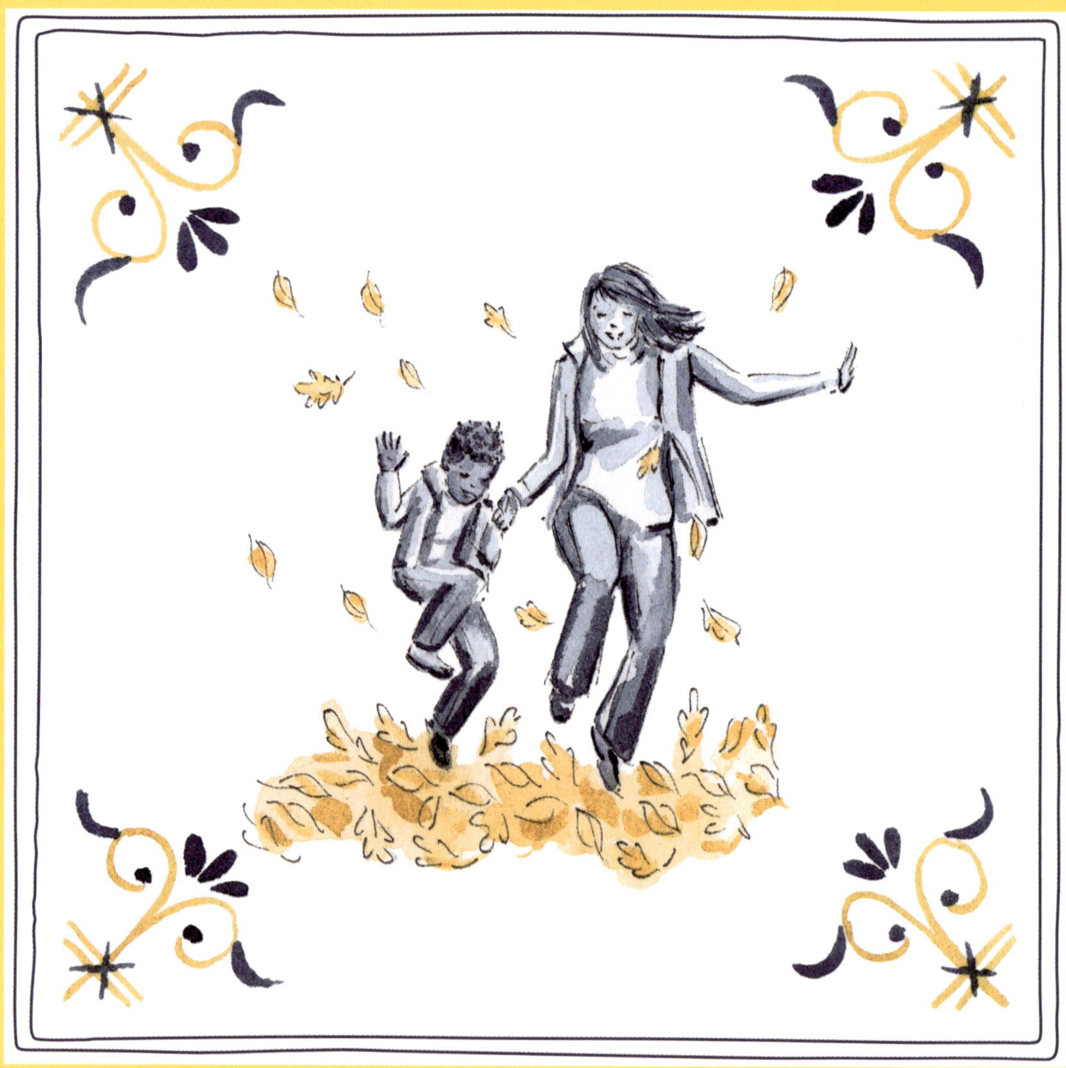

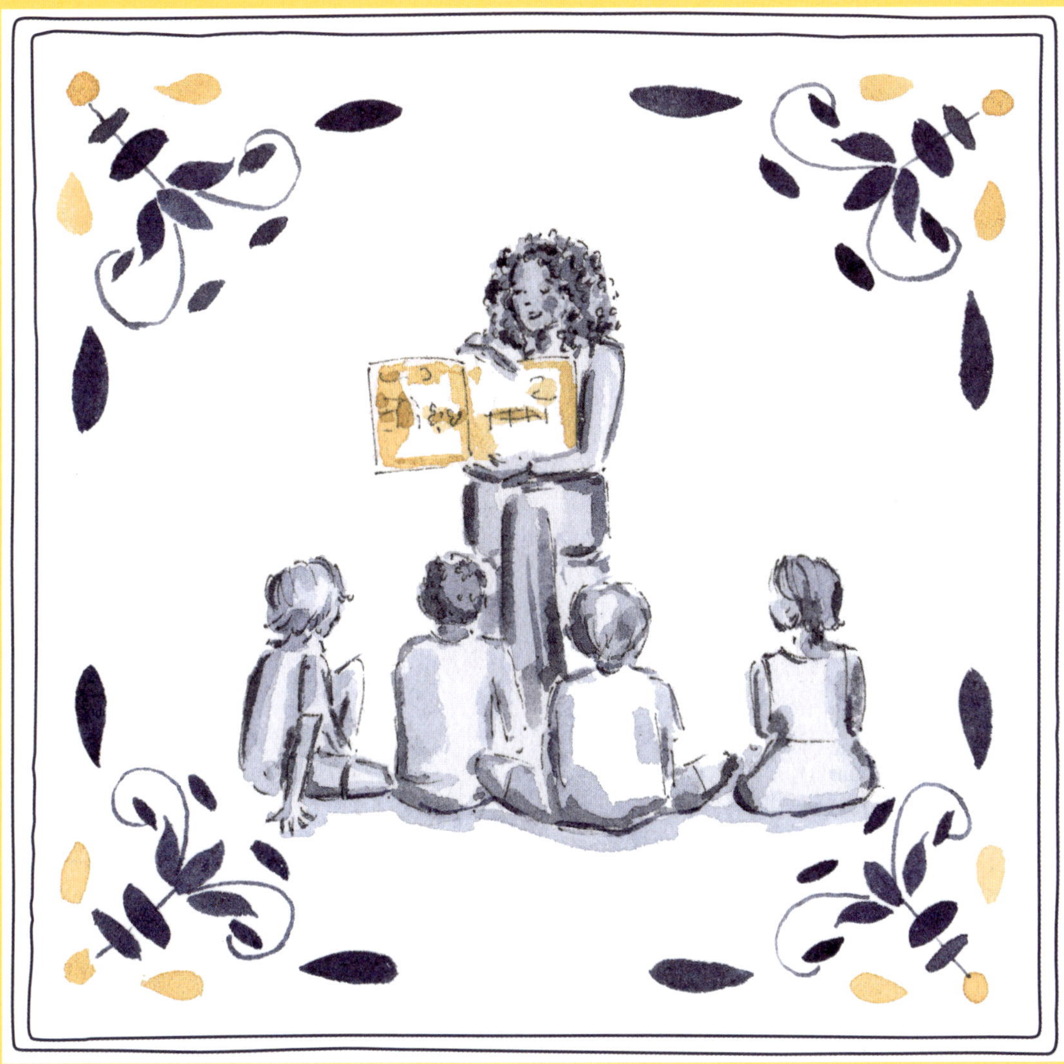

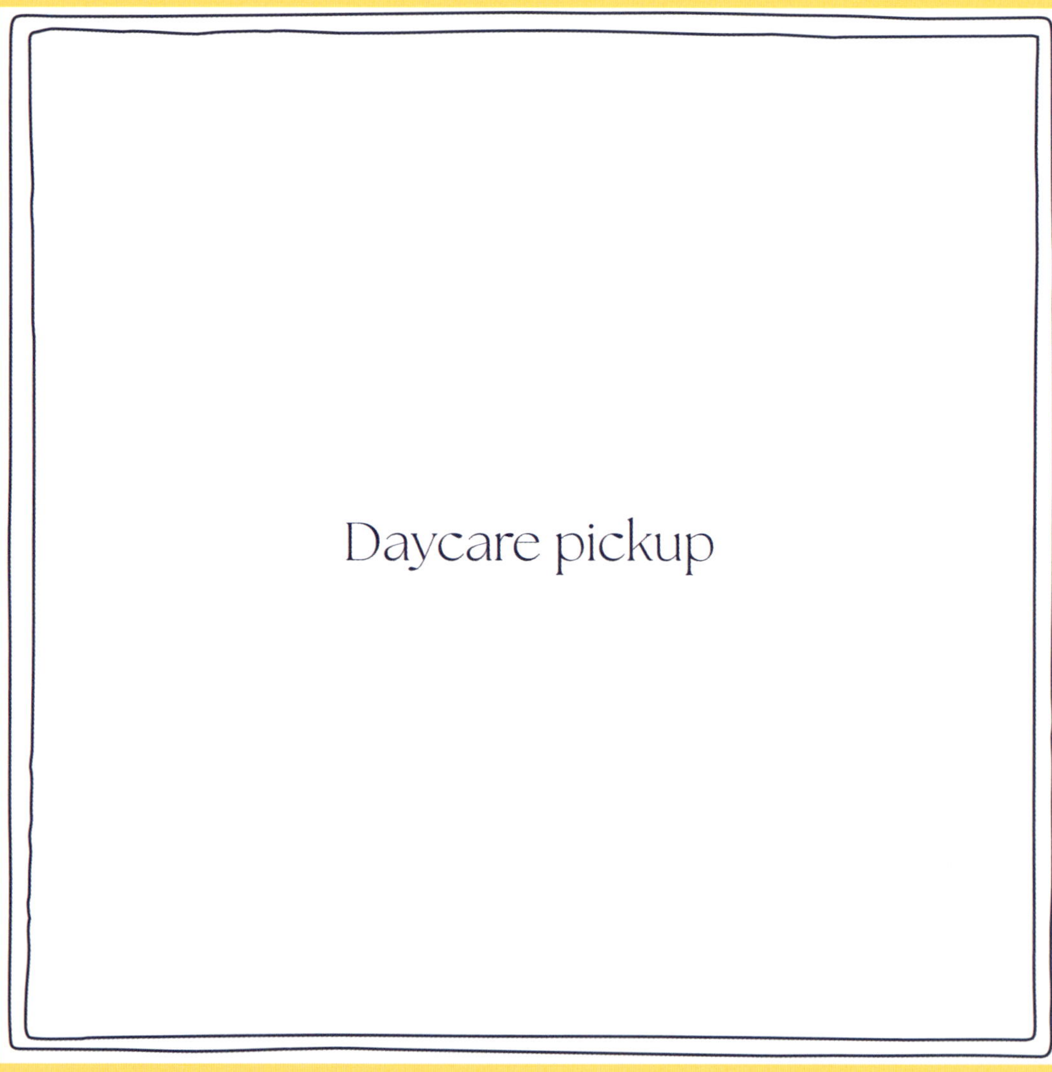

Daycare pickup

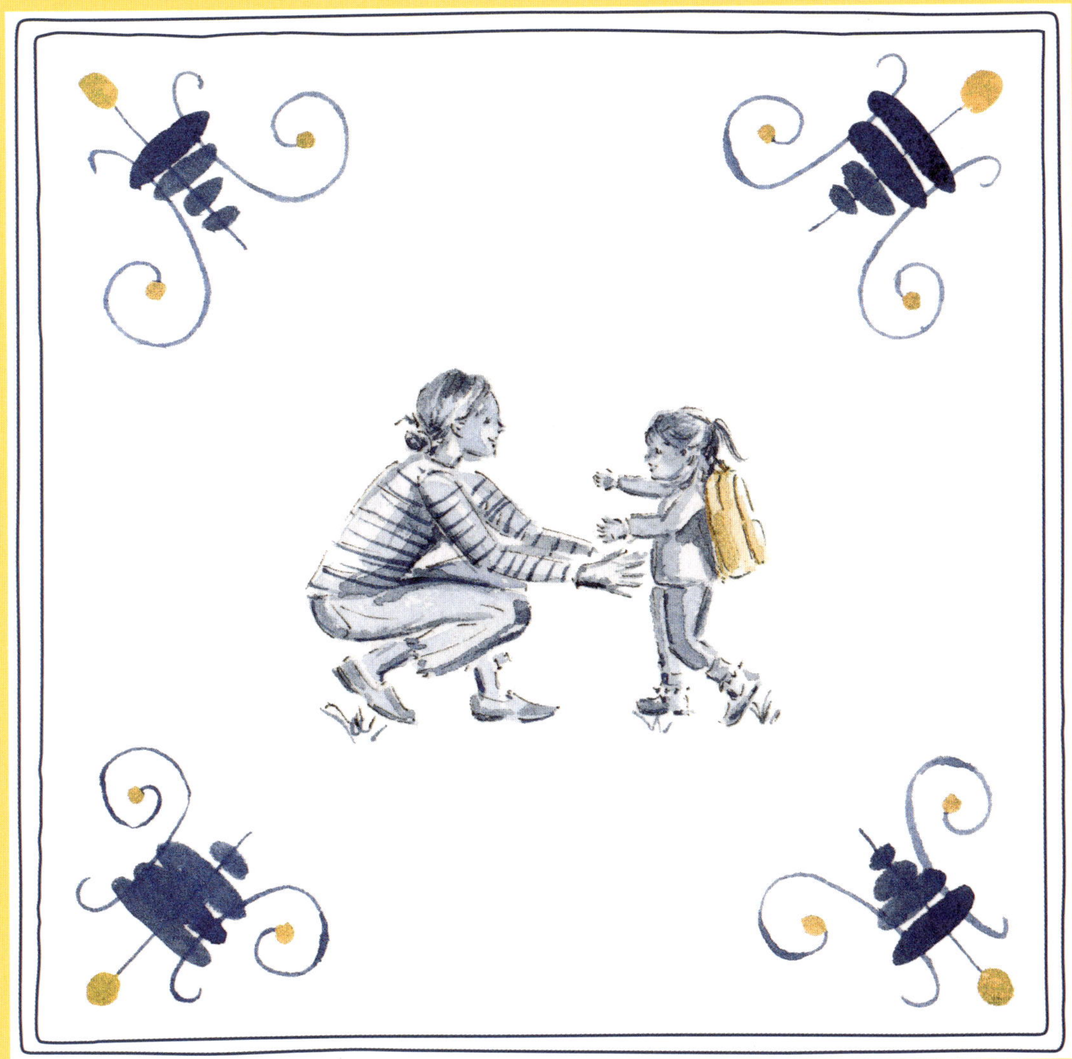

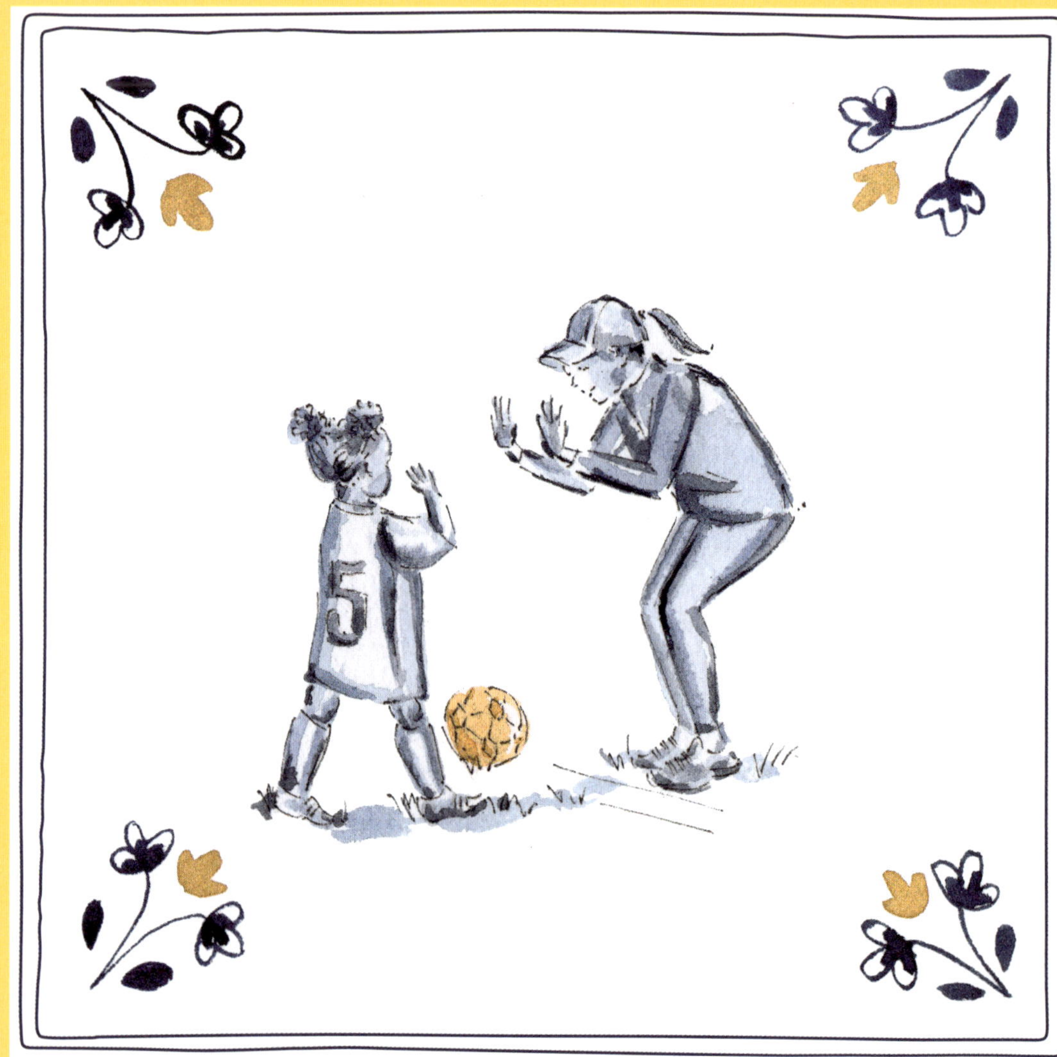

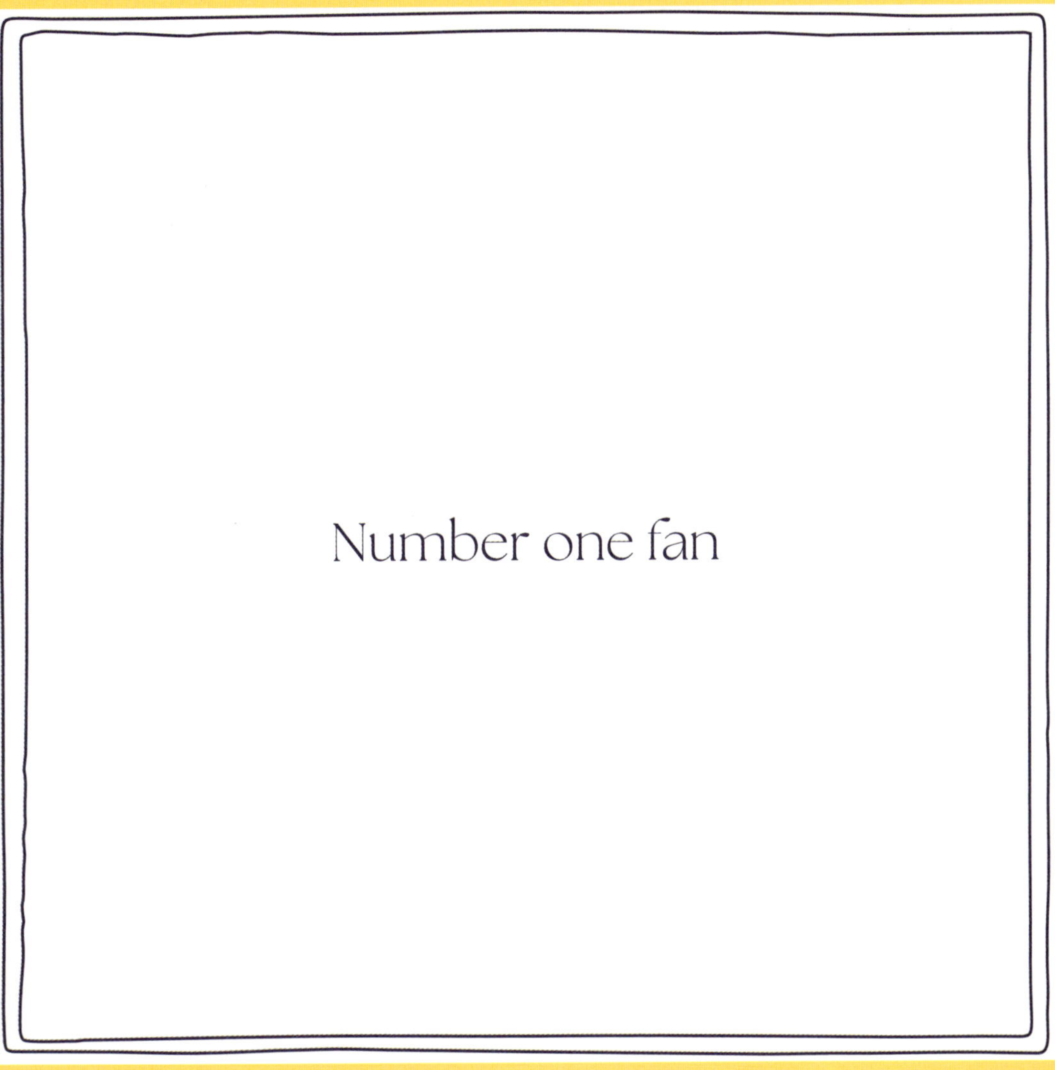
Number one fan

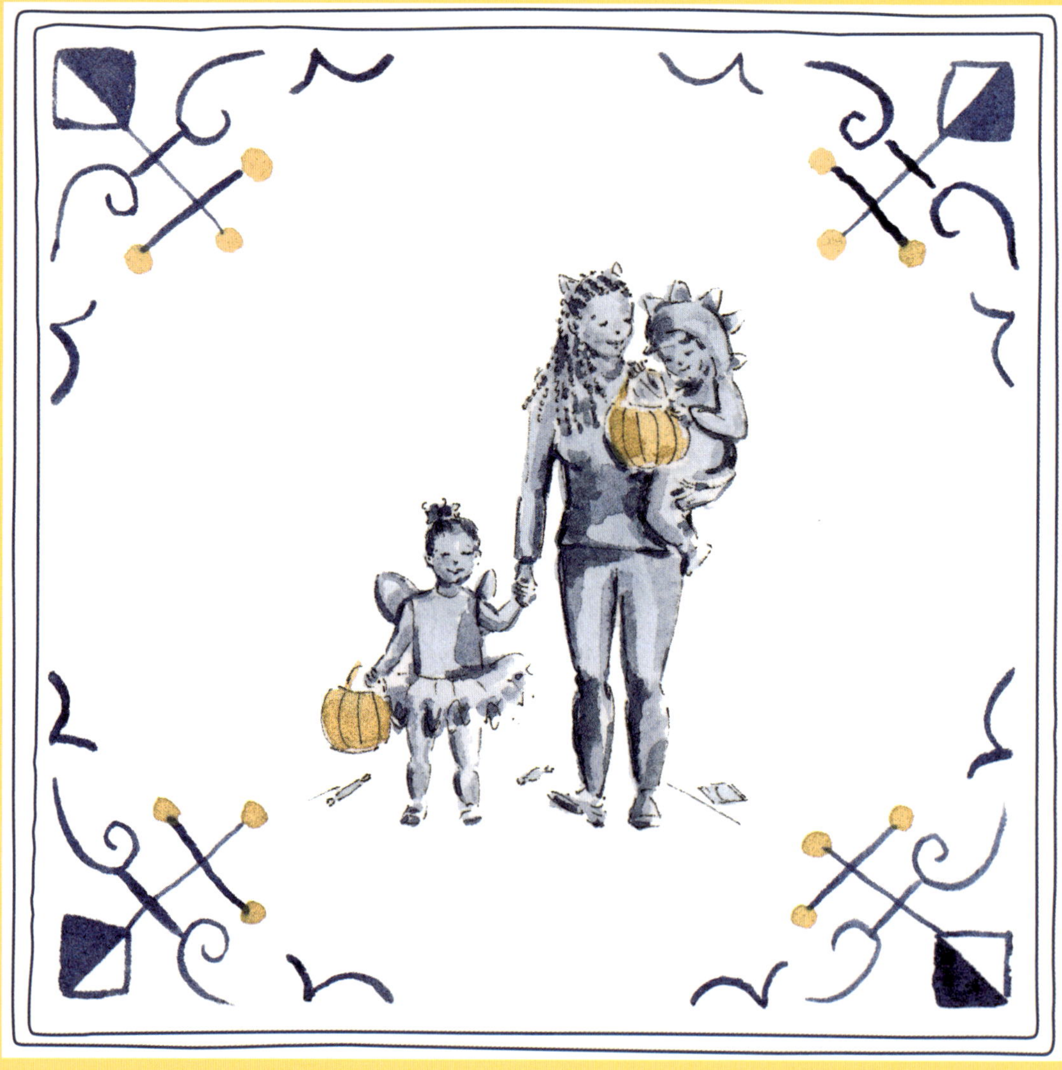

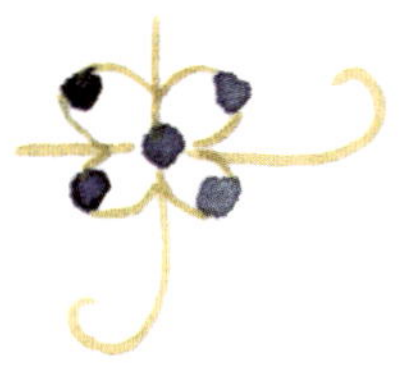
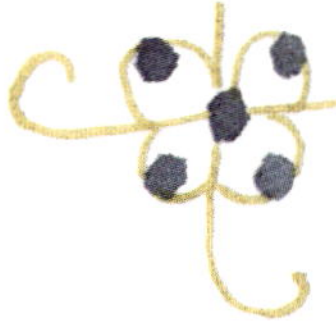
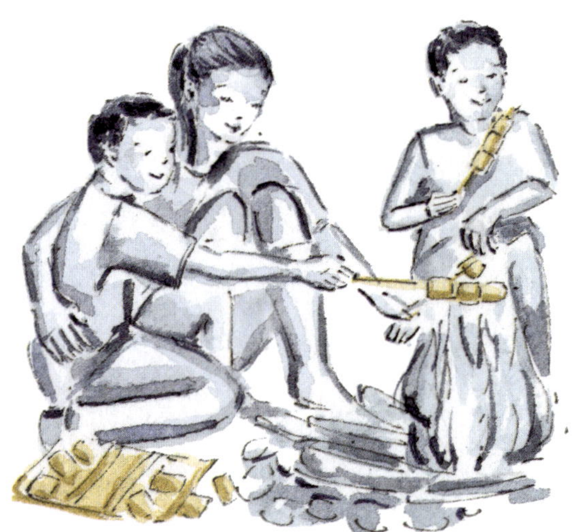
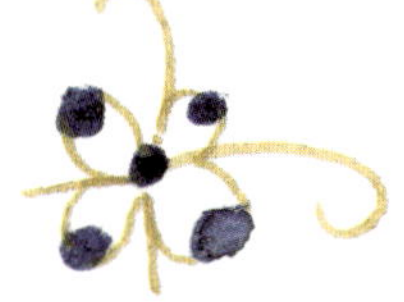
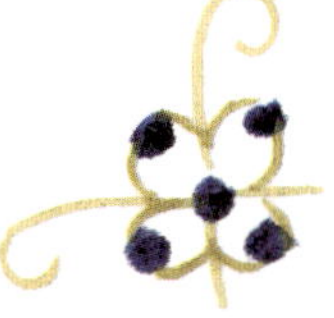

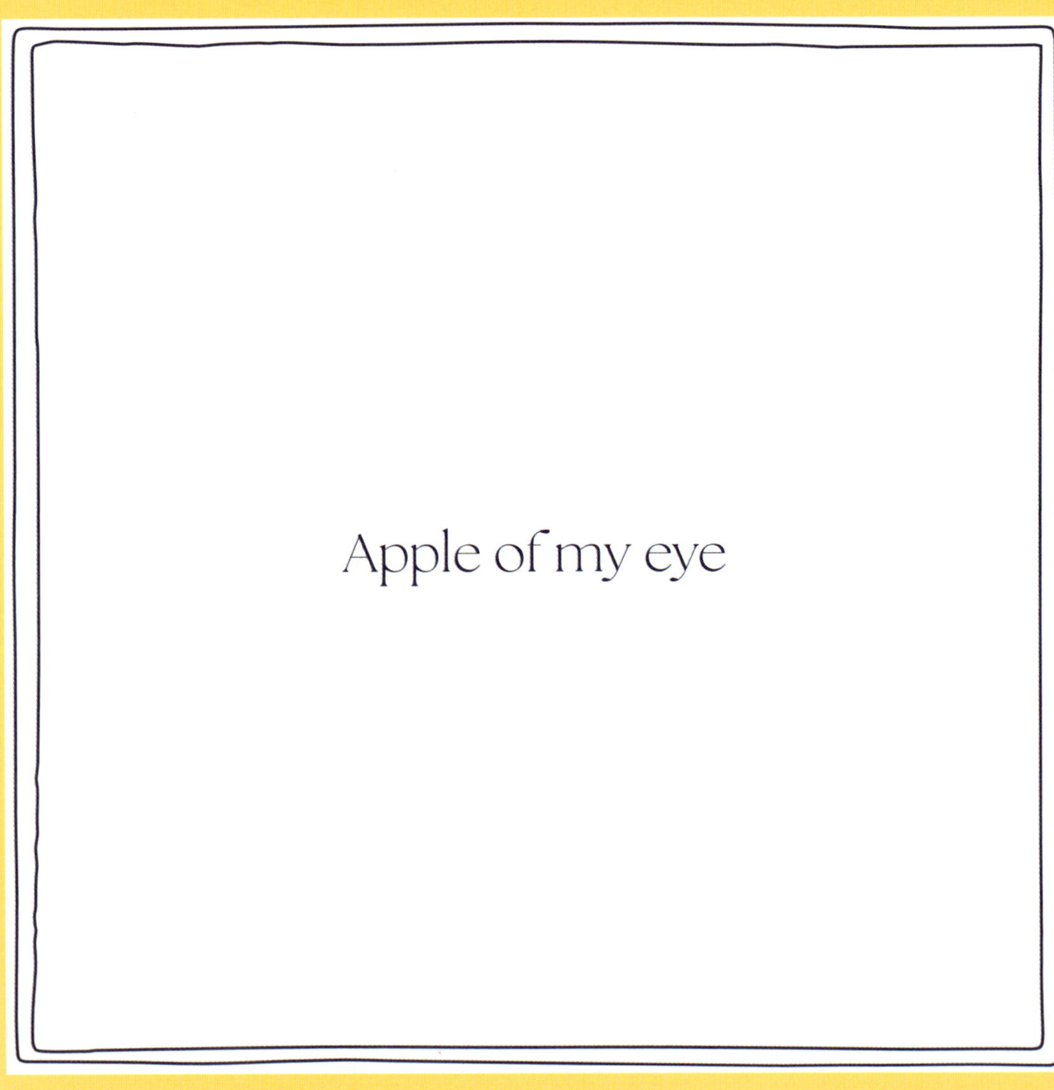

Apple of my eye

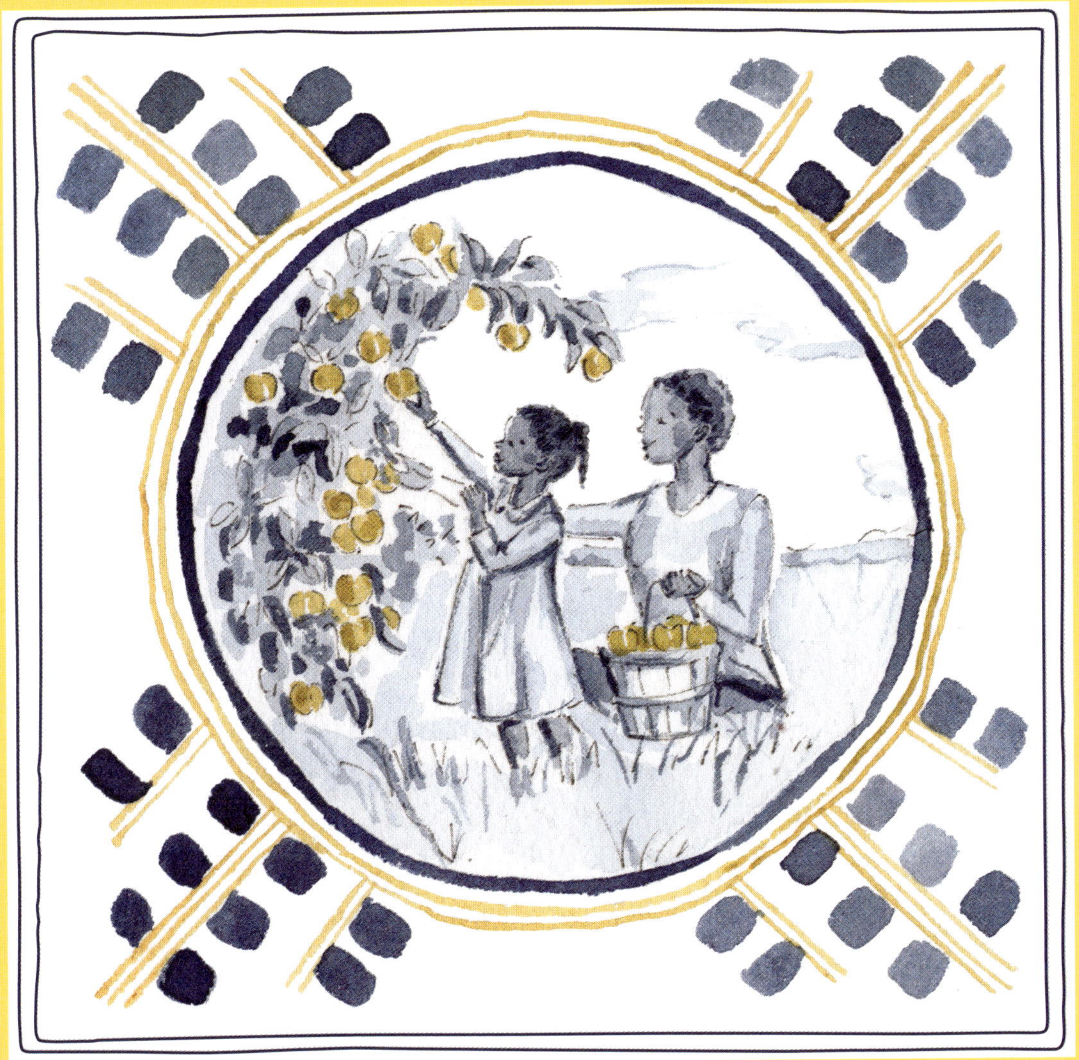

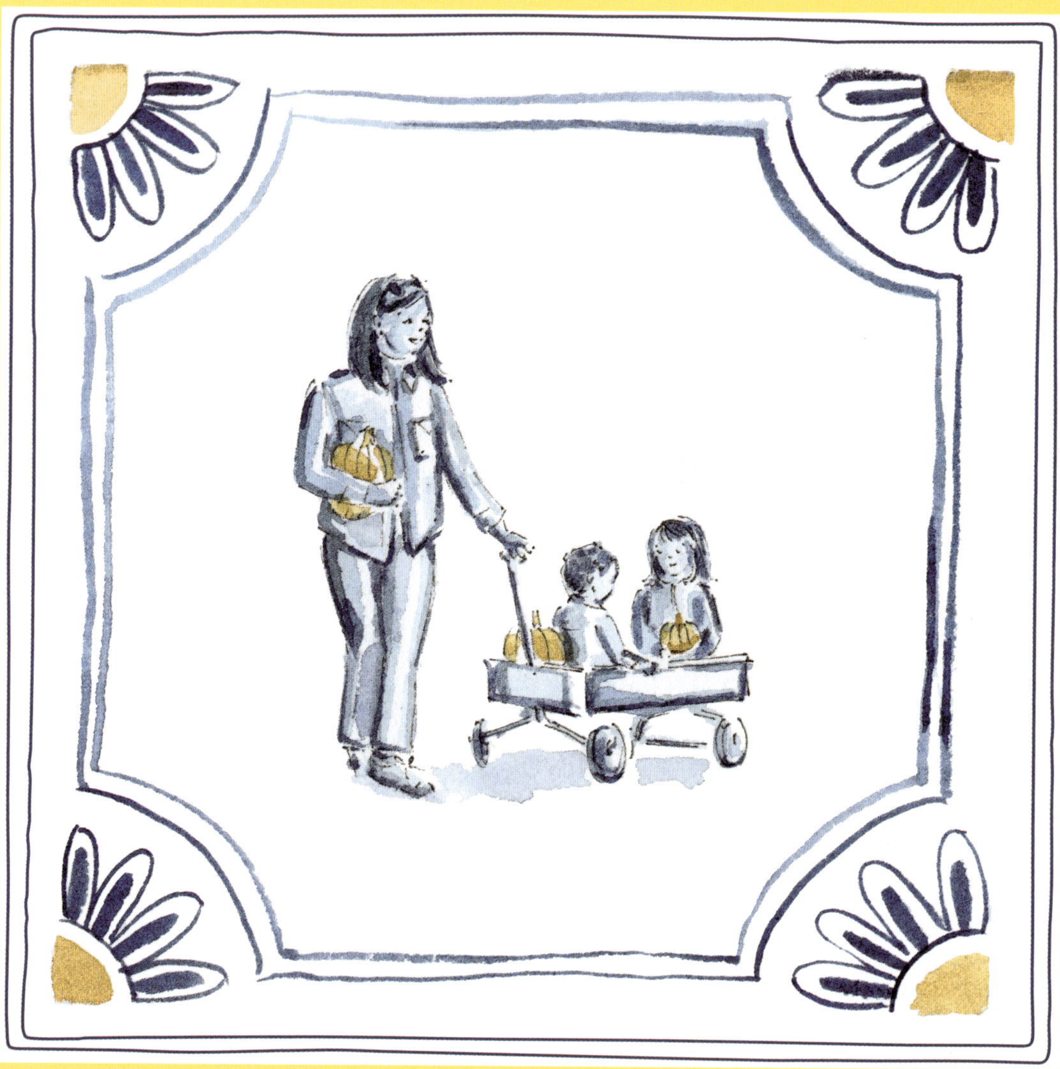

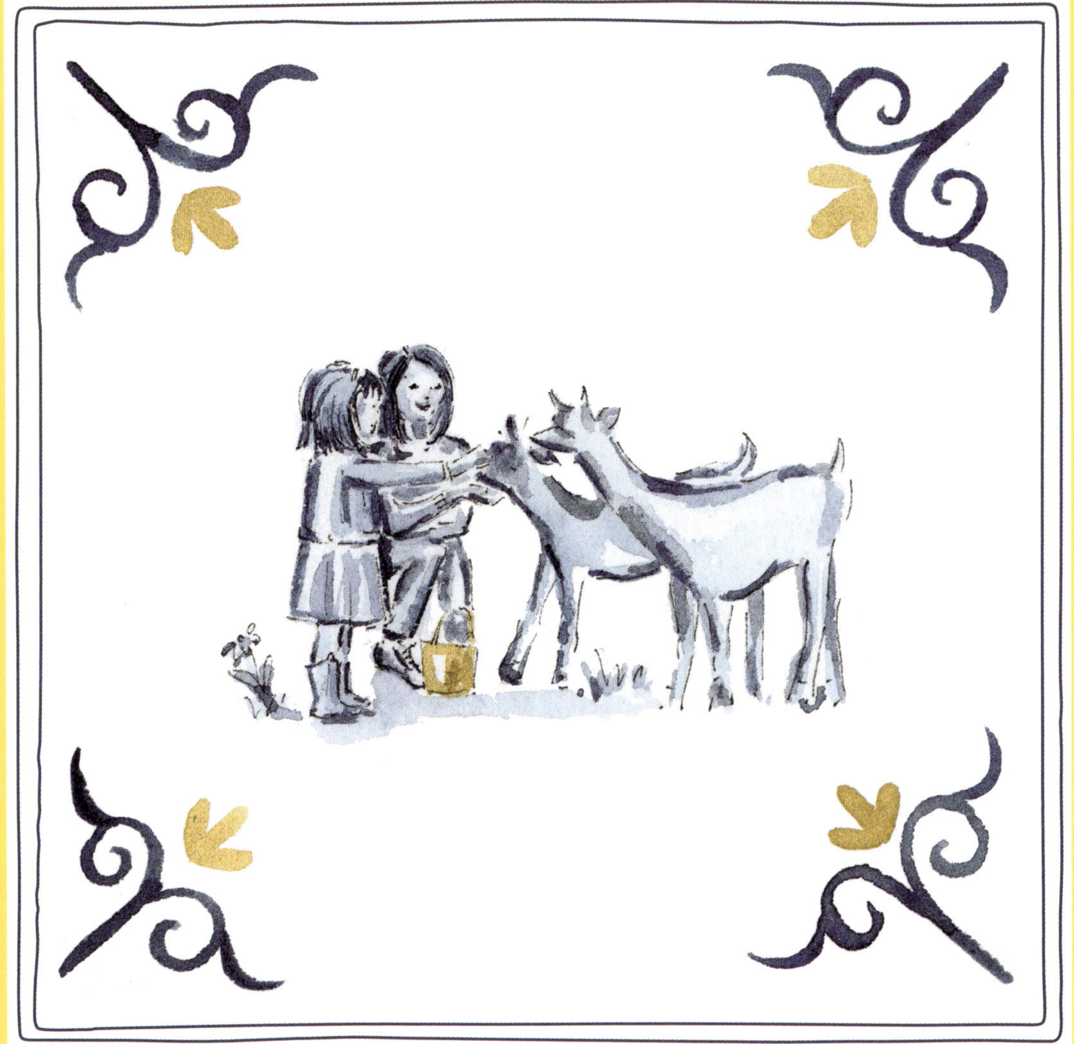

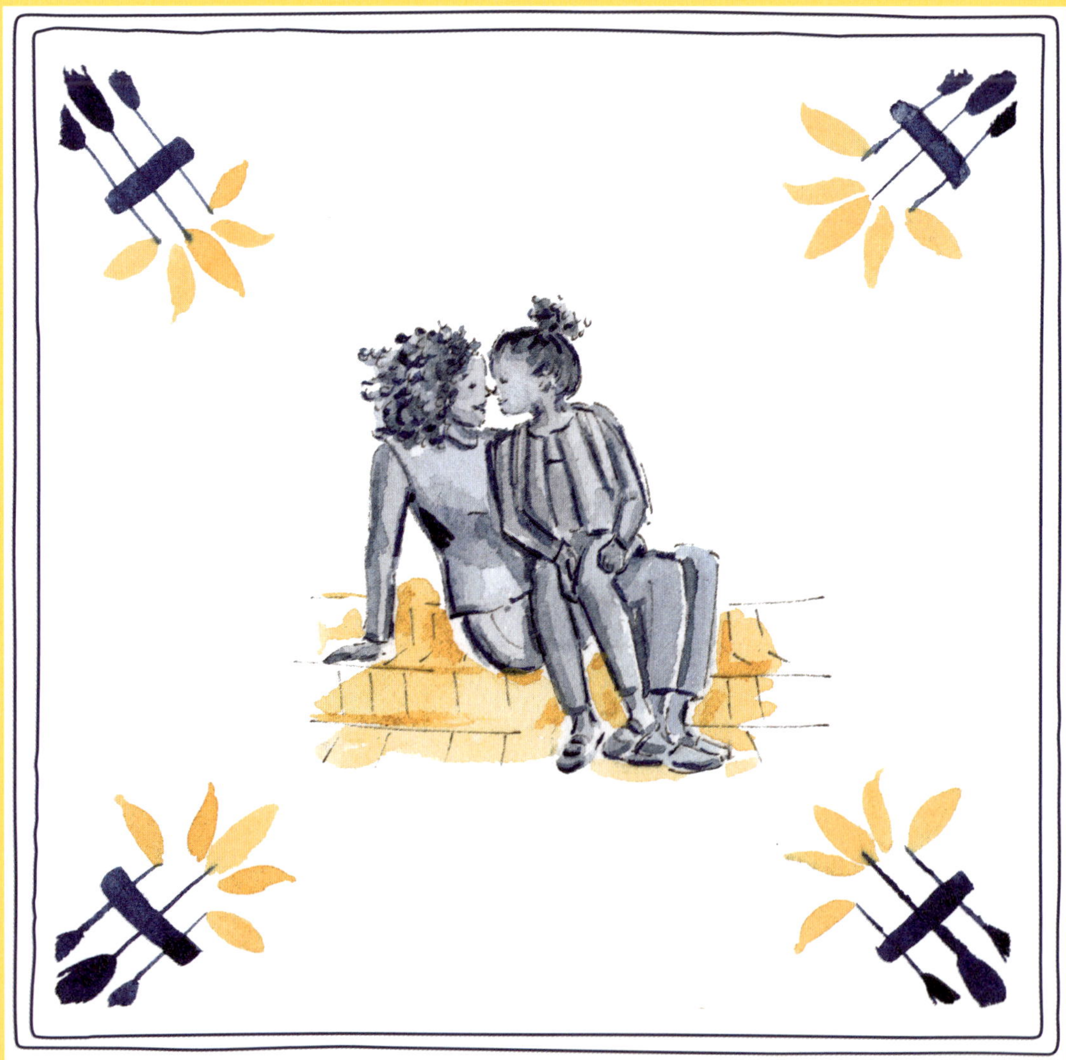

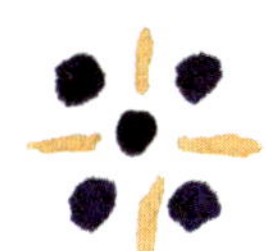
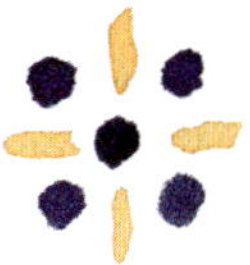
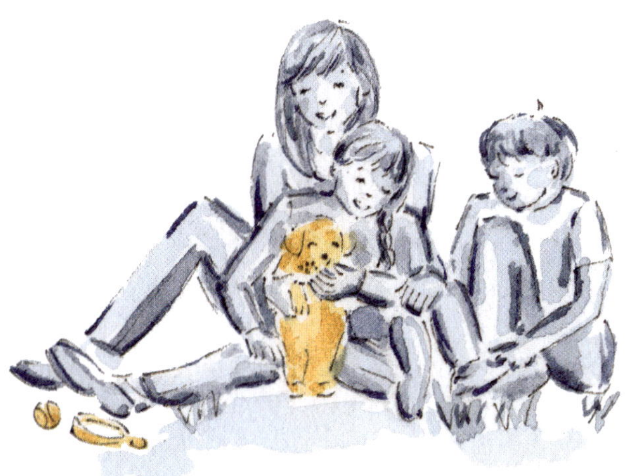
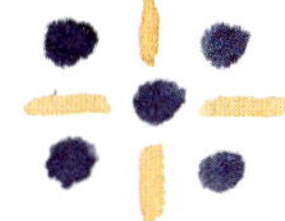
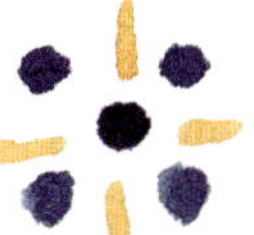

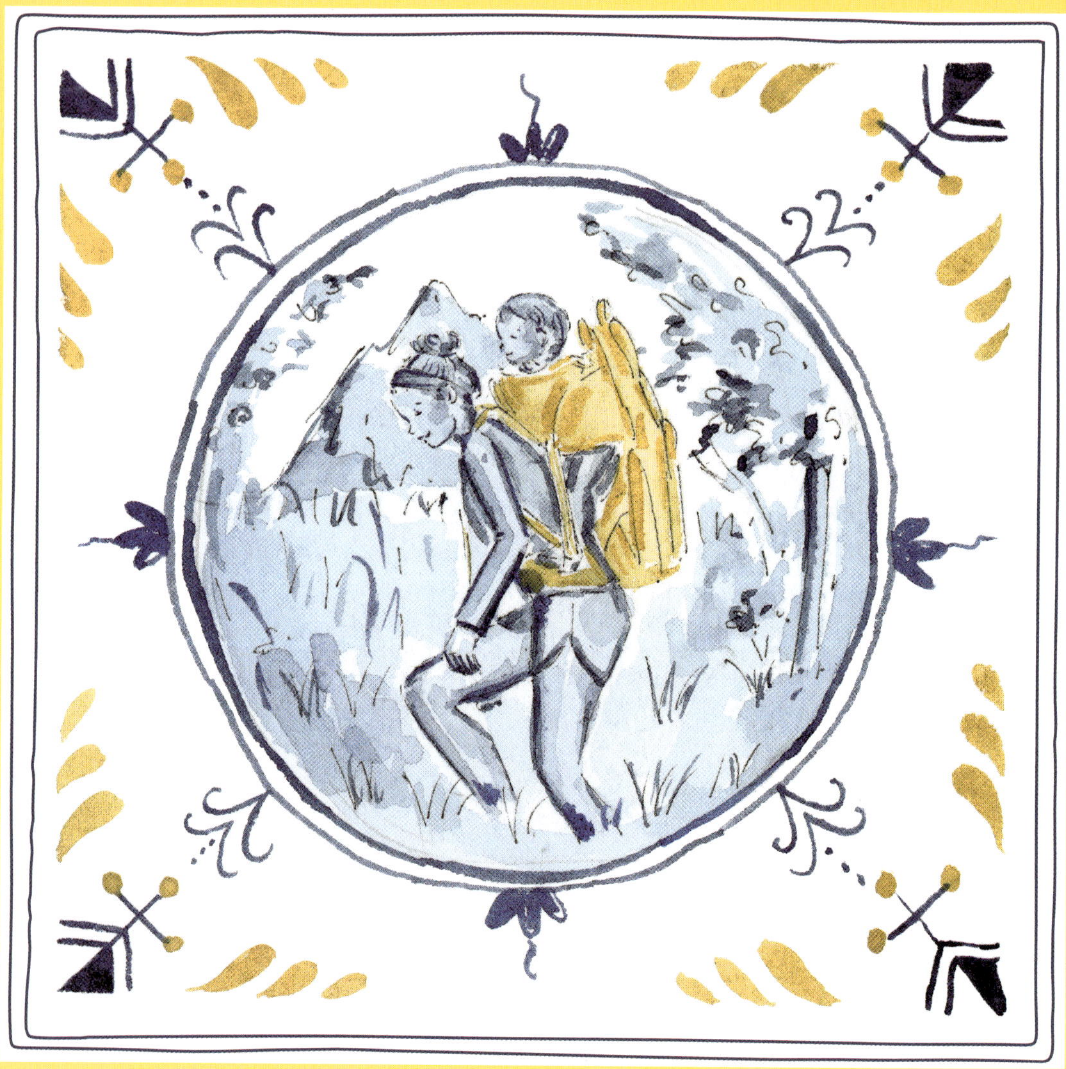

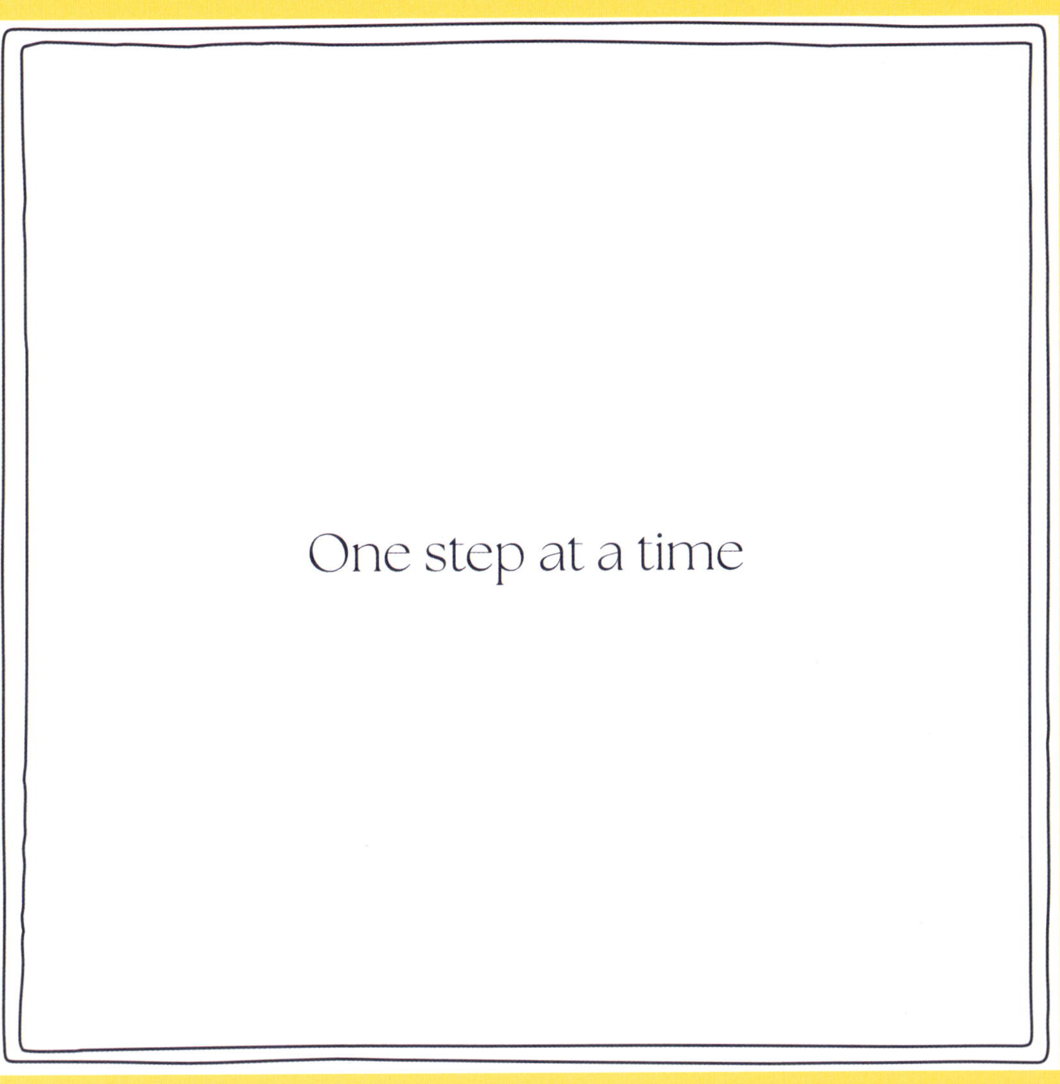
One step at a time

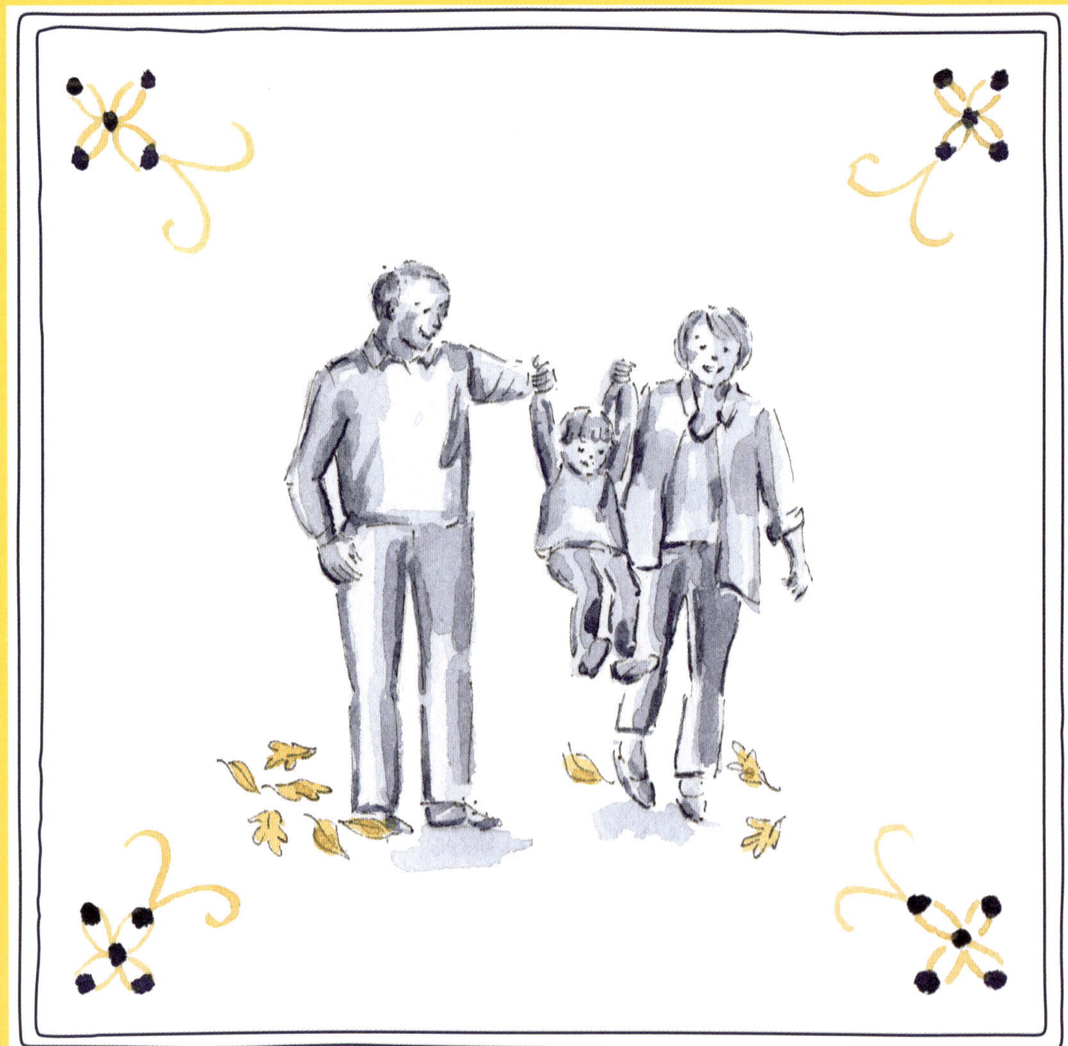

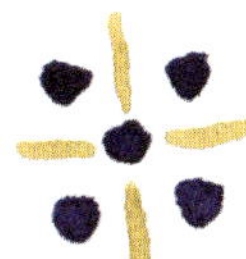
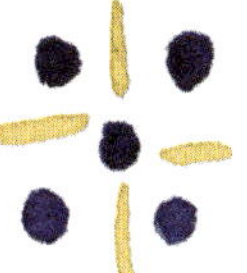
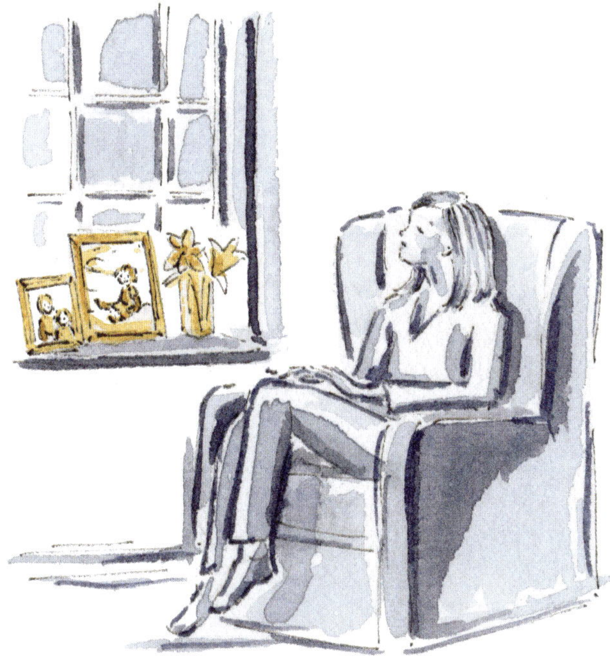
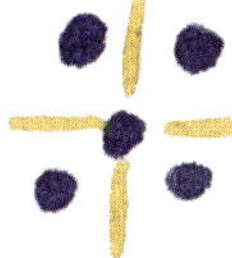
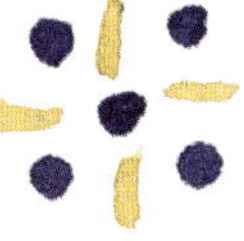

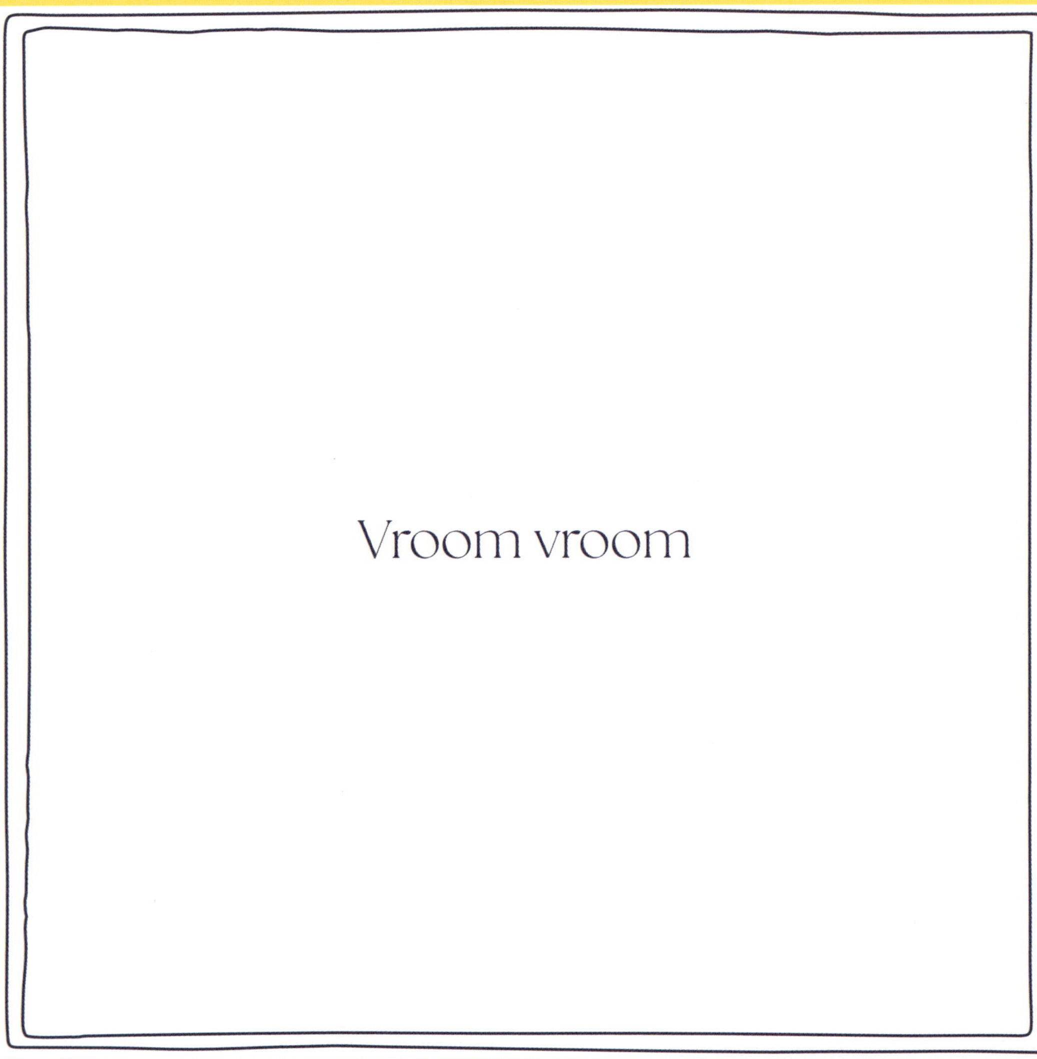

Vroom vroom

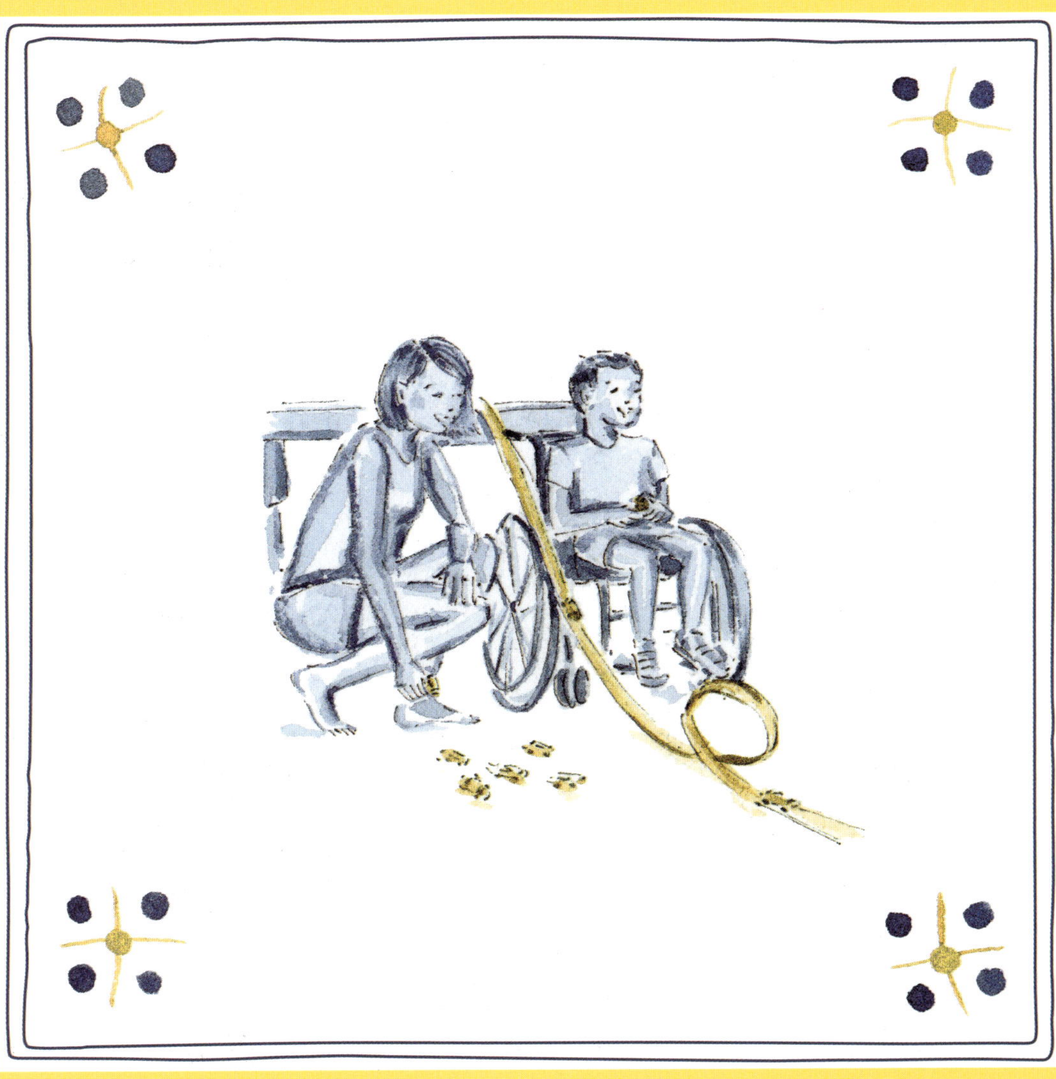

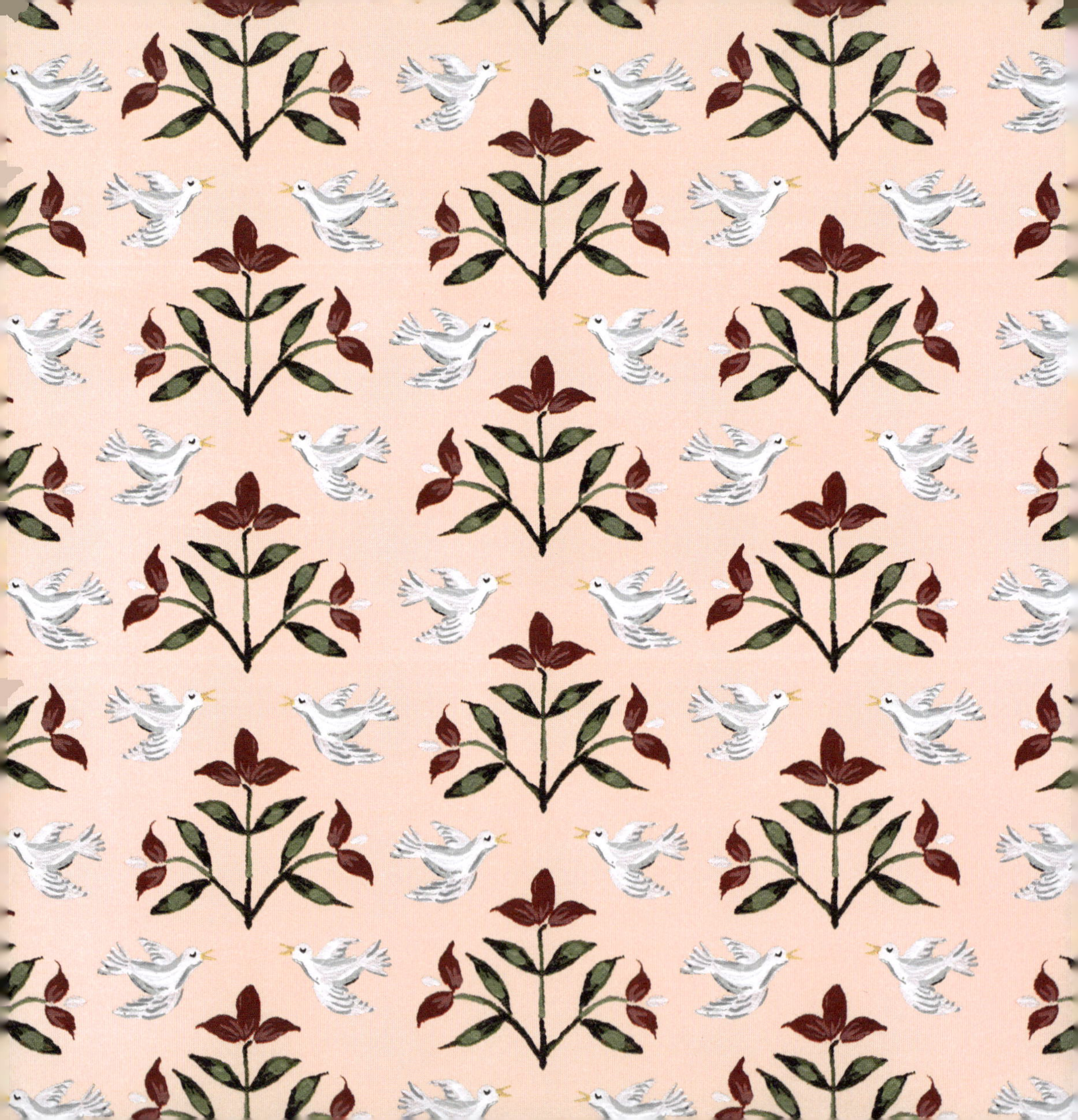

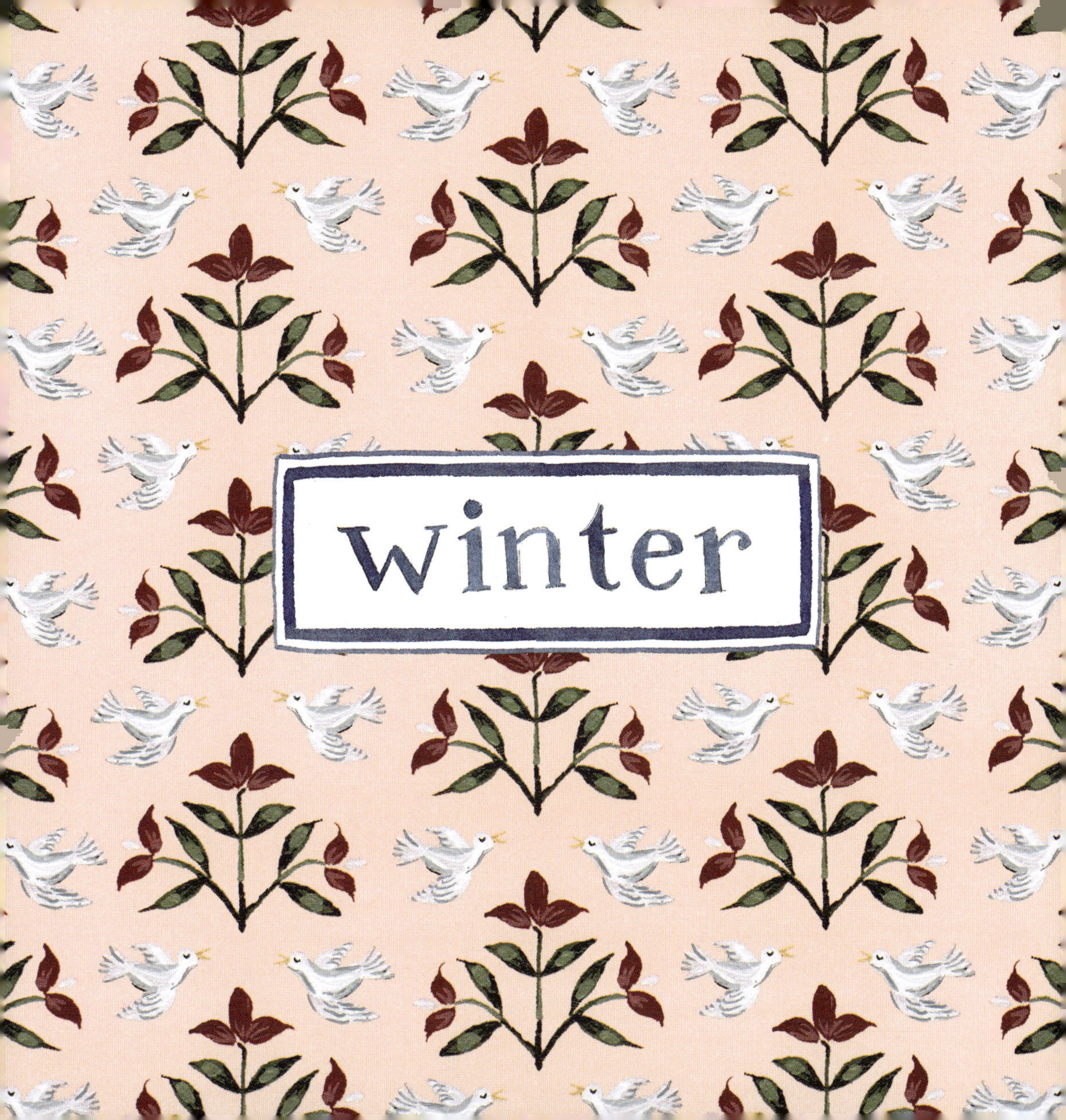

winter

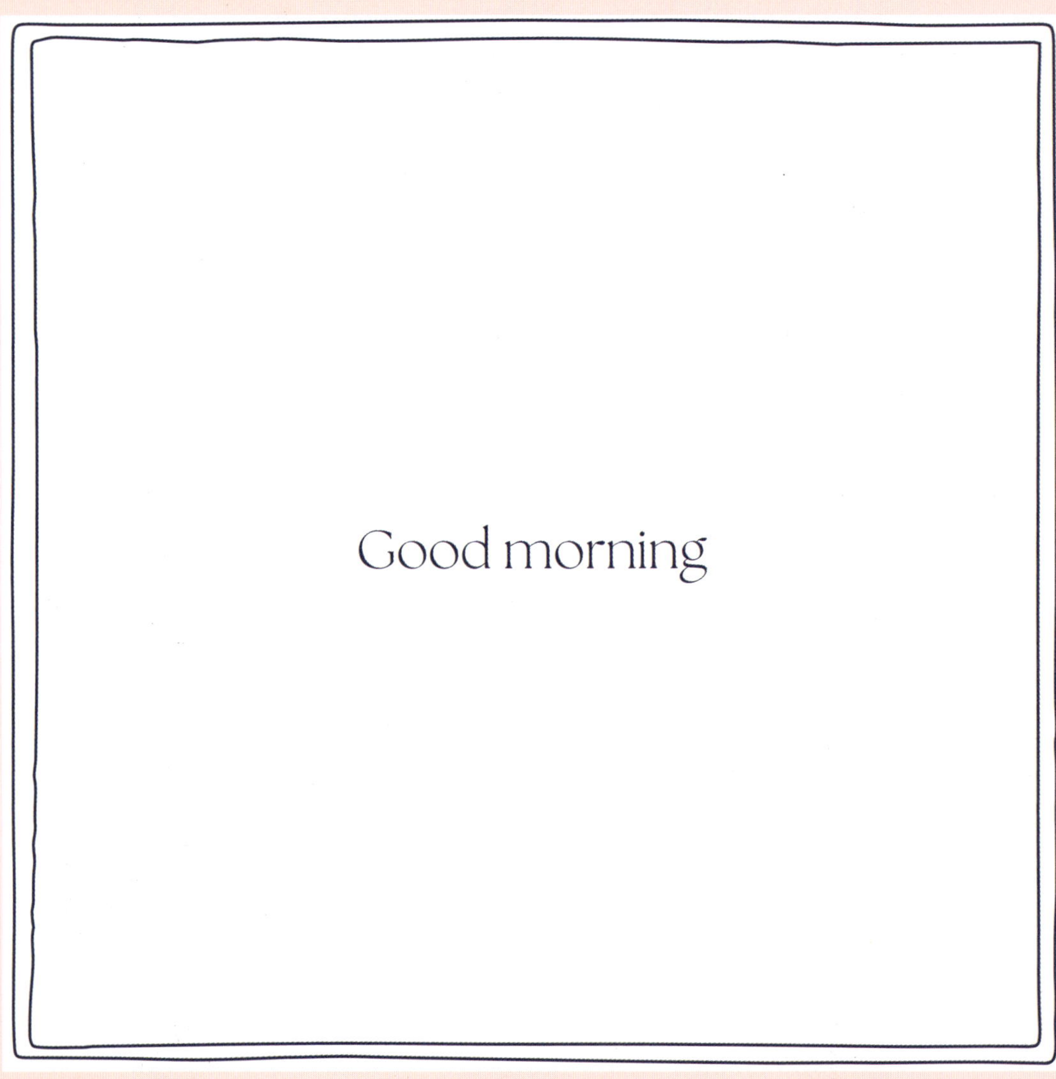
Good morning

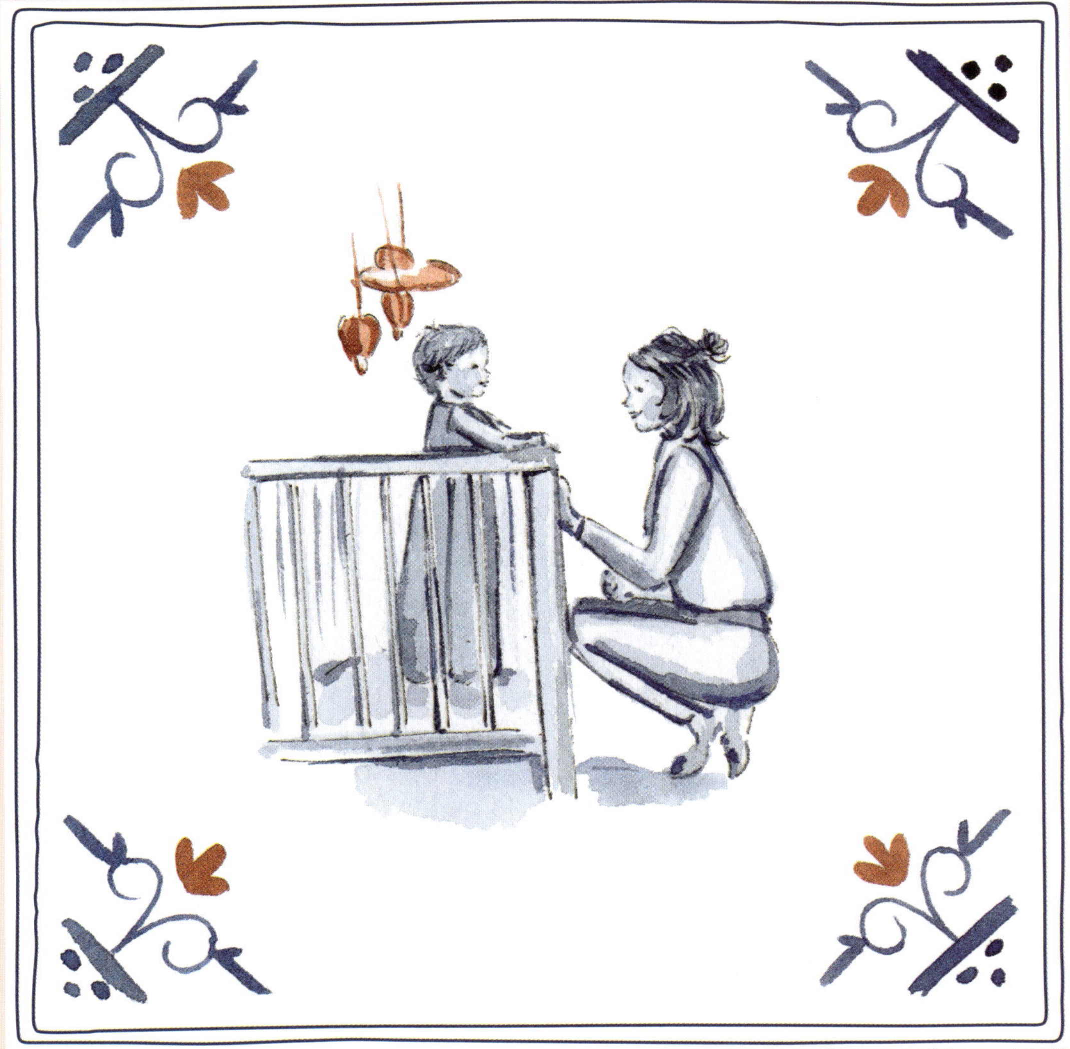

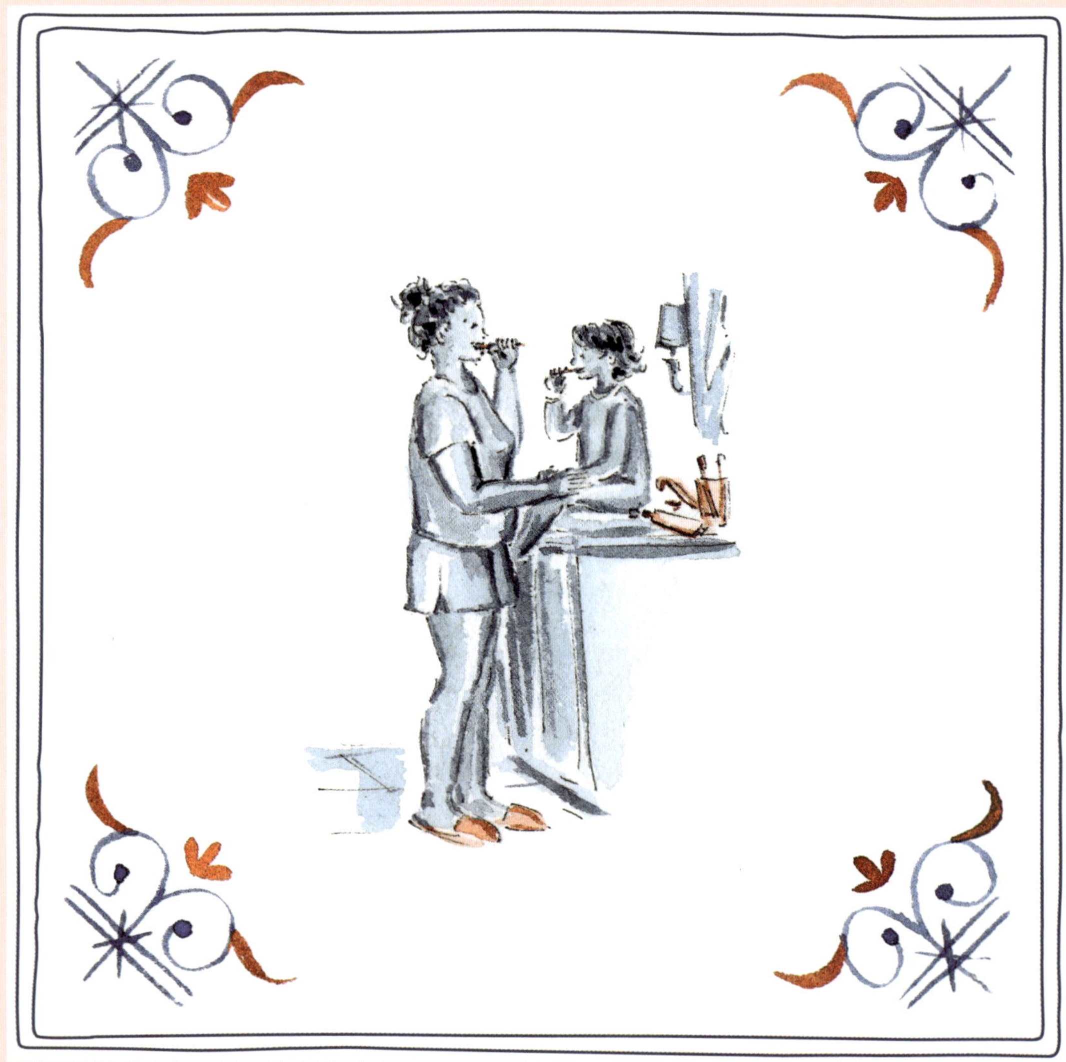

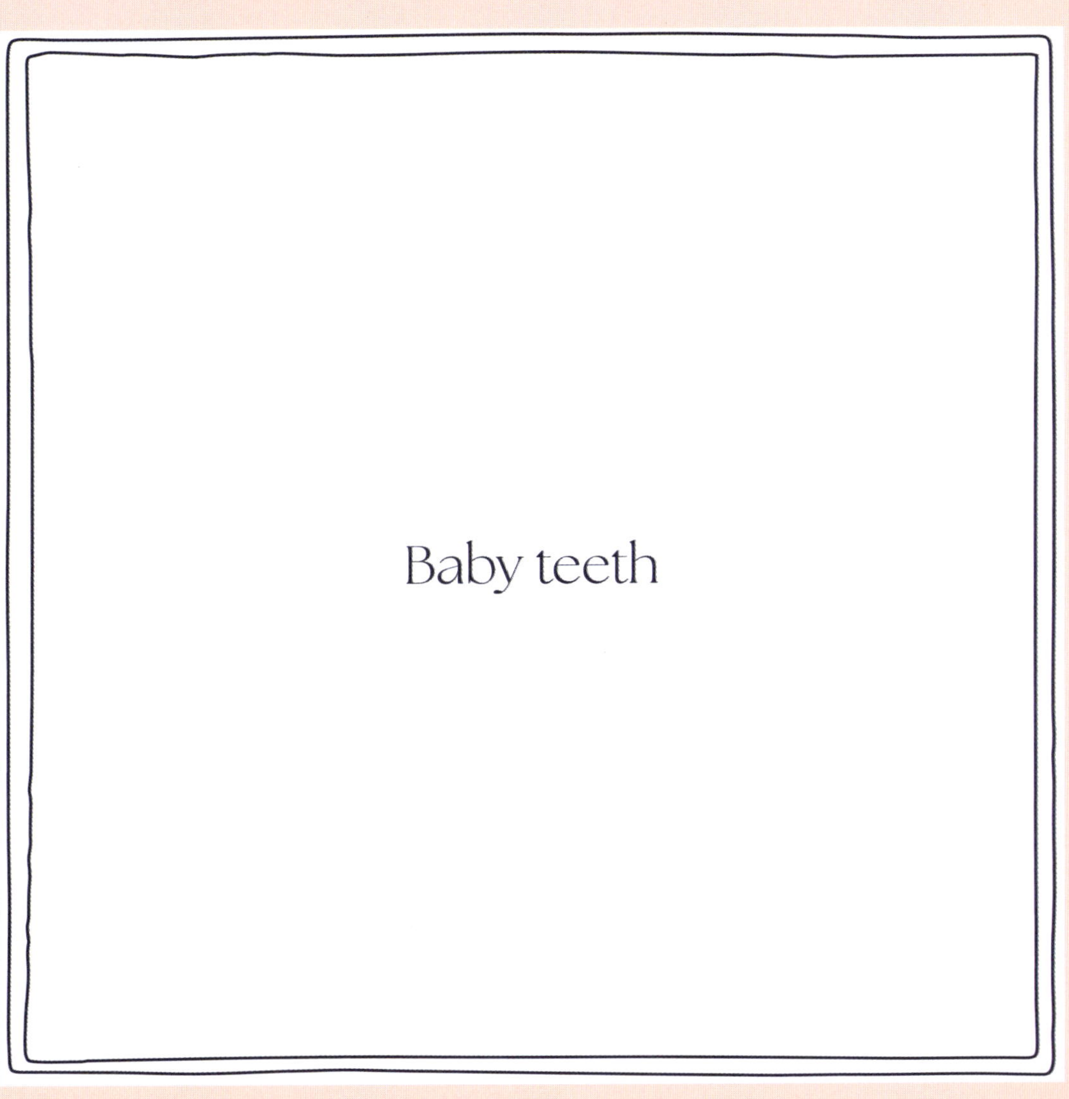

Baby teeth

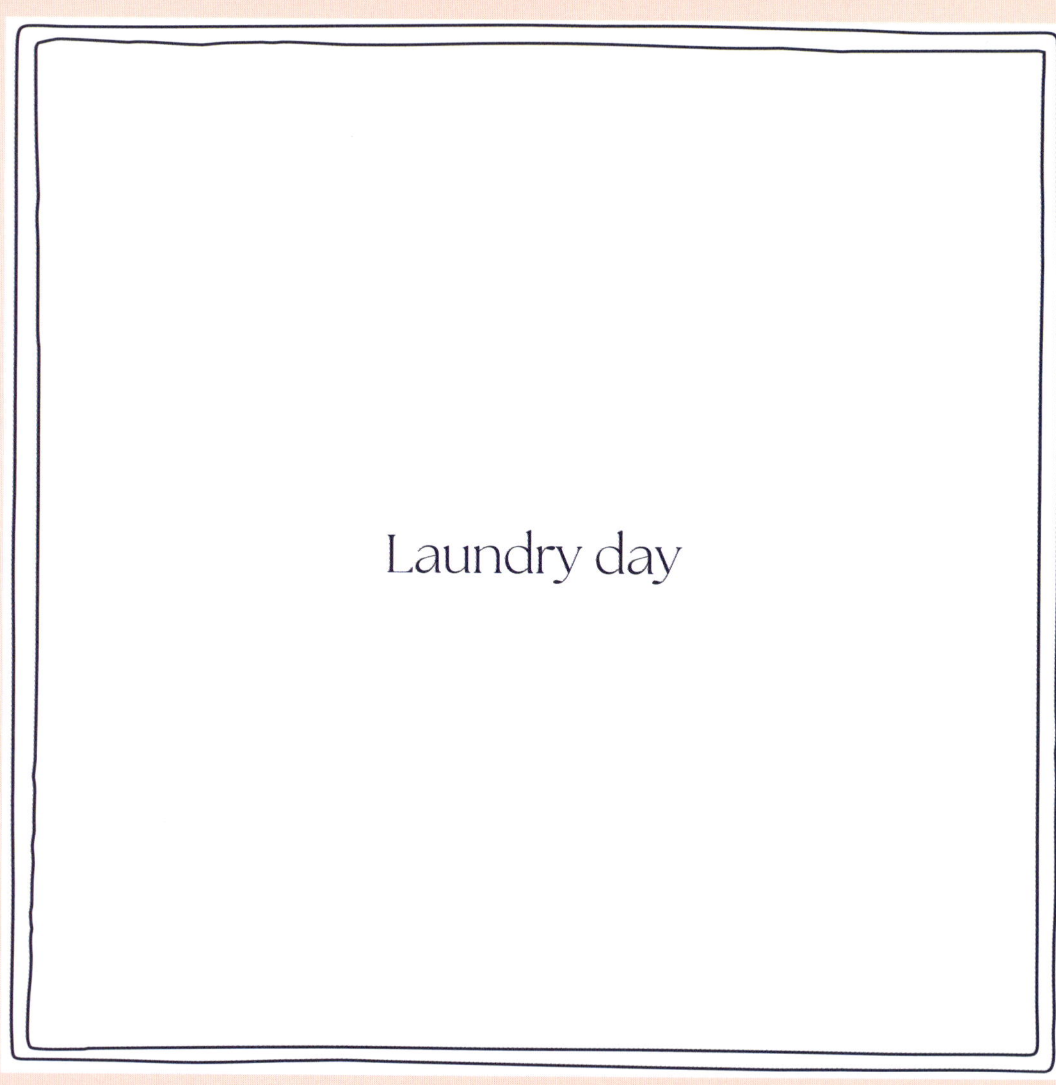
Laundry day

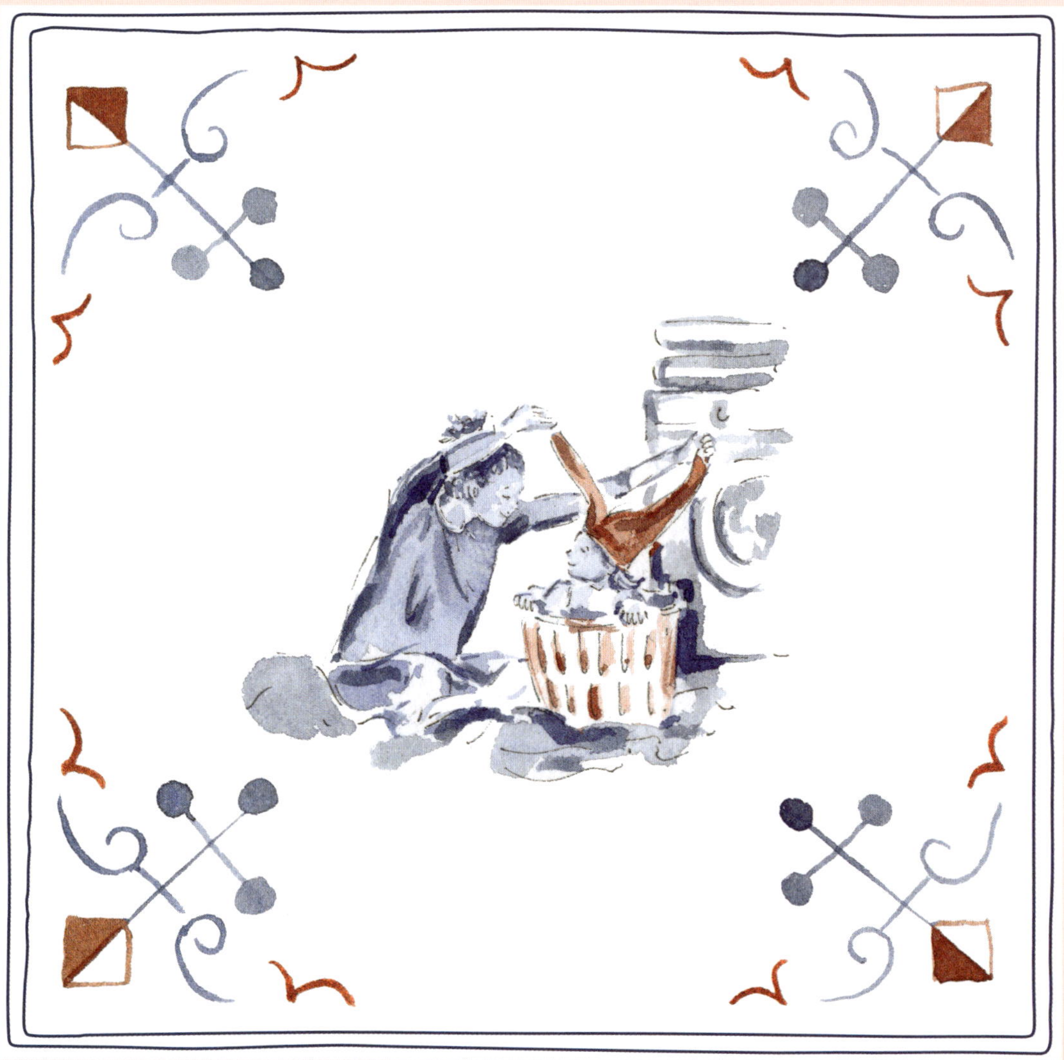

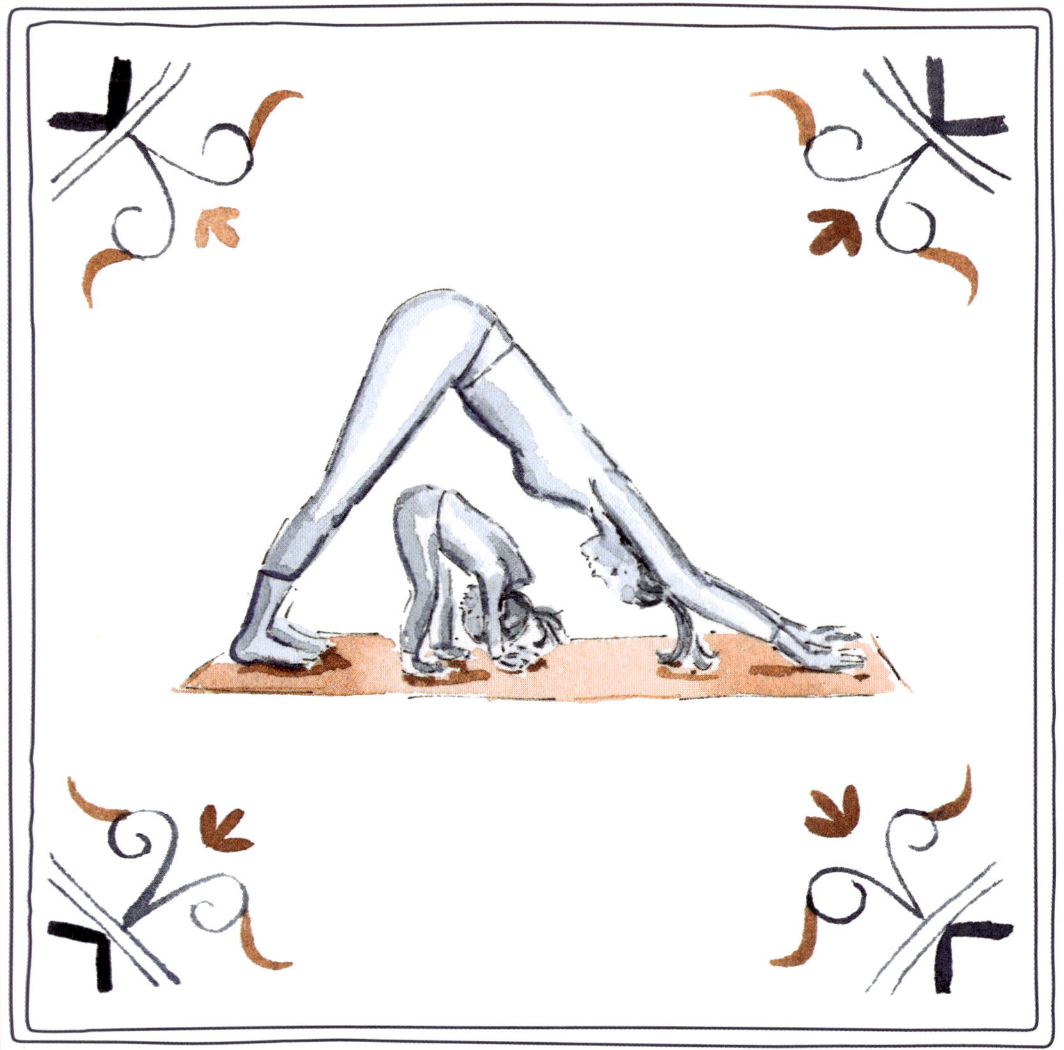

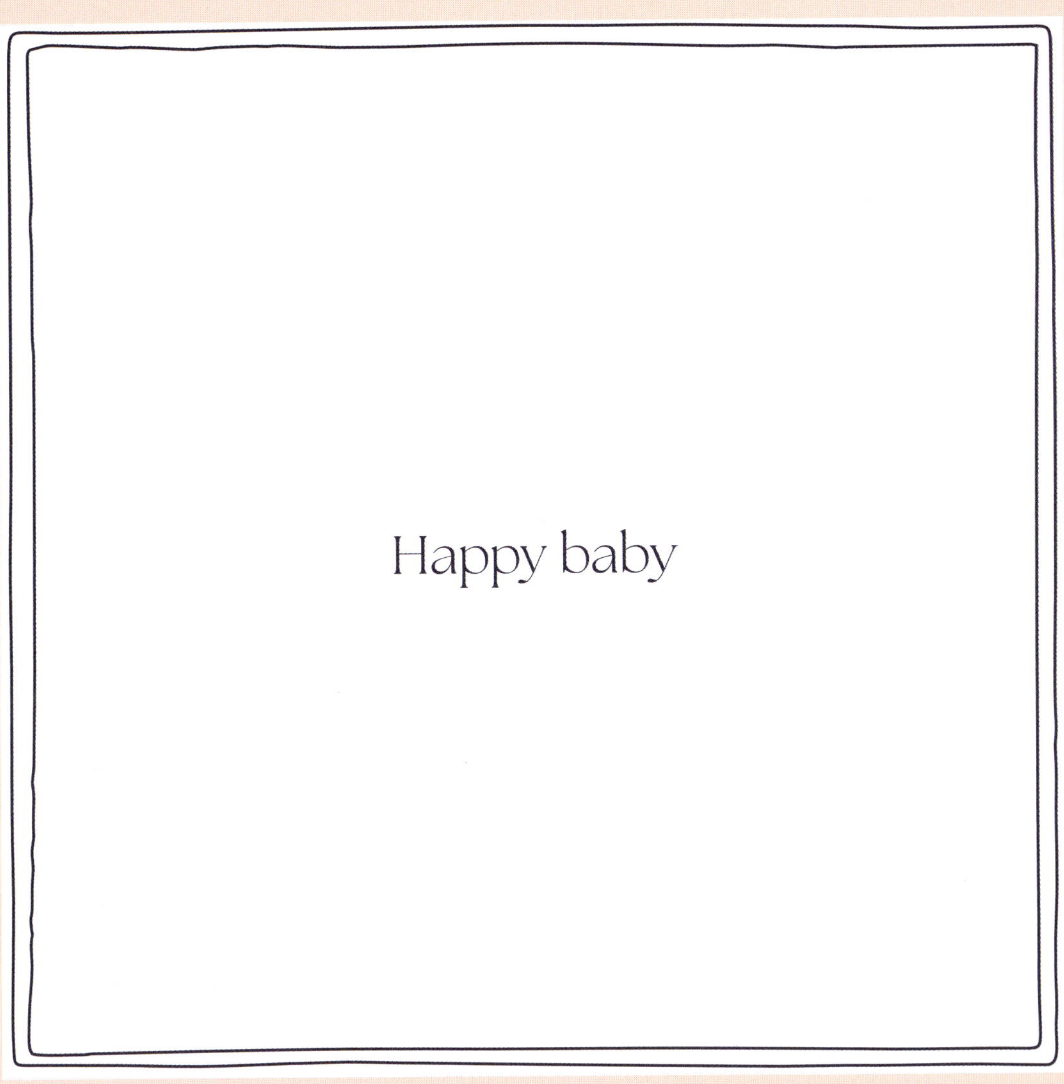

Happy baby

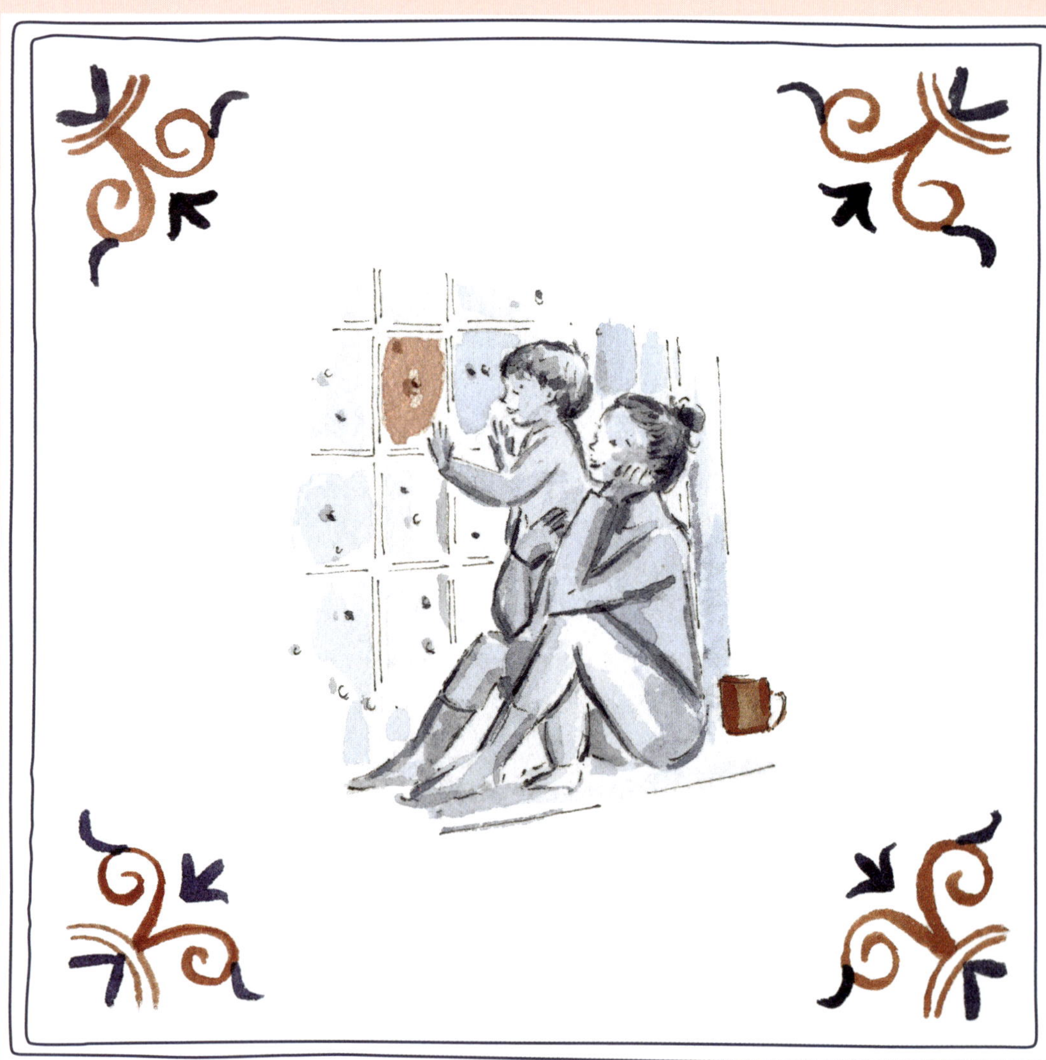

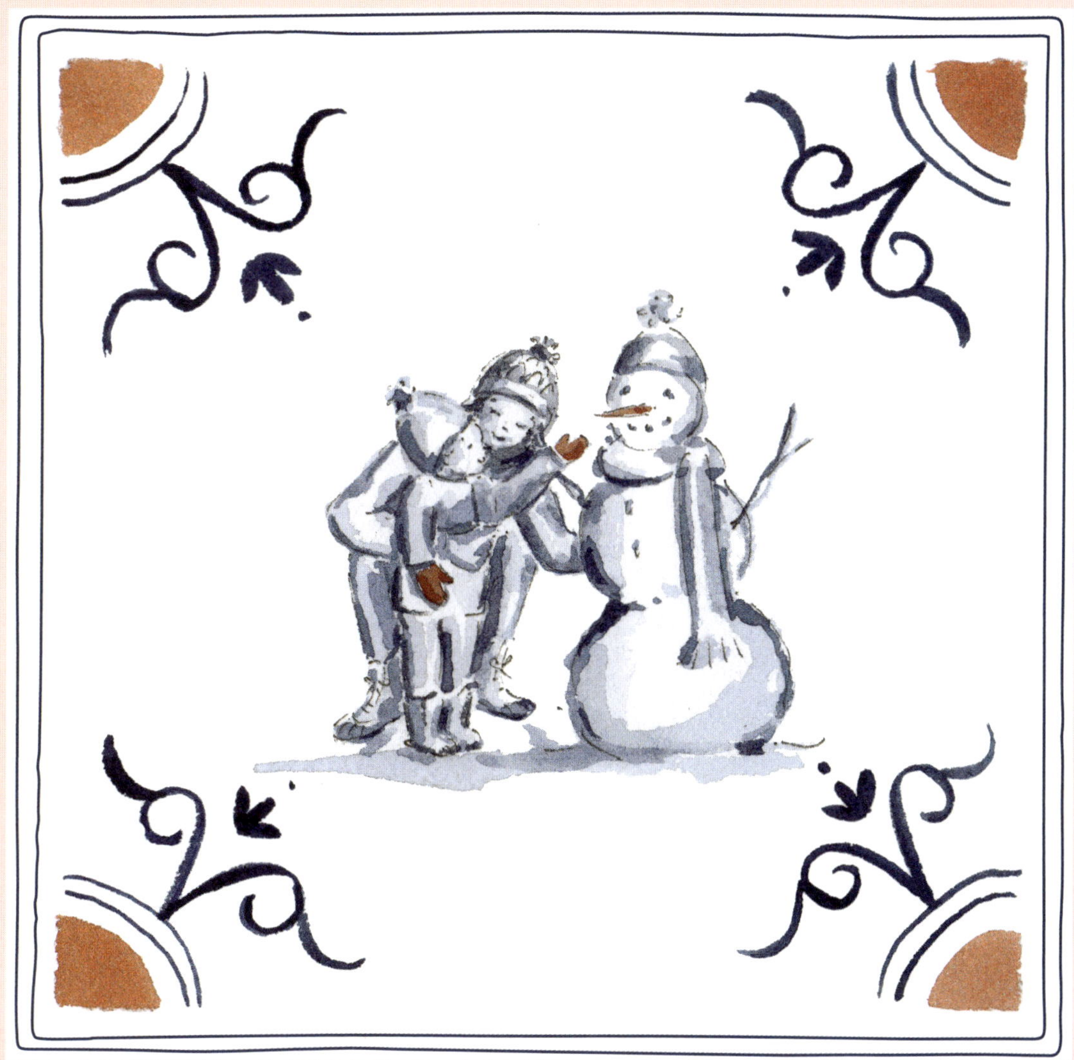

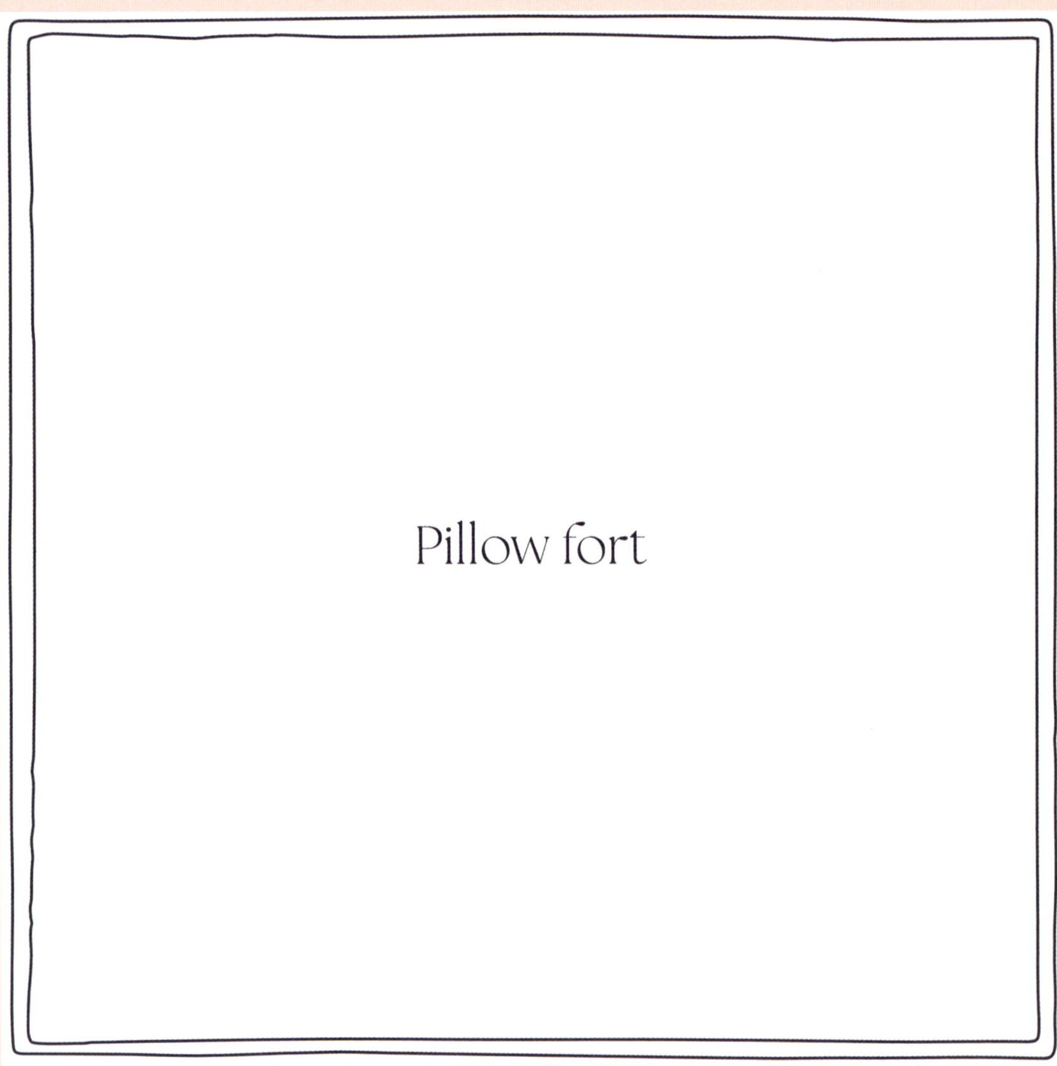

Pillow fort

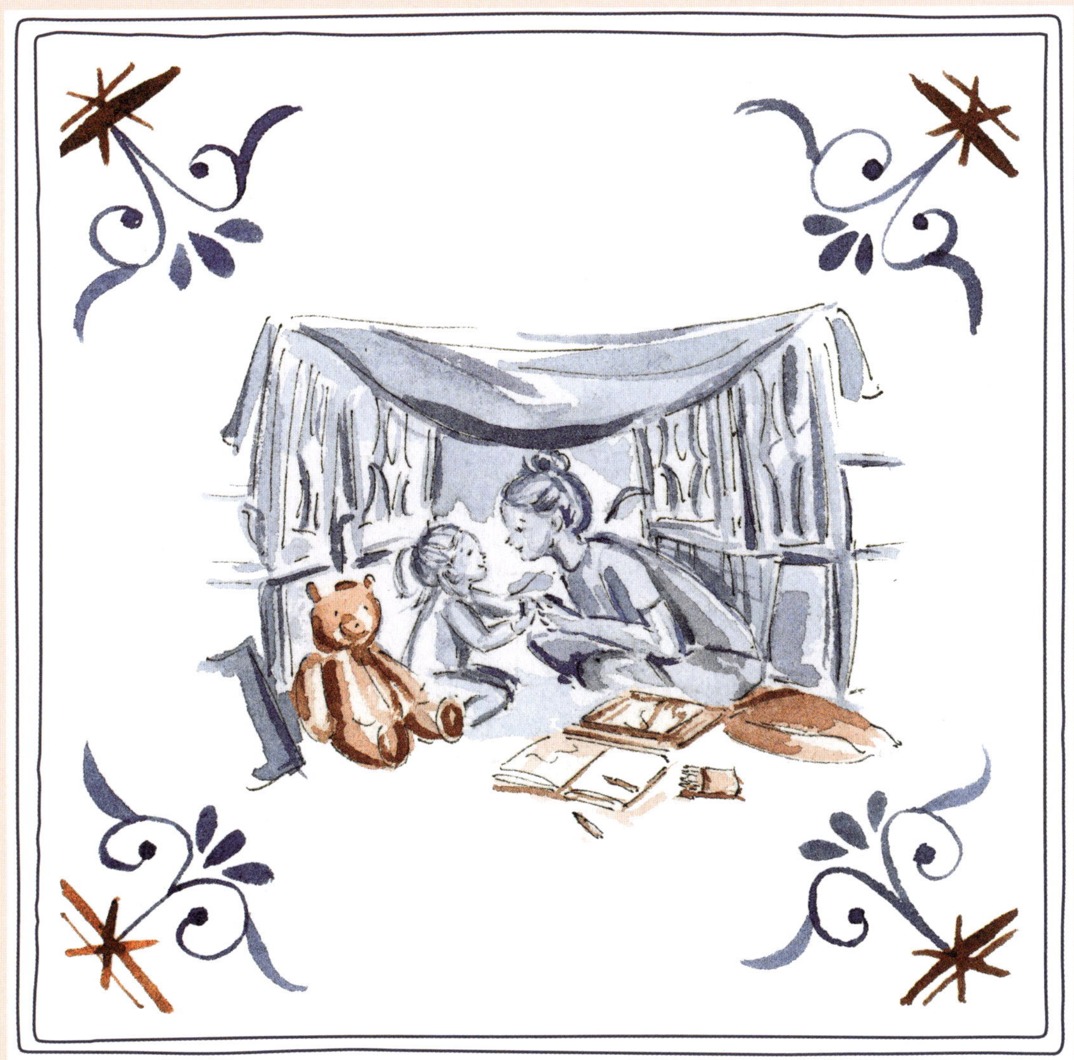

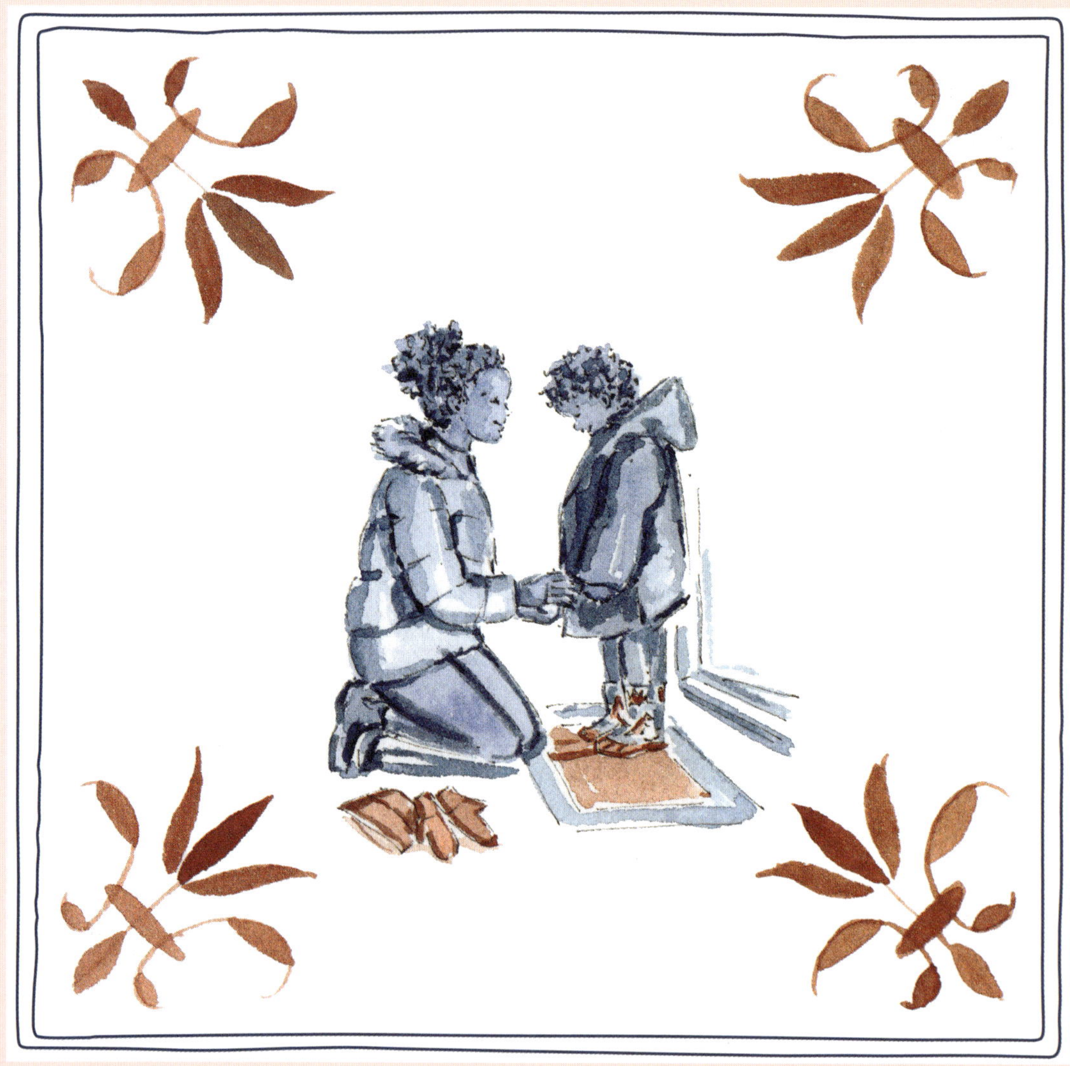

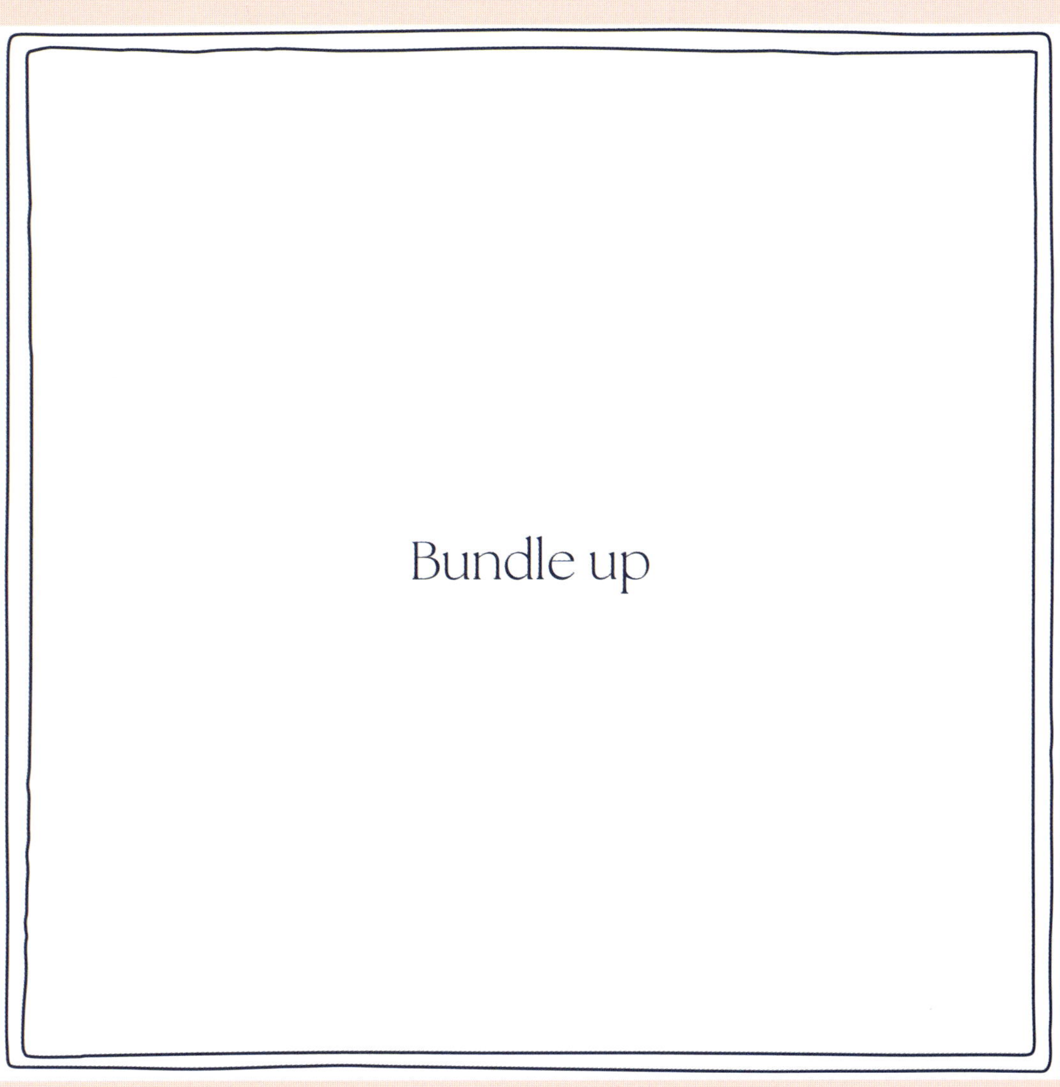

Bundle up

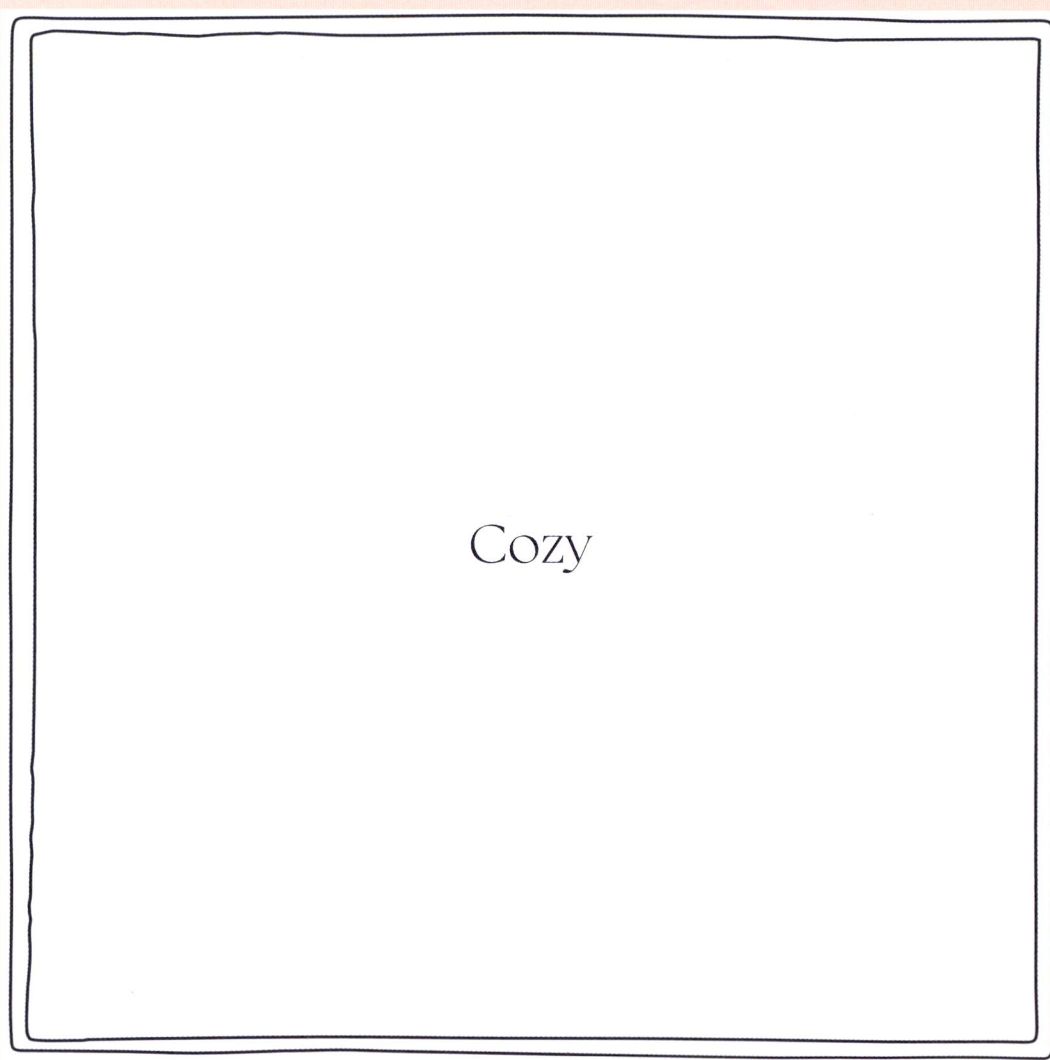

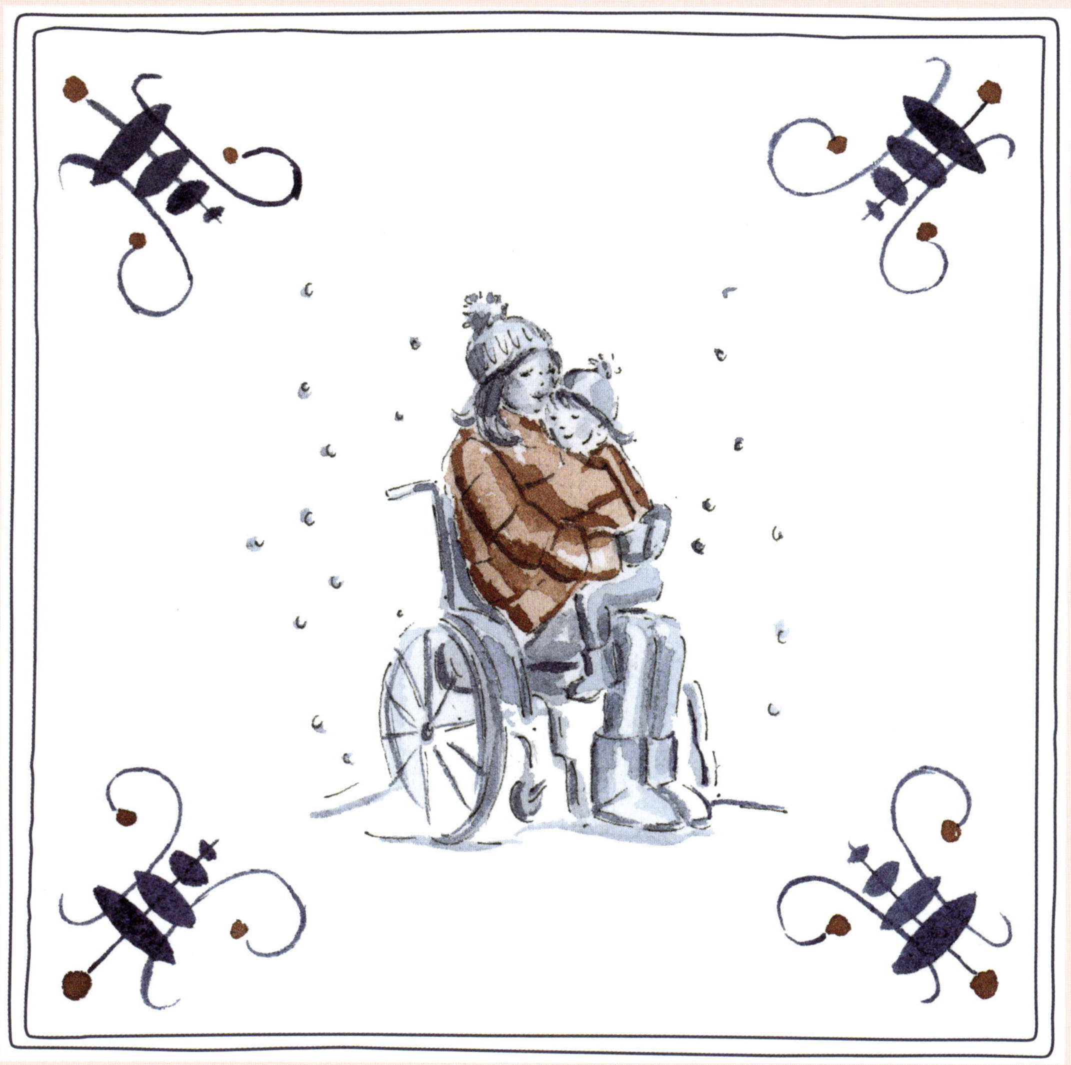

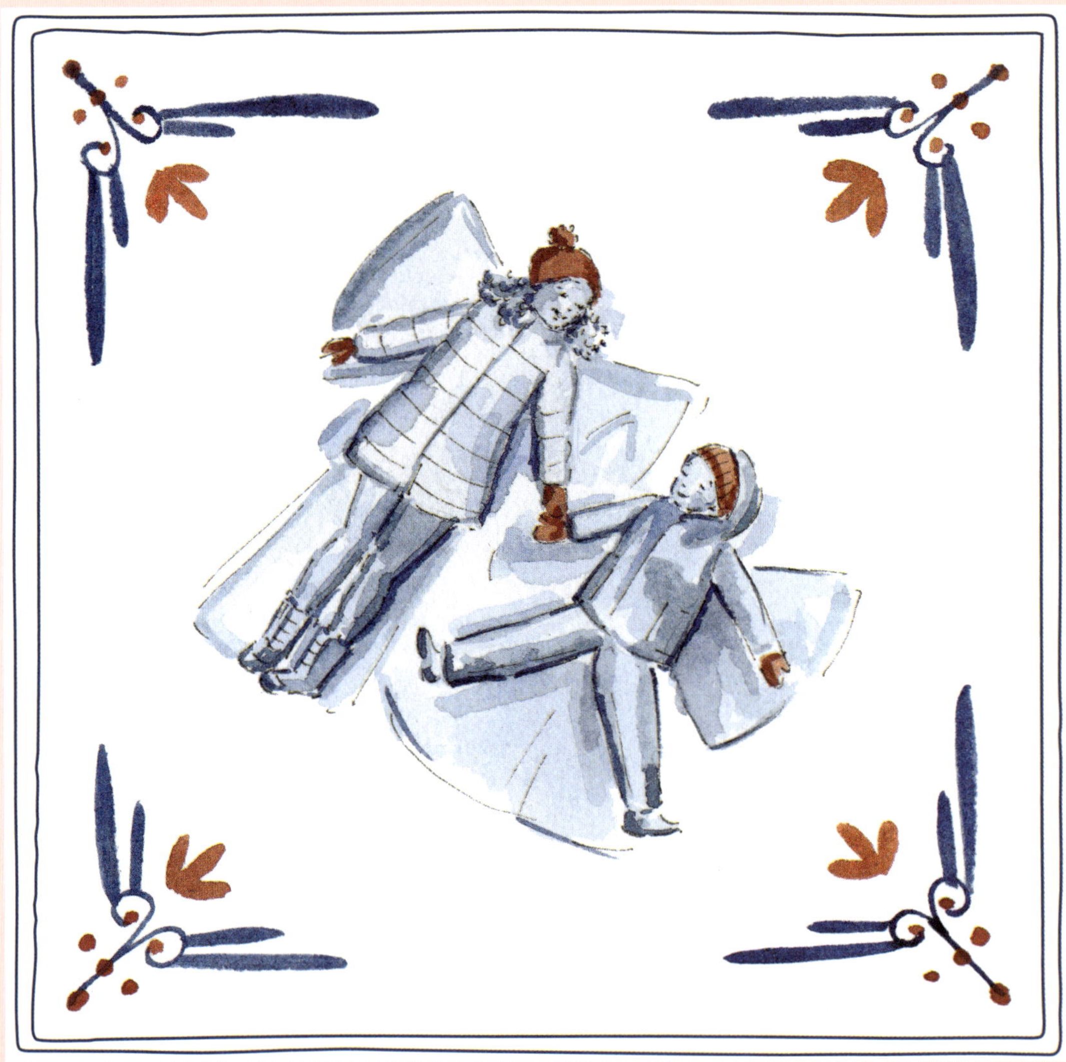

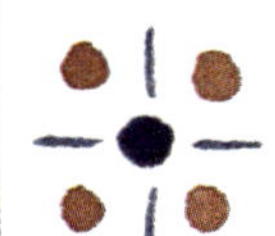
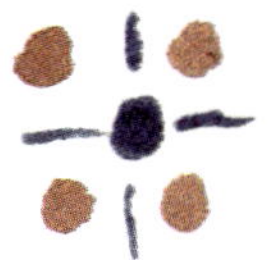
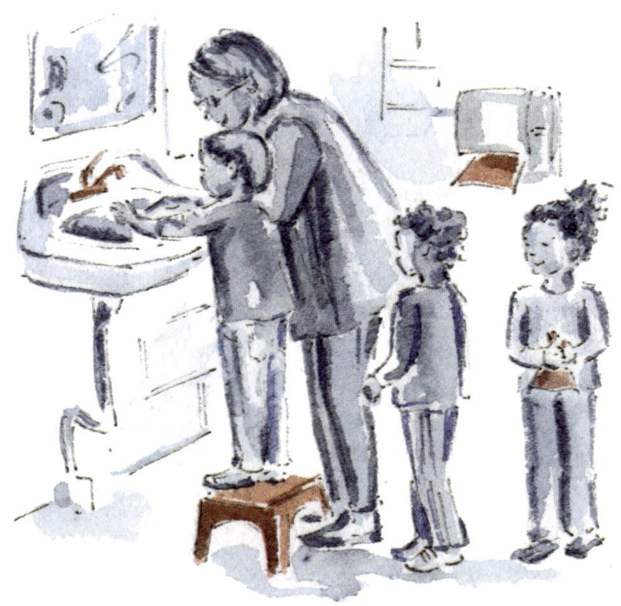
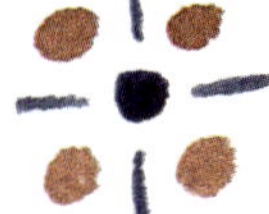
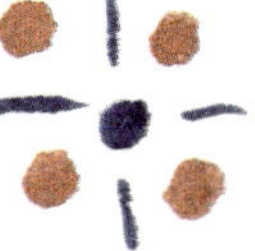

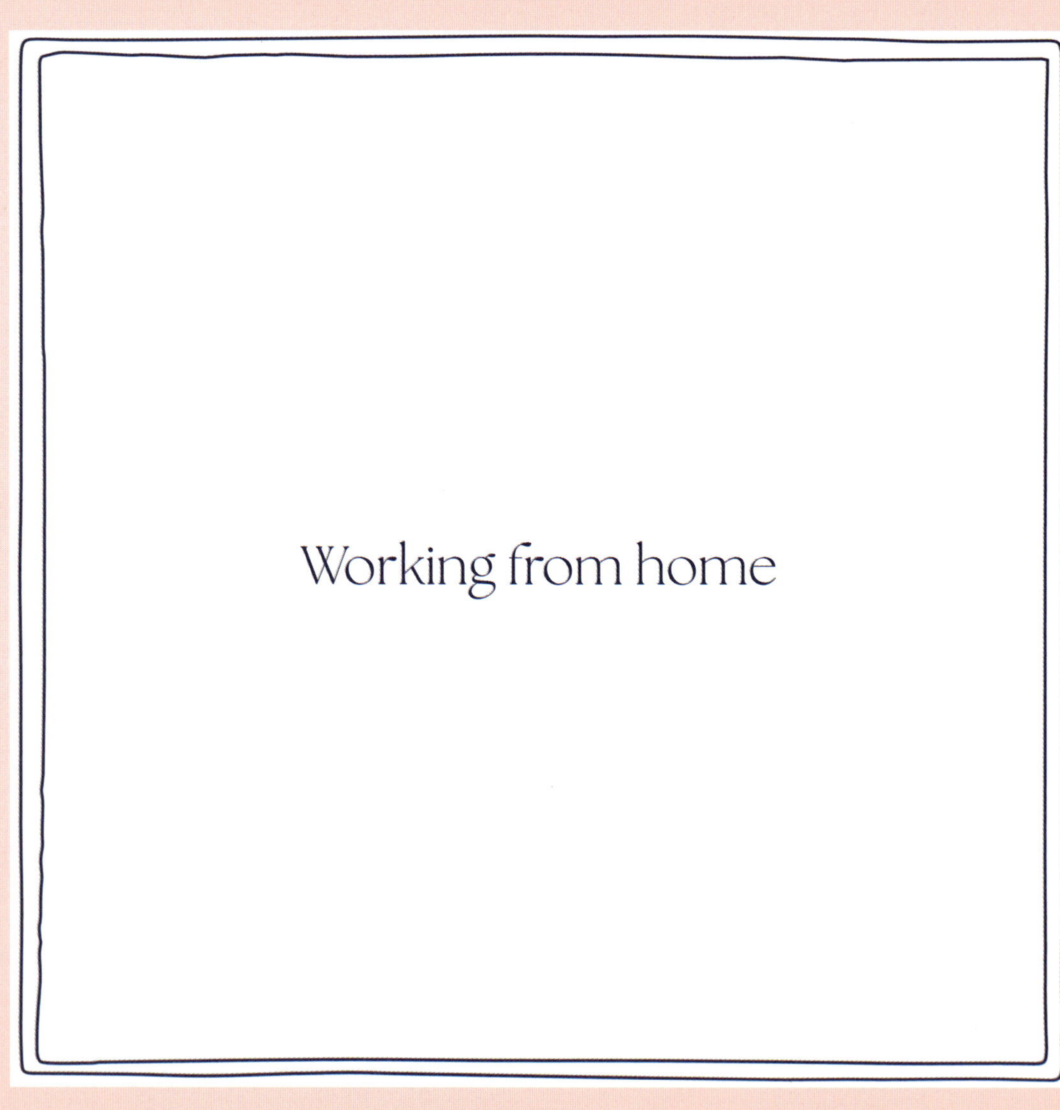
Working from home

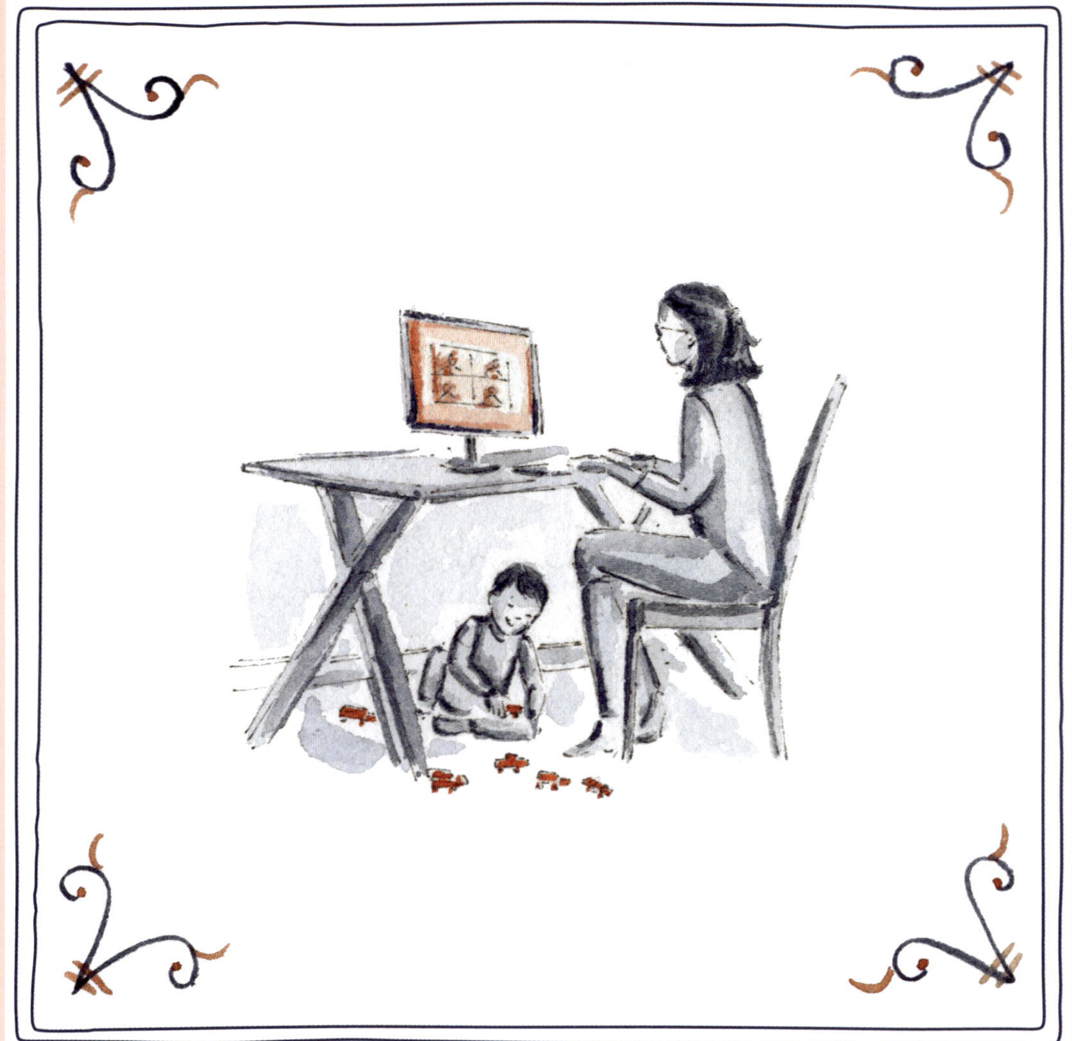

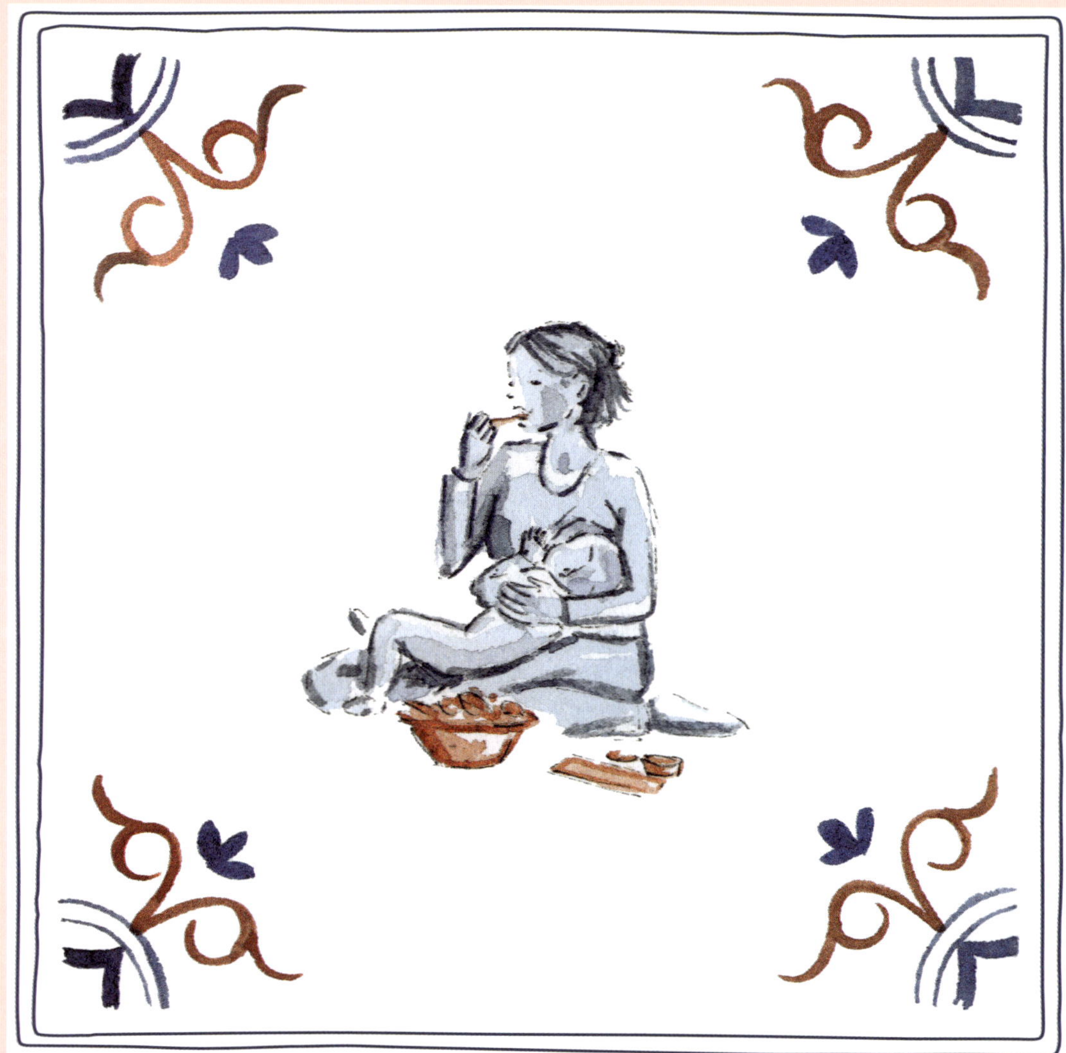

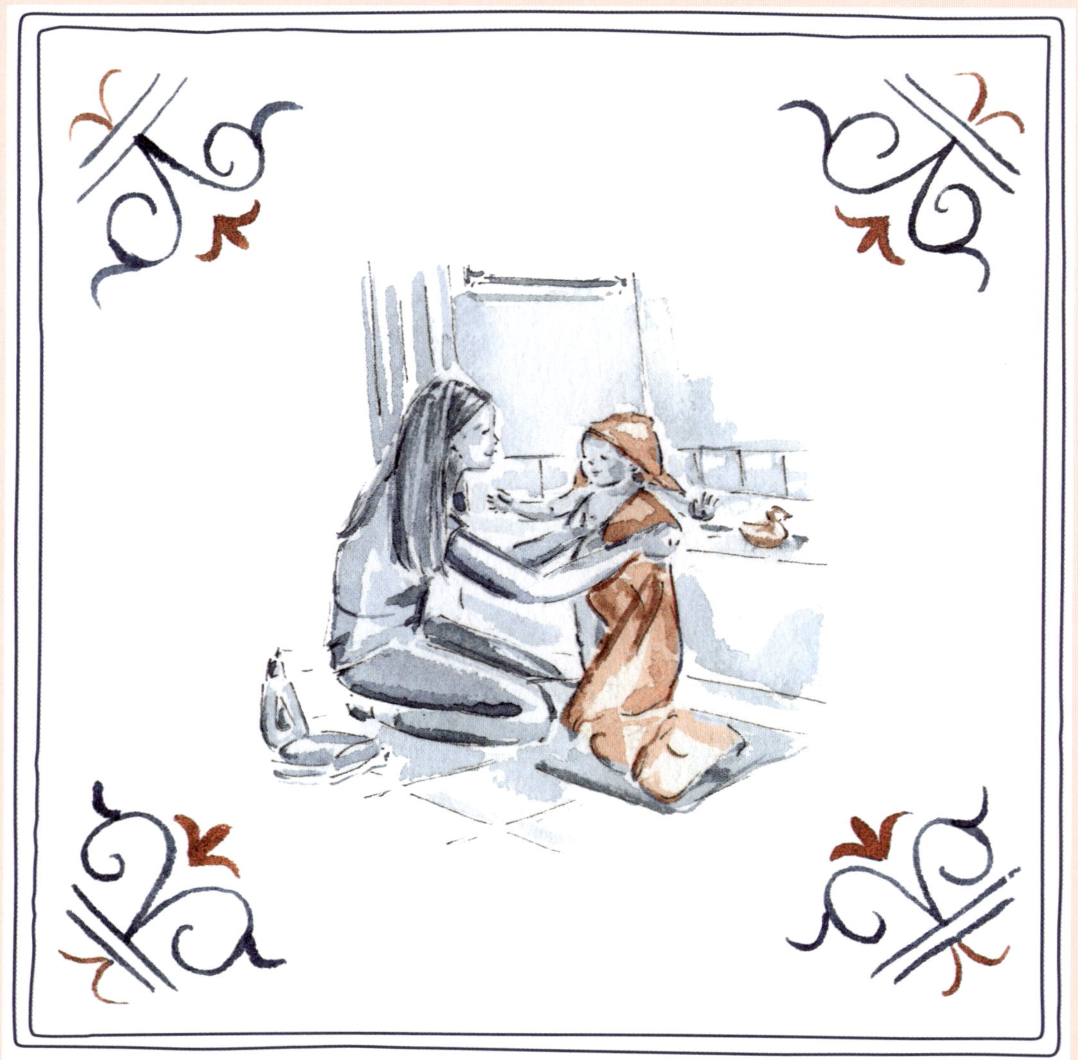

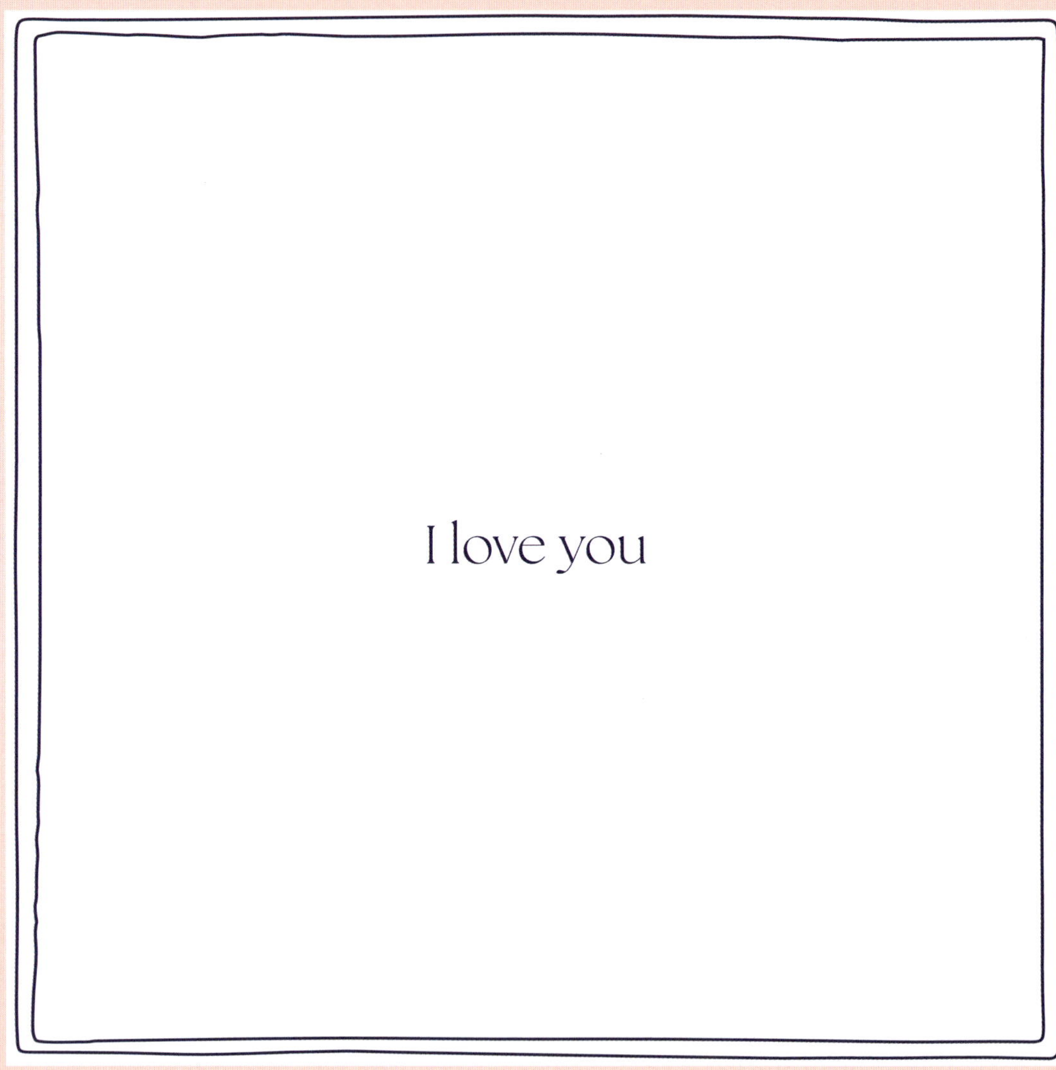

I love you

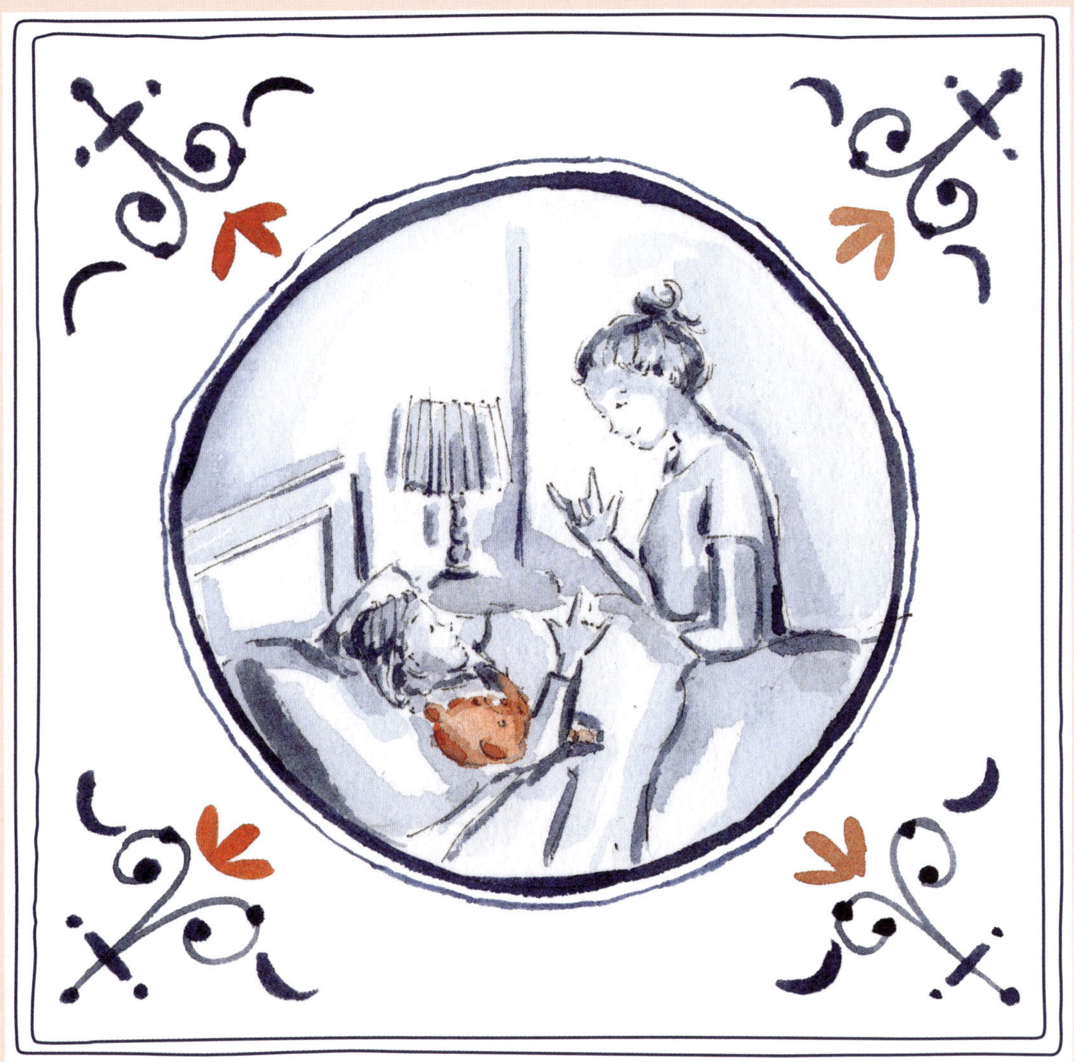

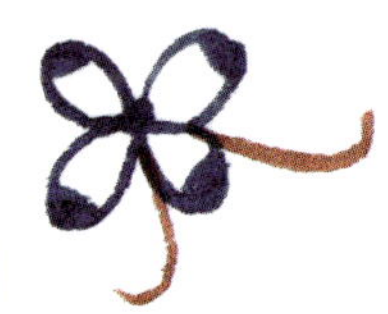
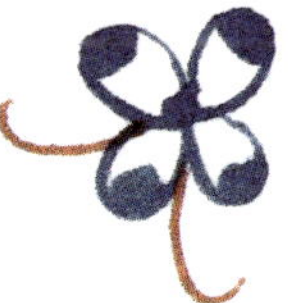
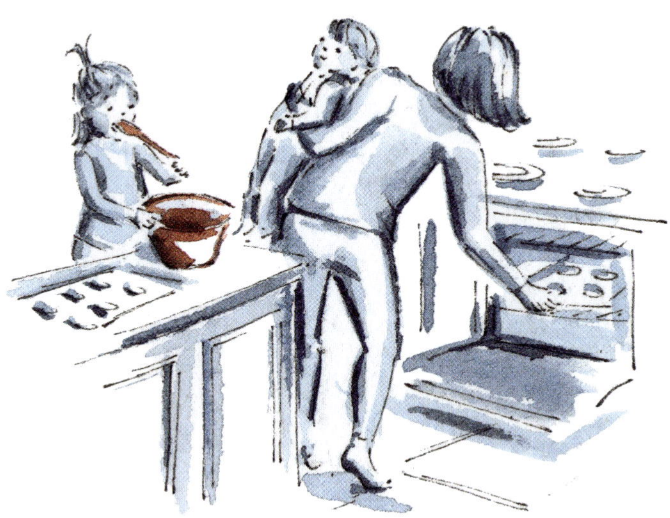
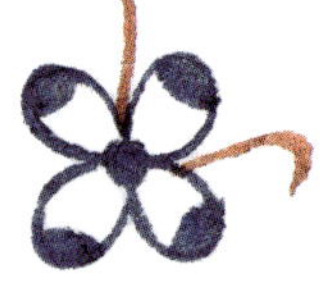
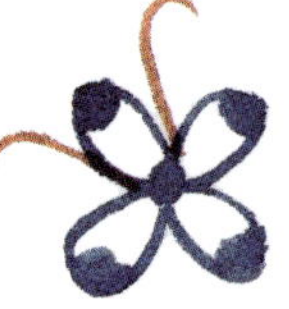

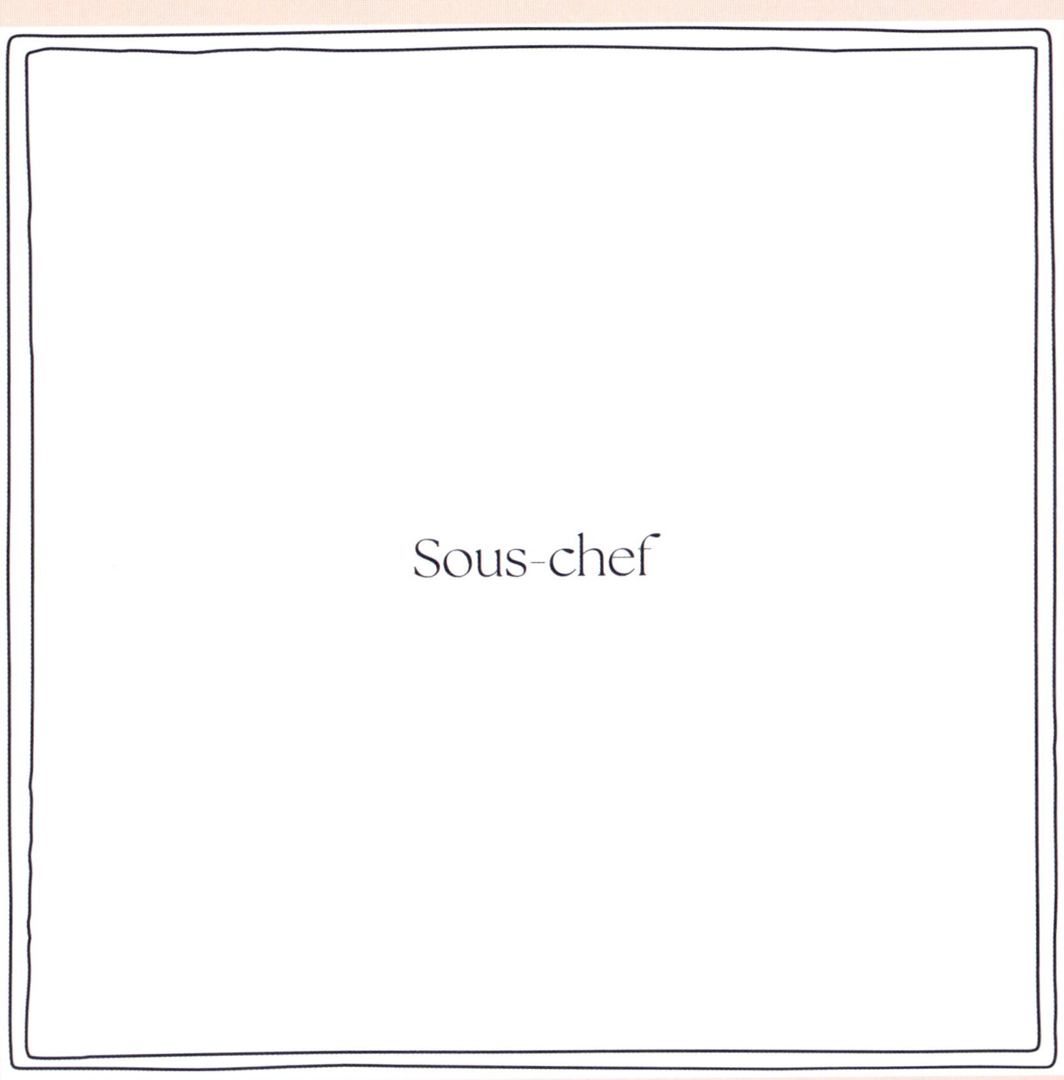

Sous-chef

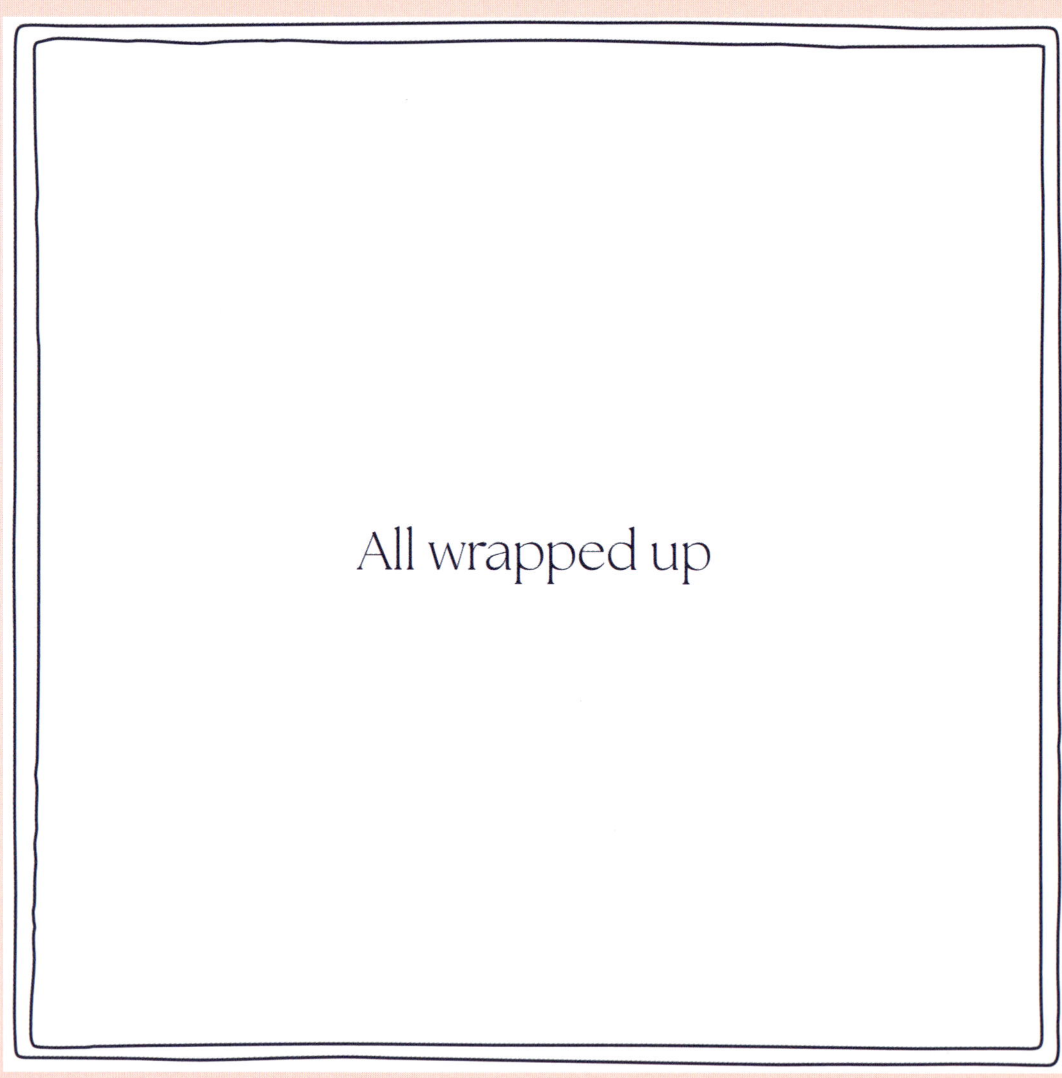
All wrapped up

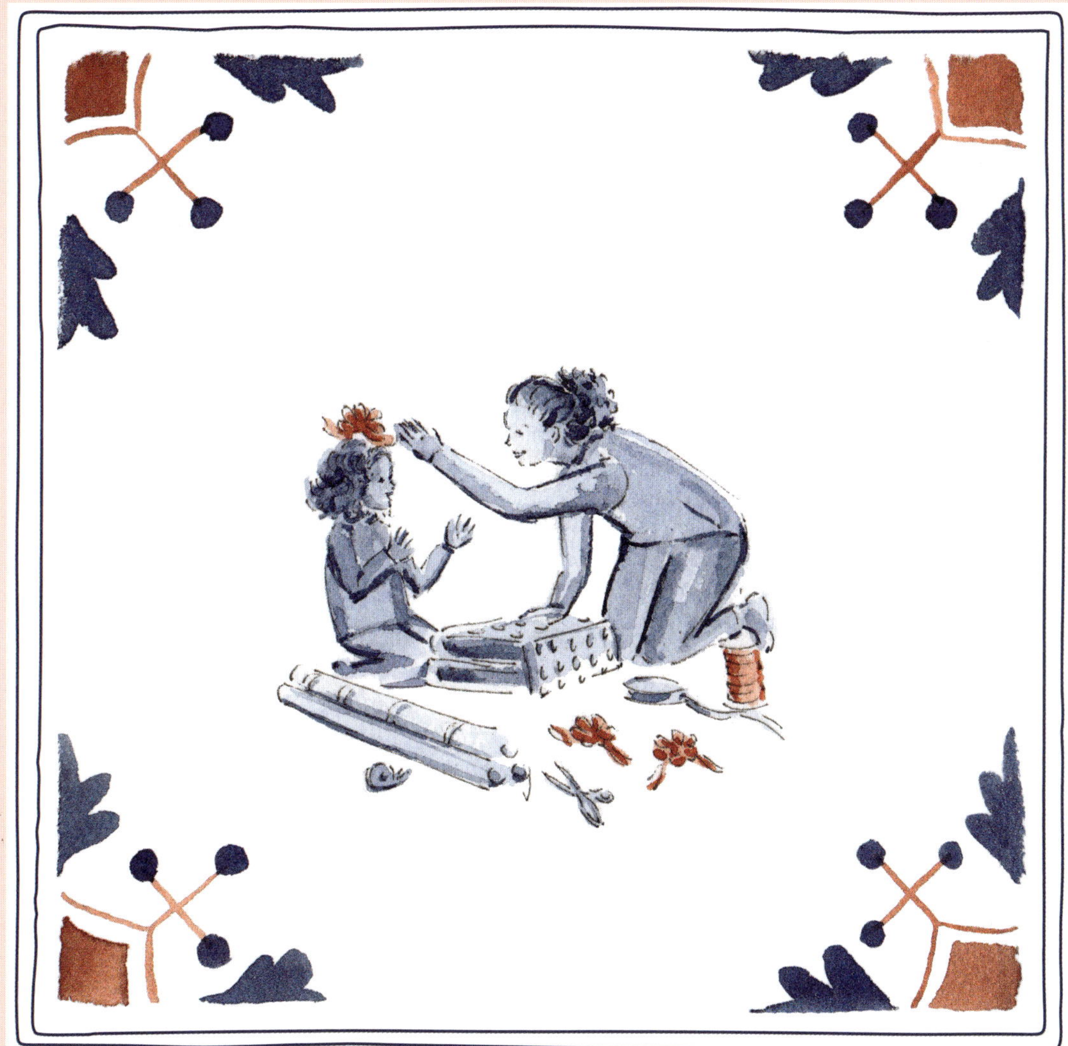

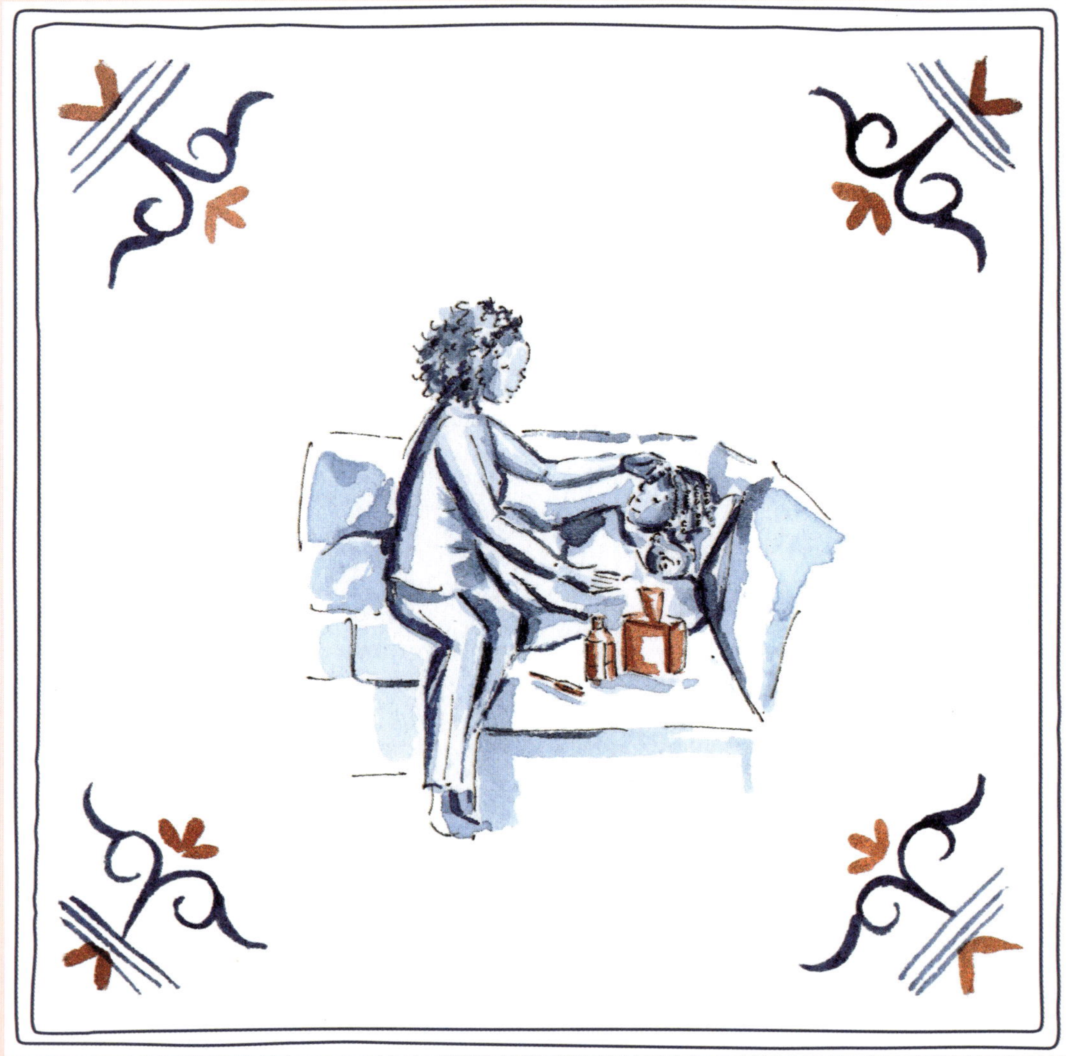

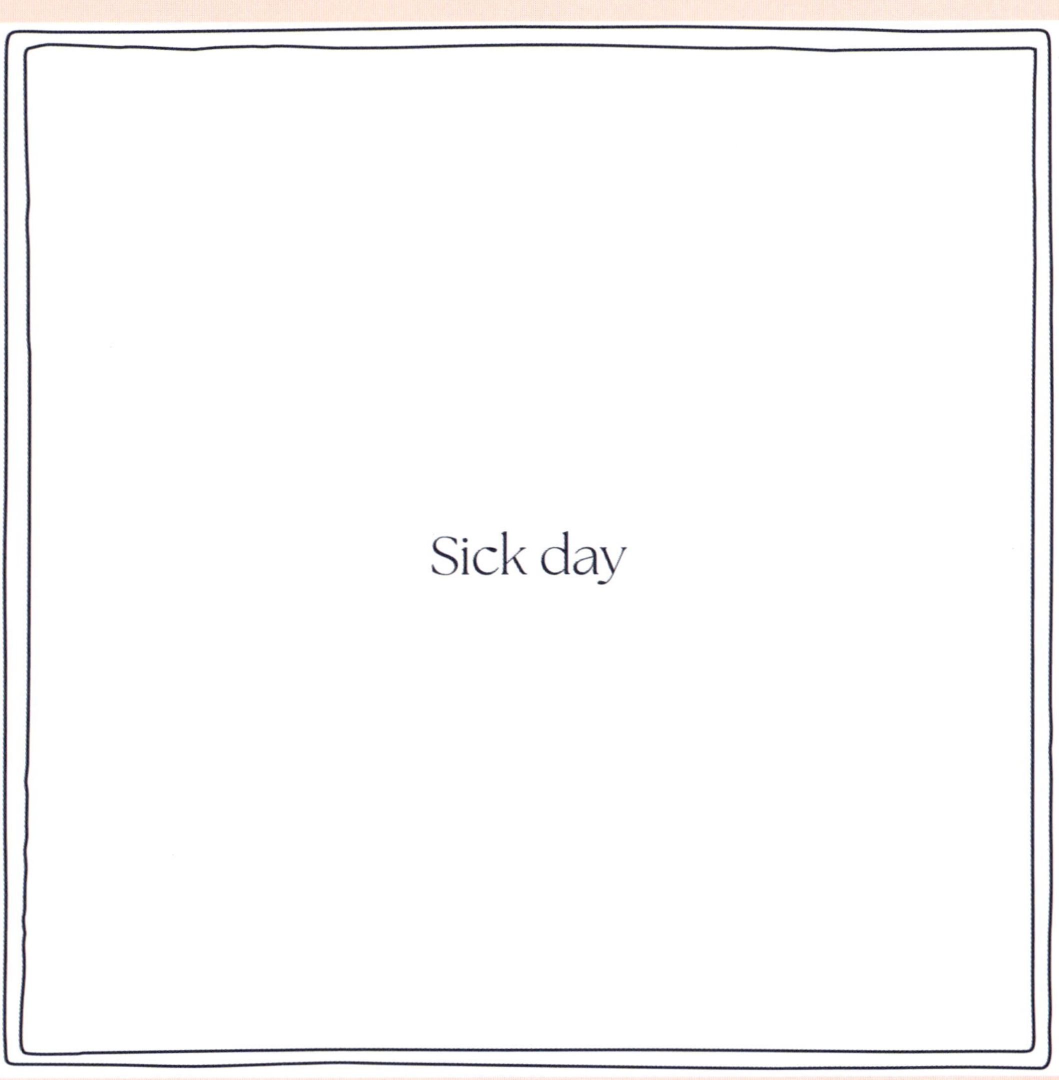
Sick day

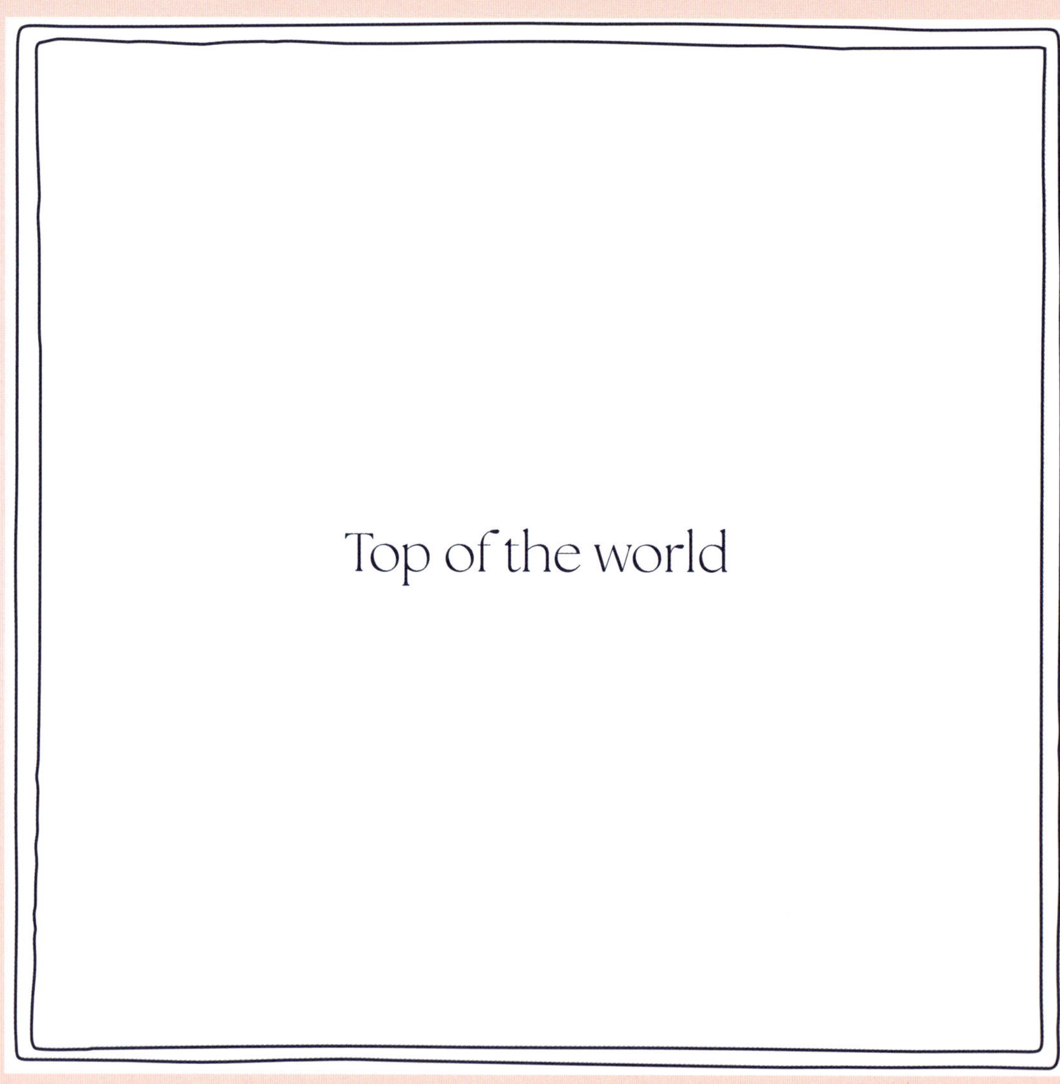

Top of the world

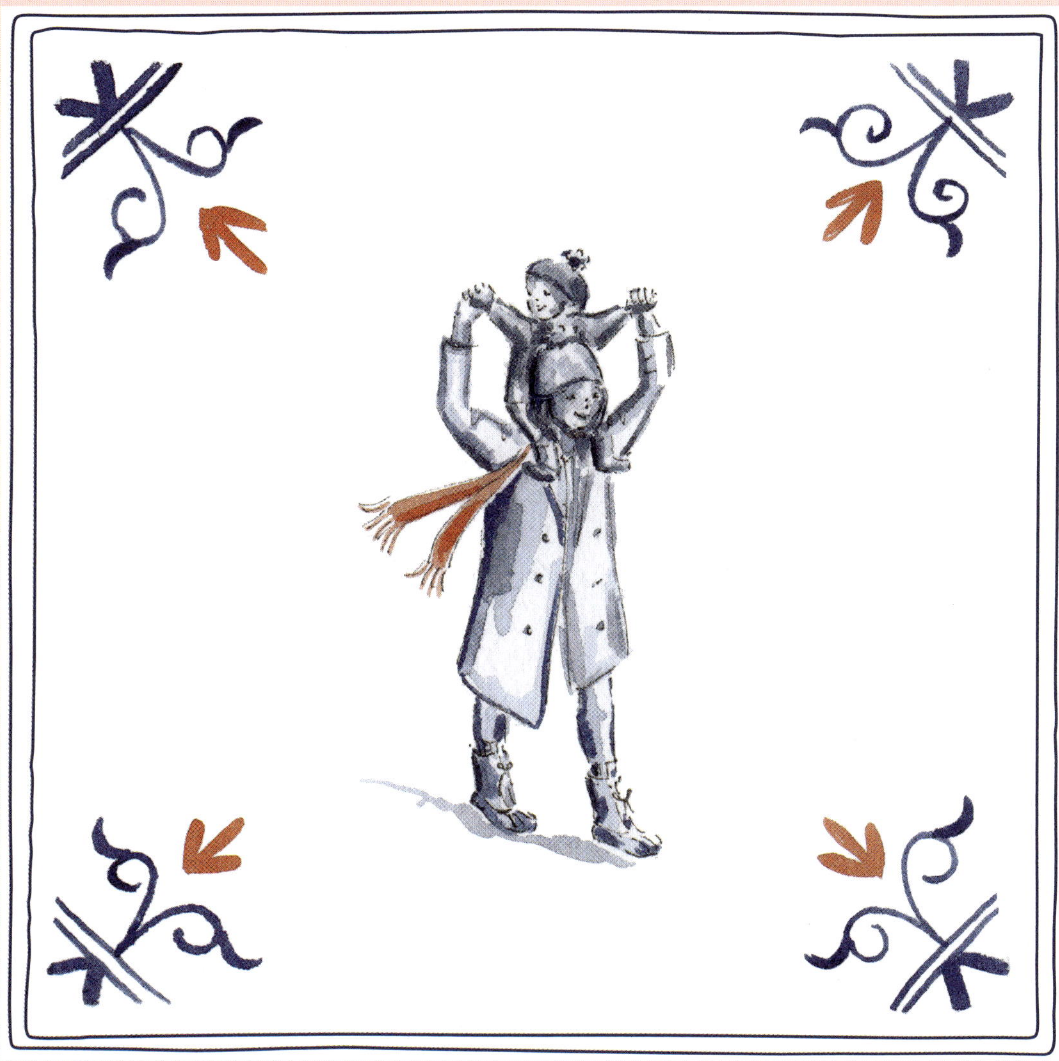

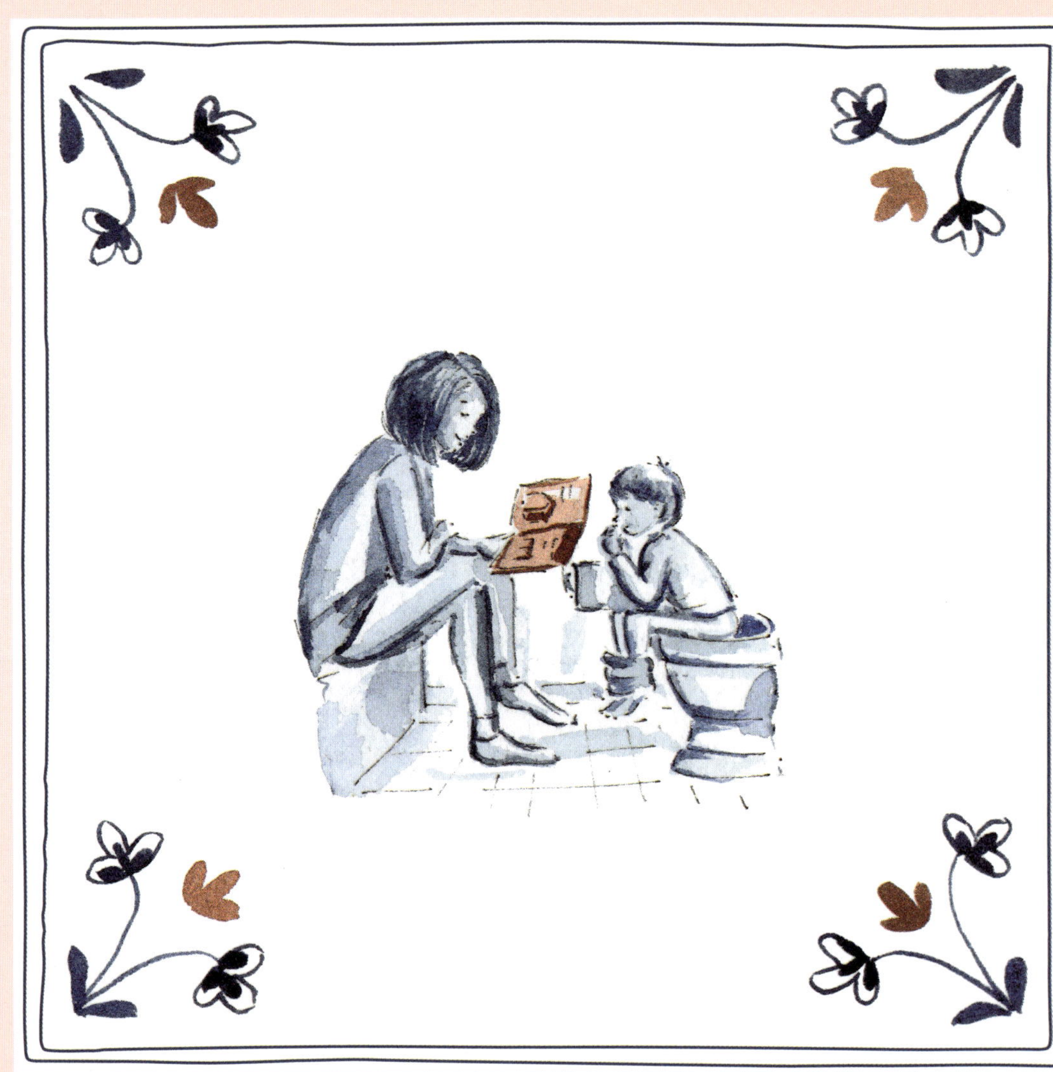

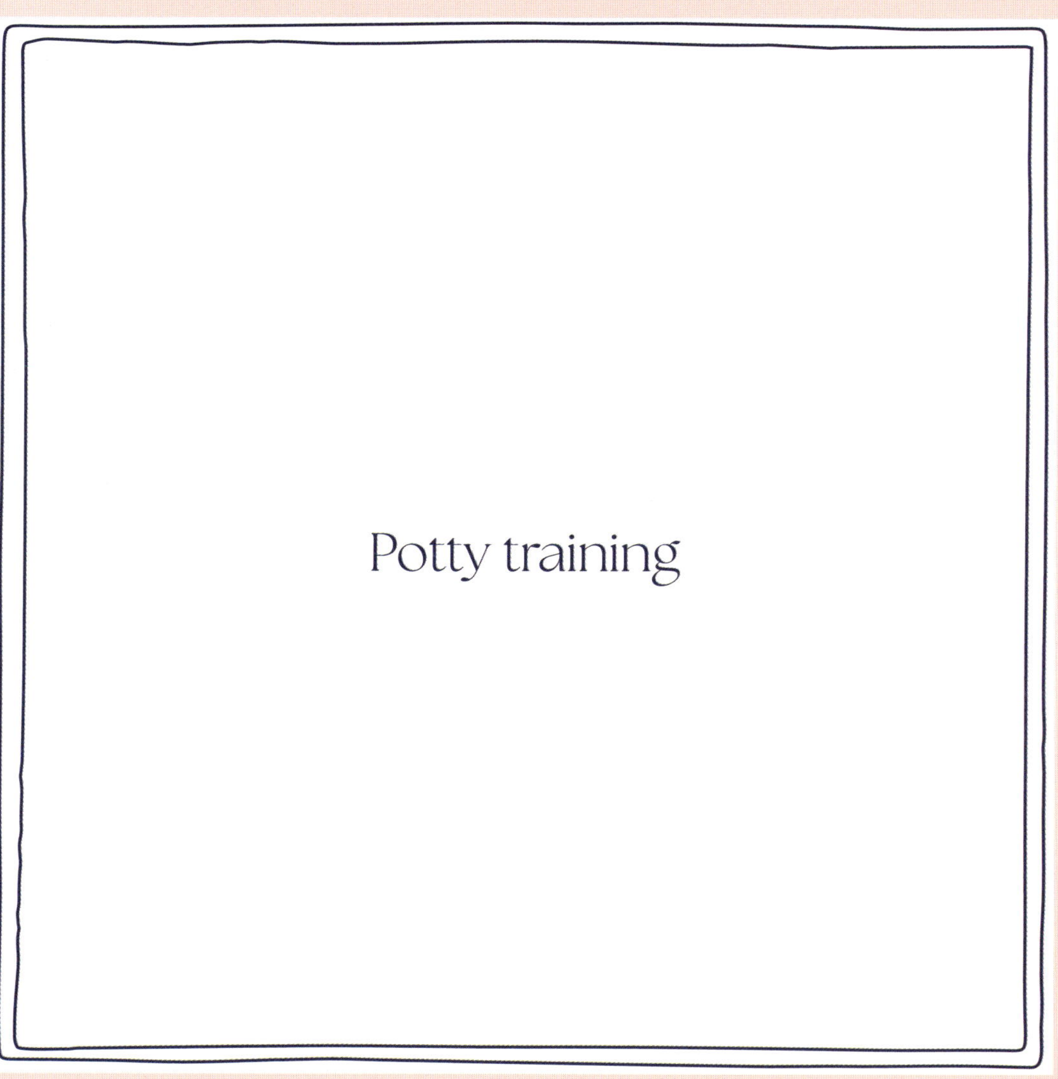

Potty training

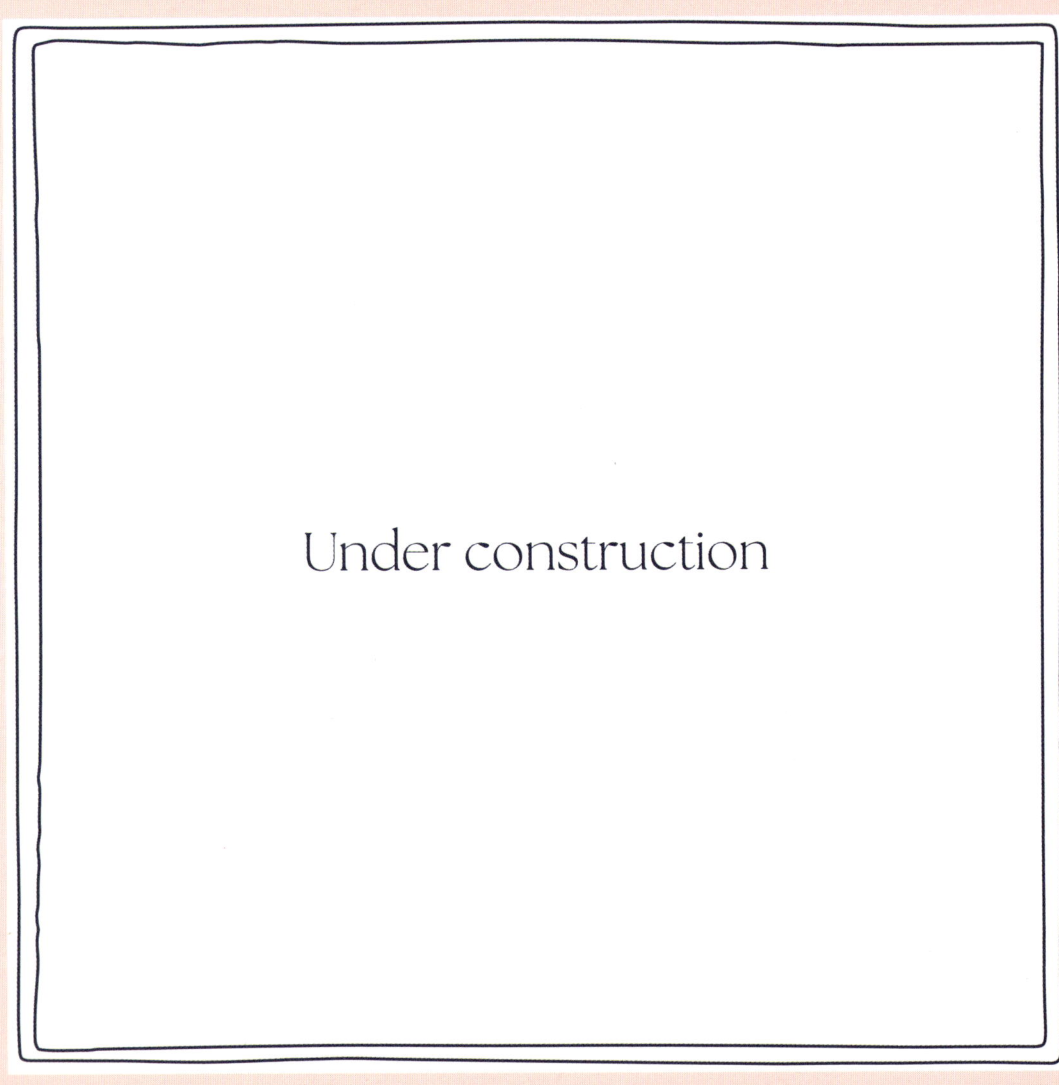
Under construction

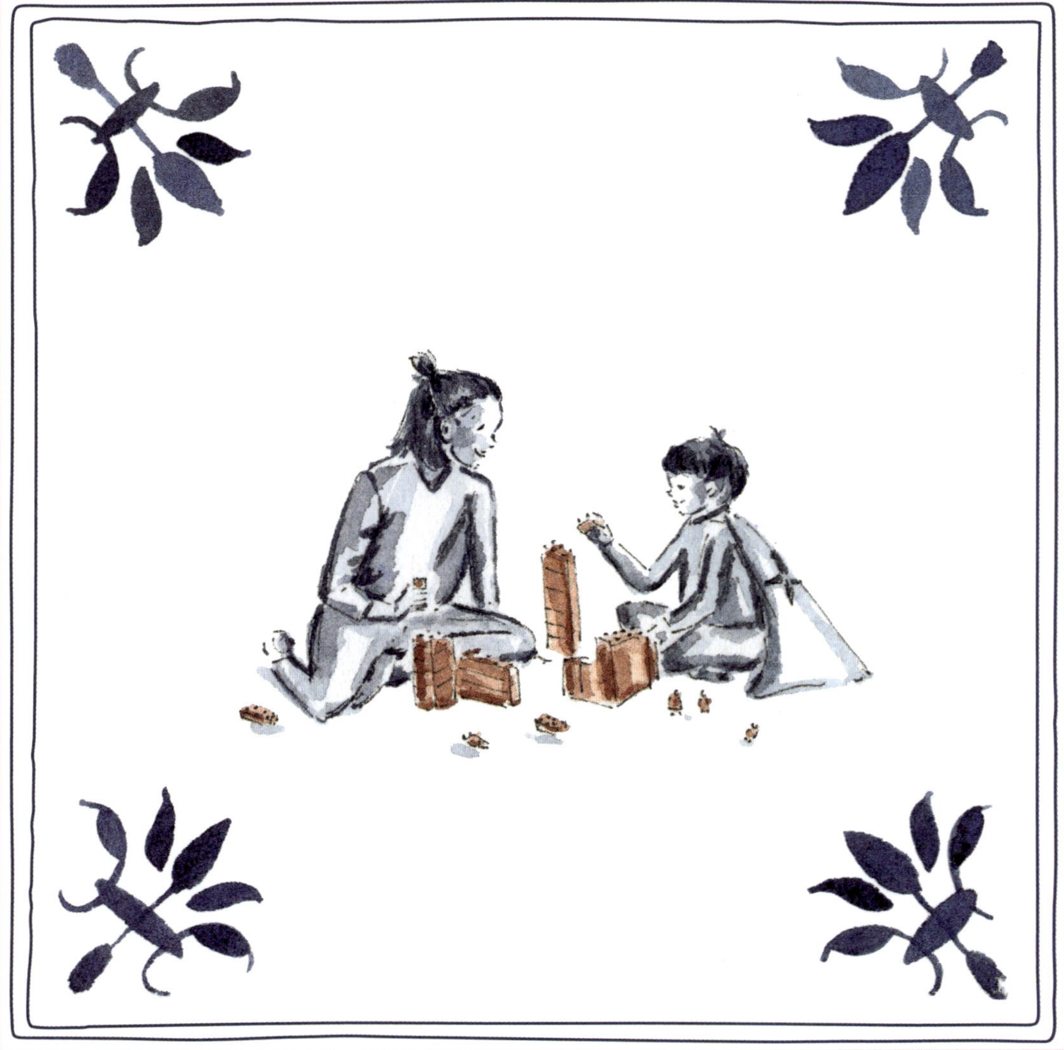

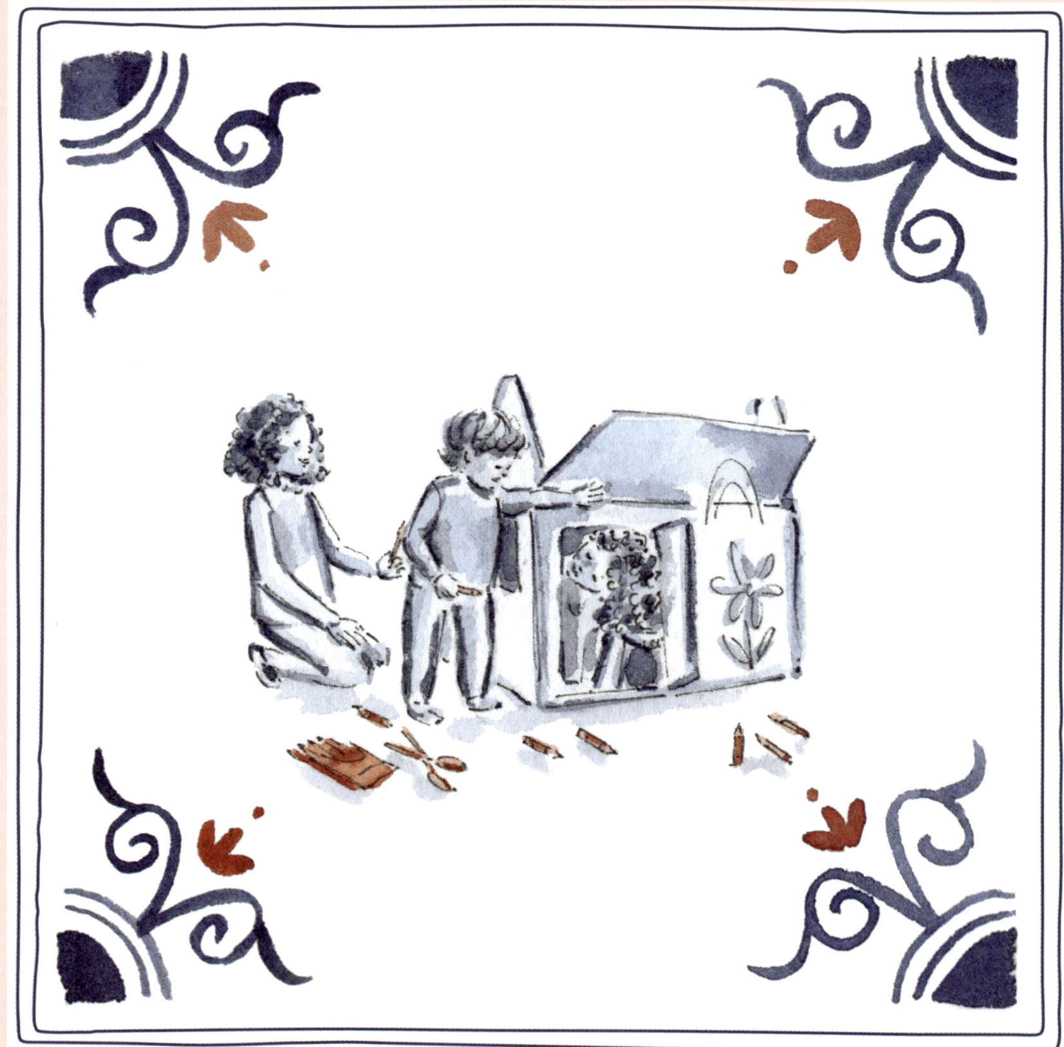

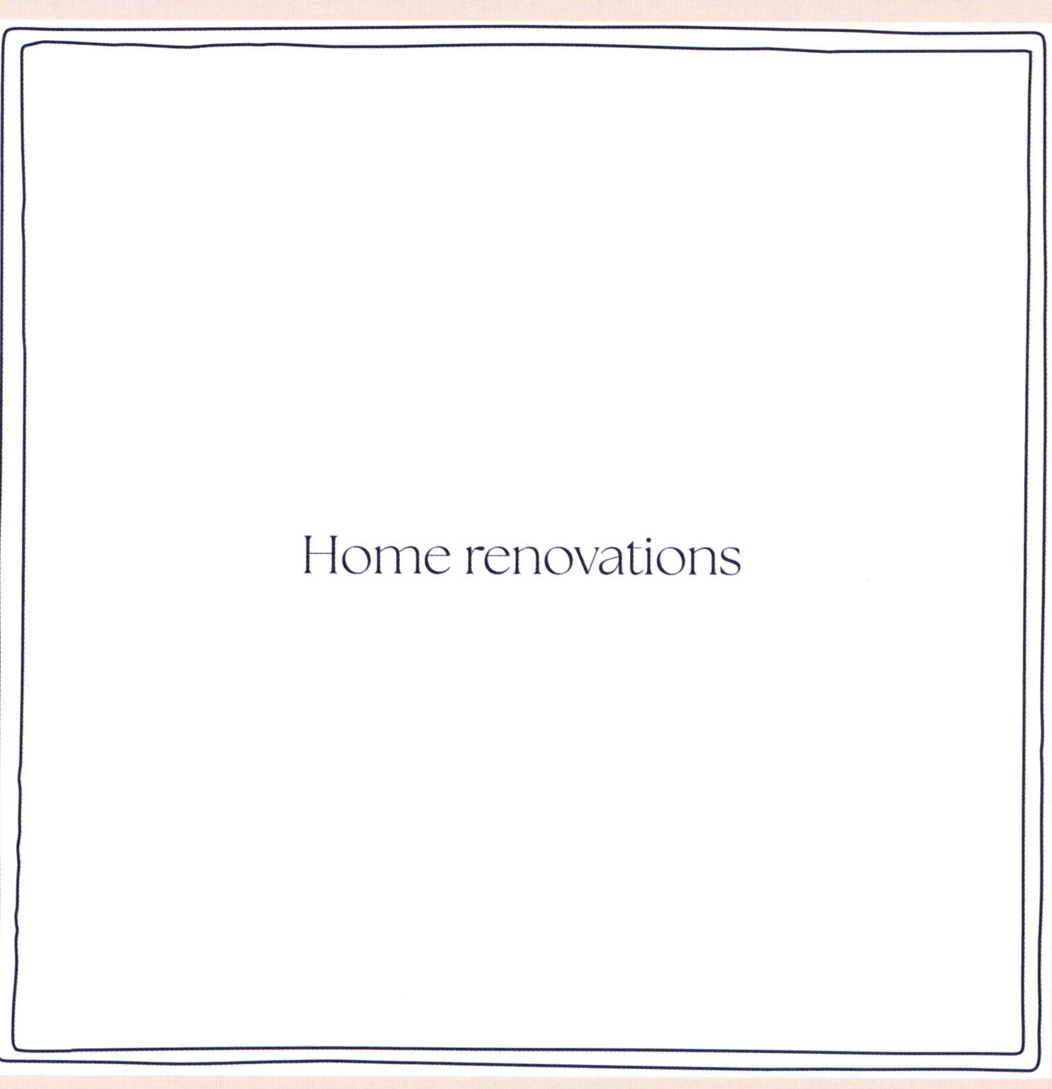

Home renovations

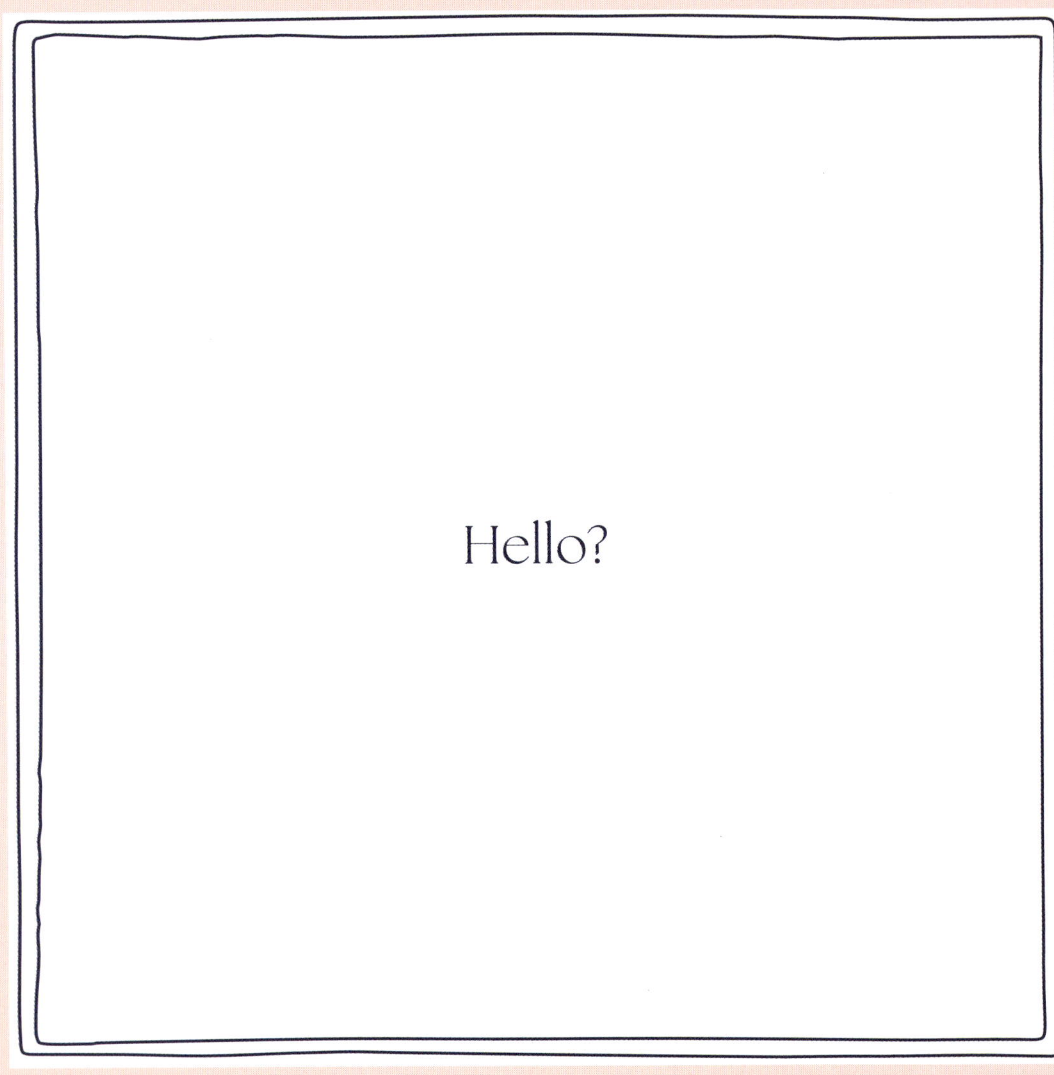

Hello?

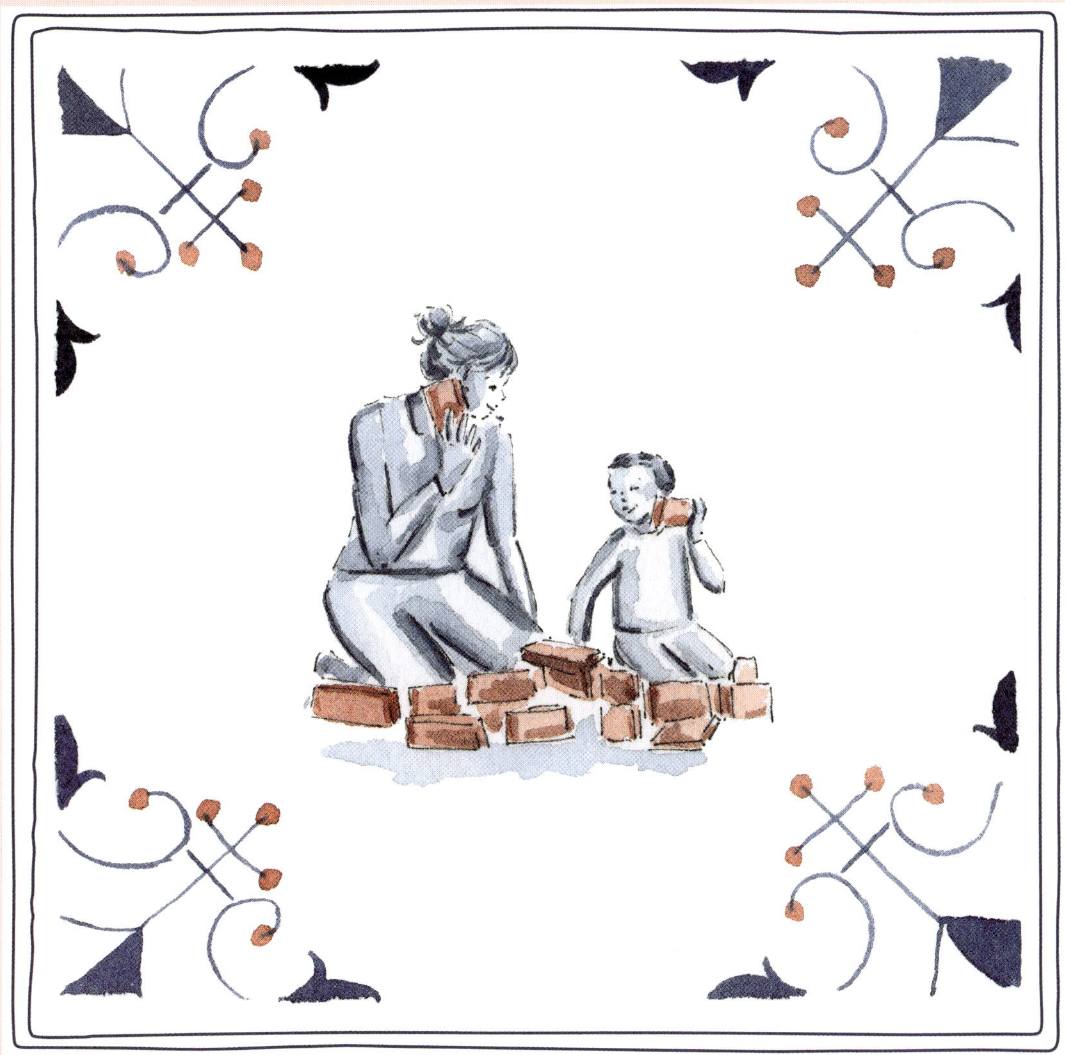

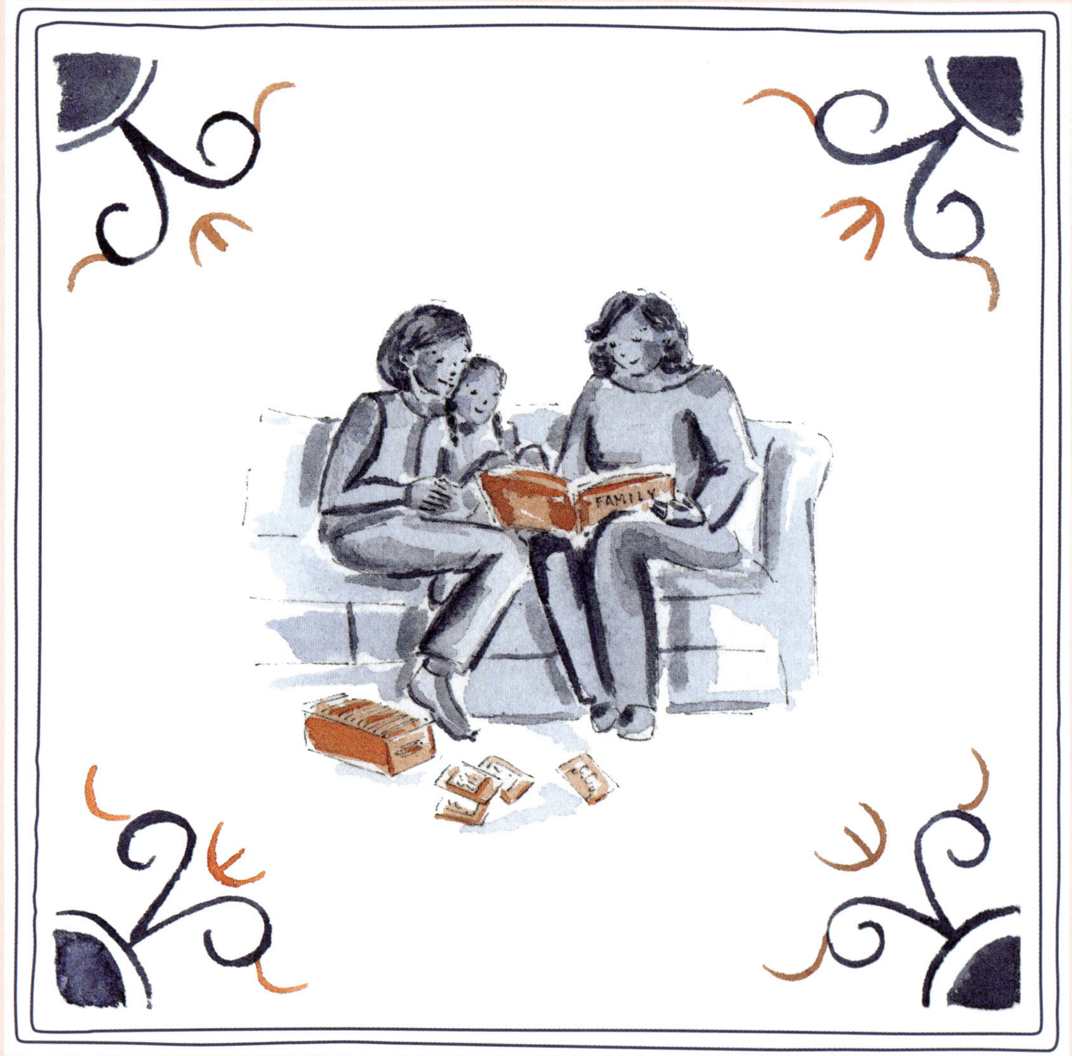

FAMILY

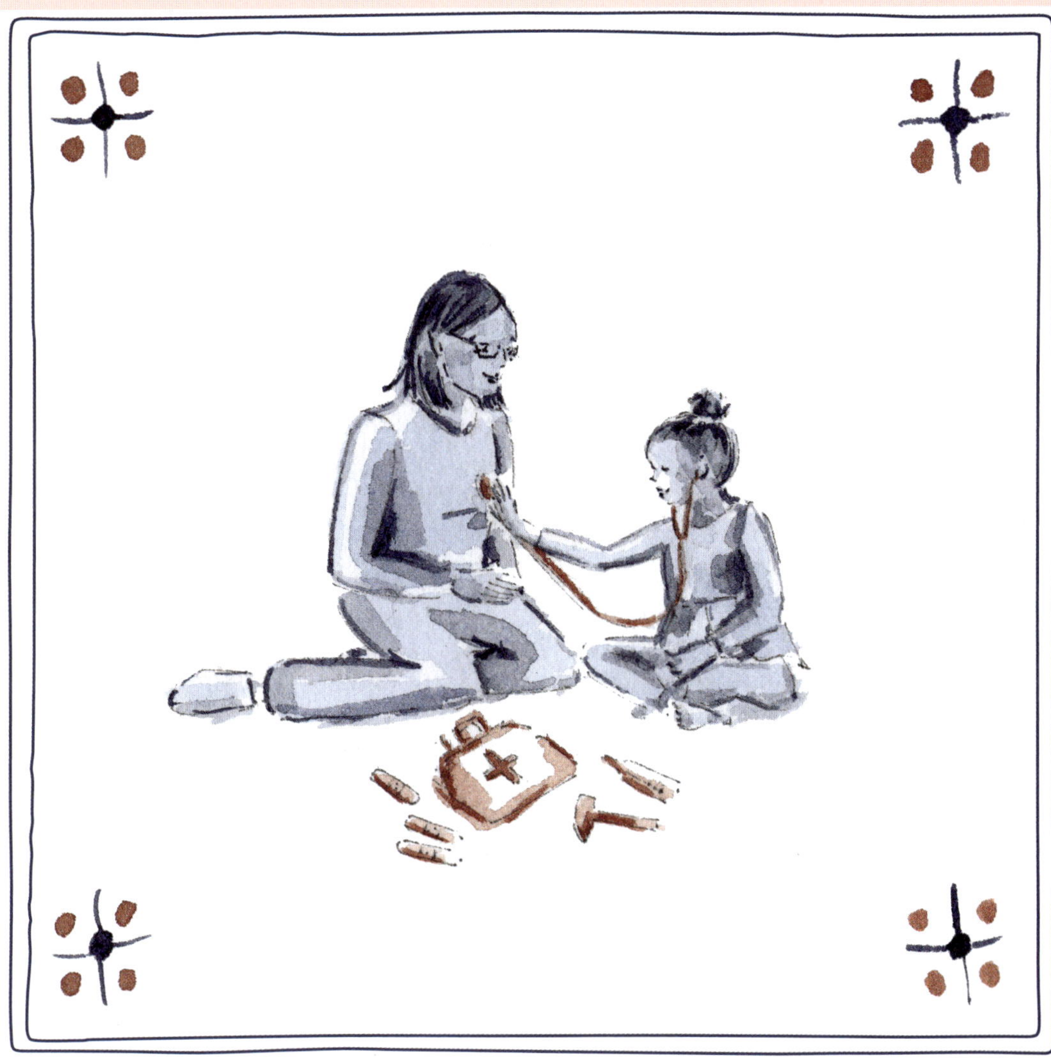

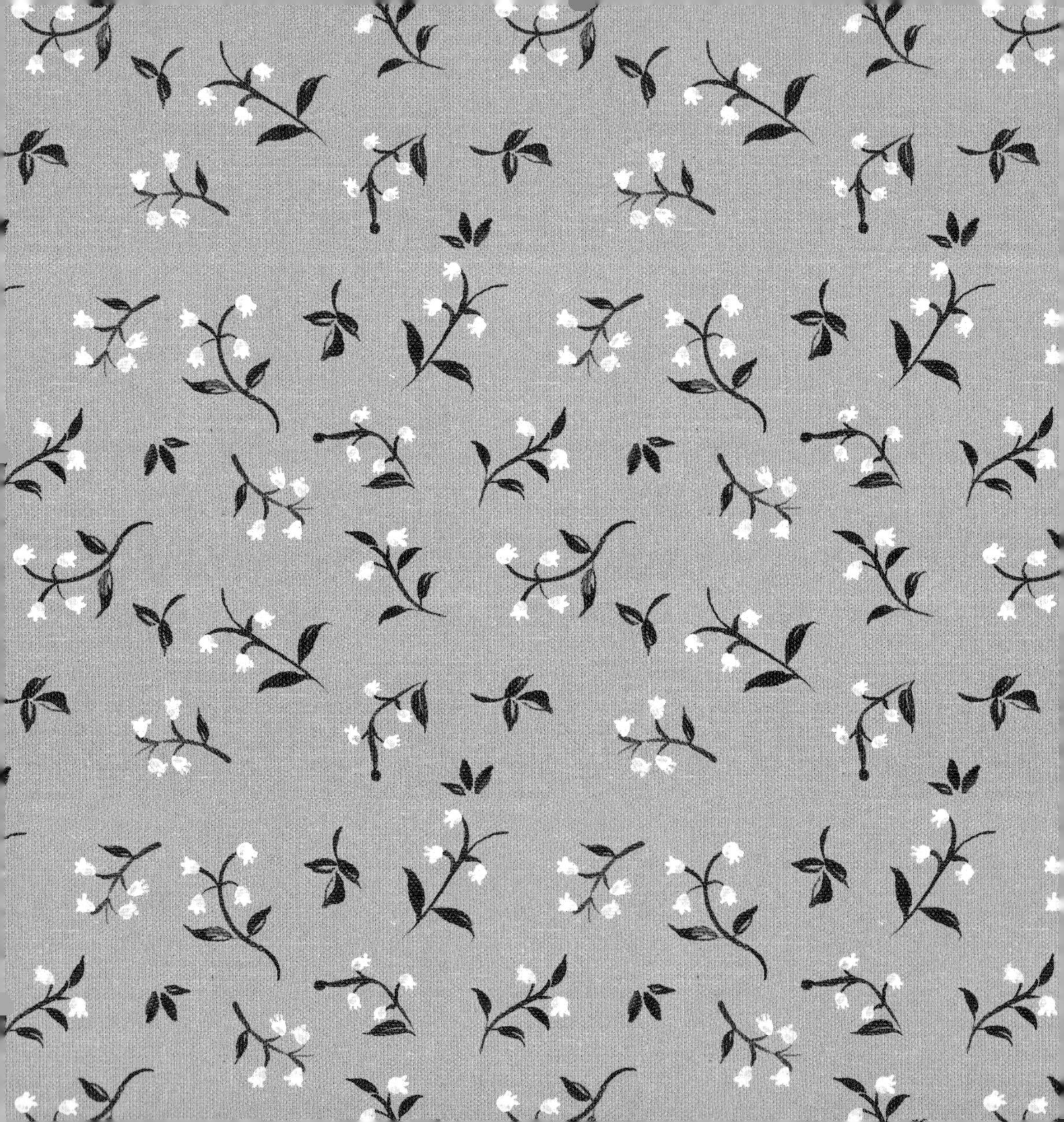

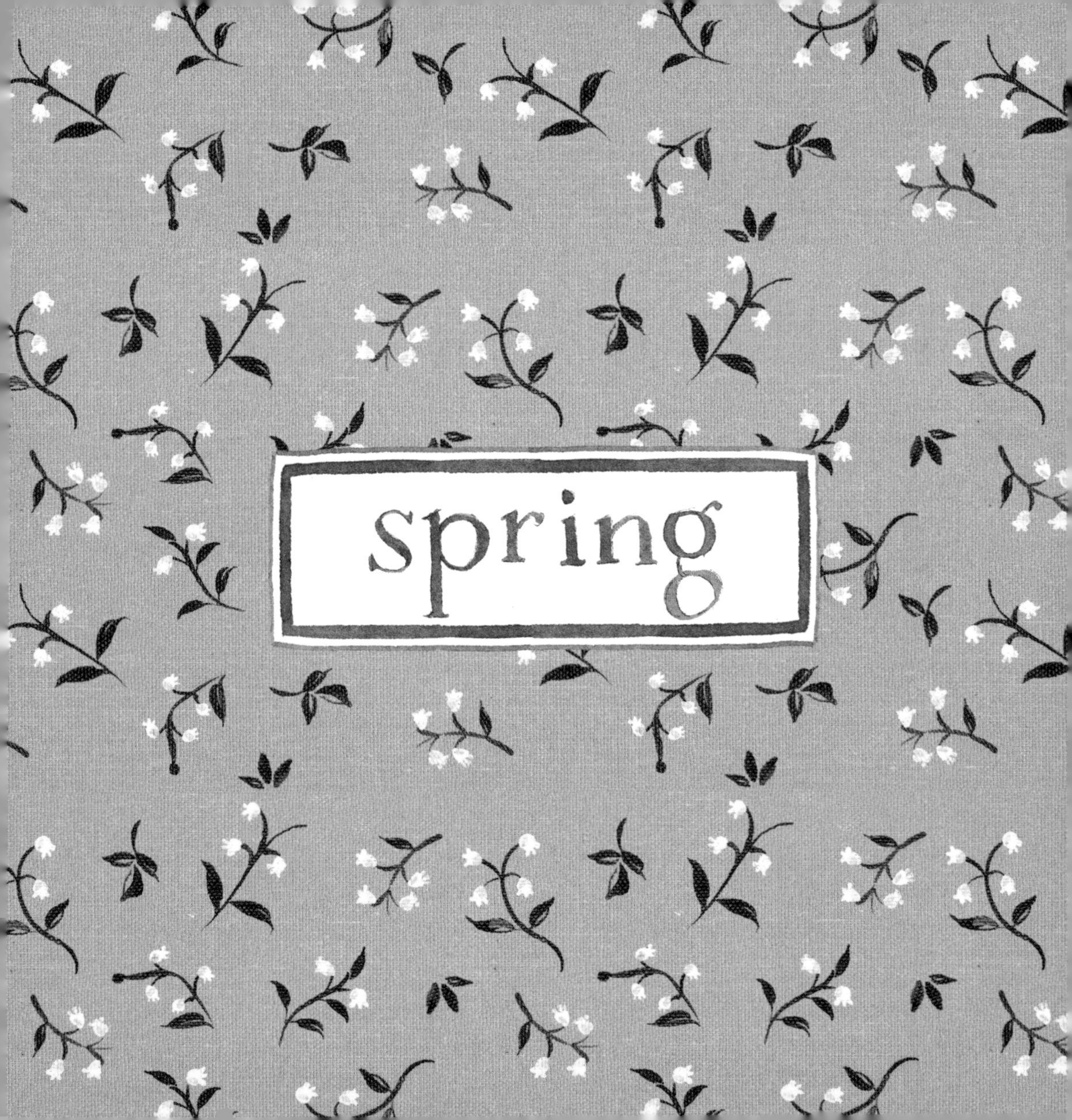
spring

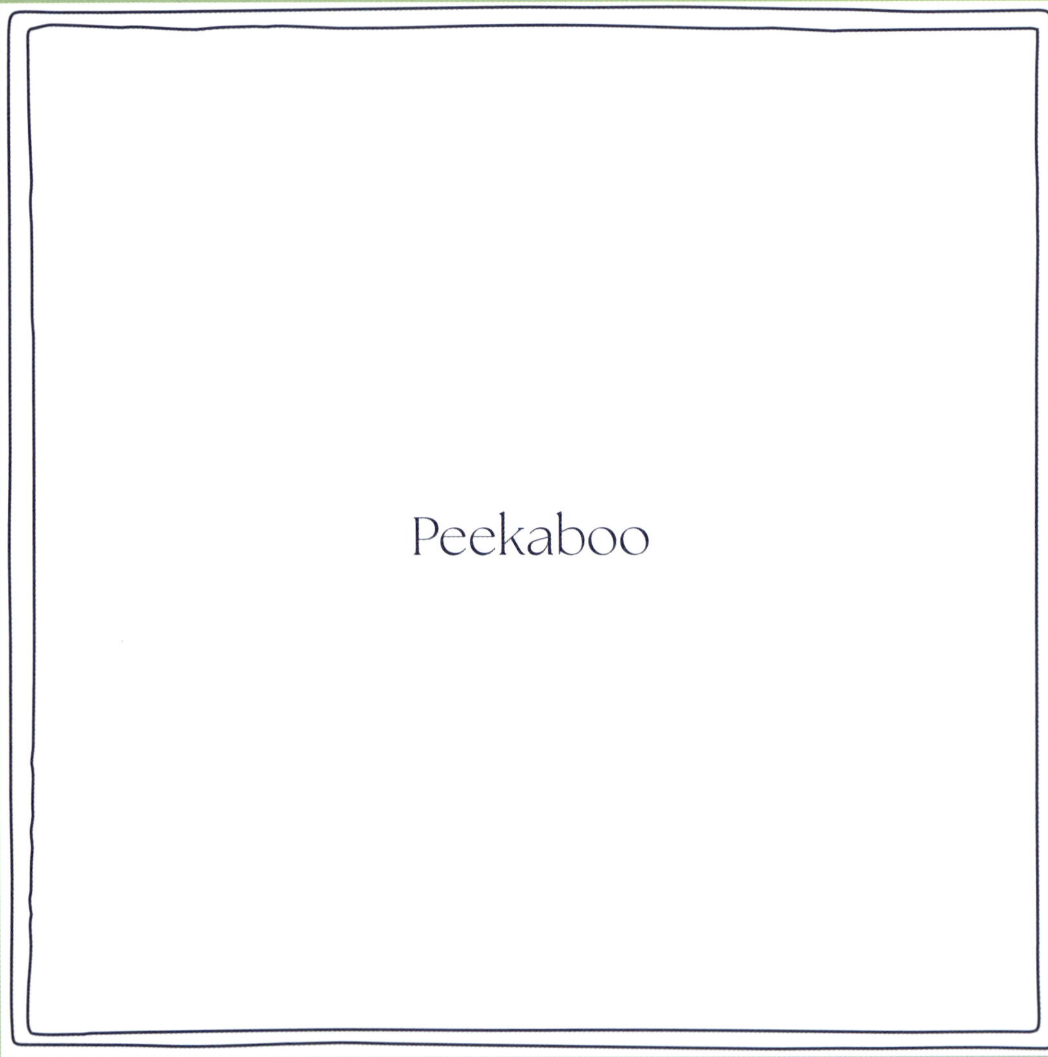

Peekaboo

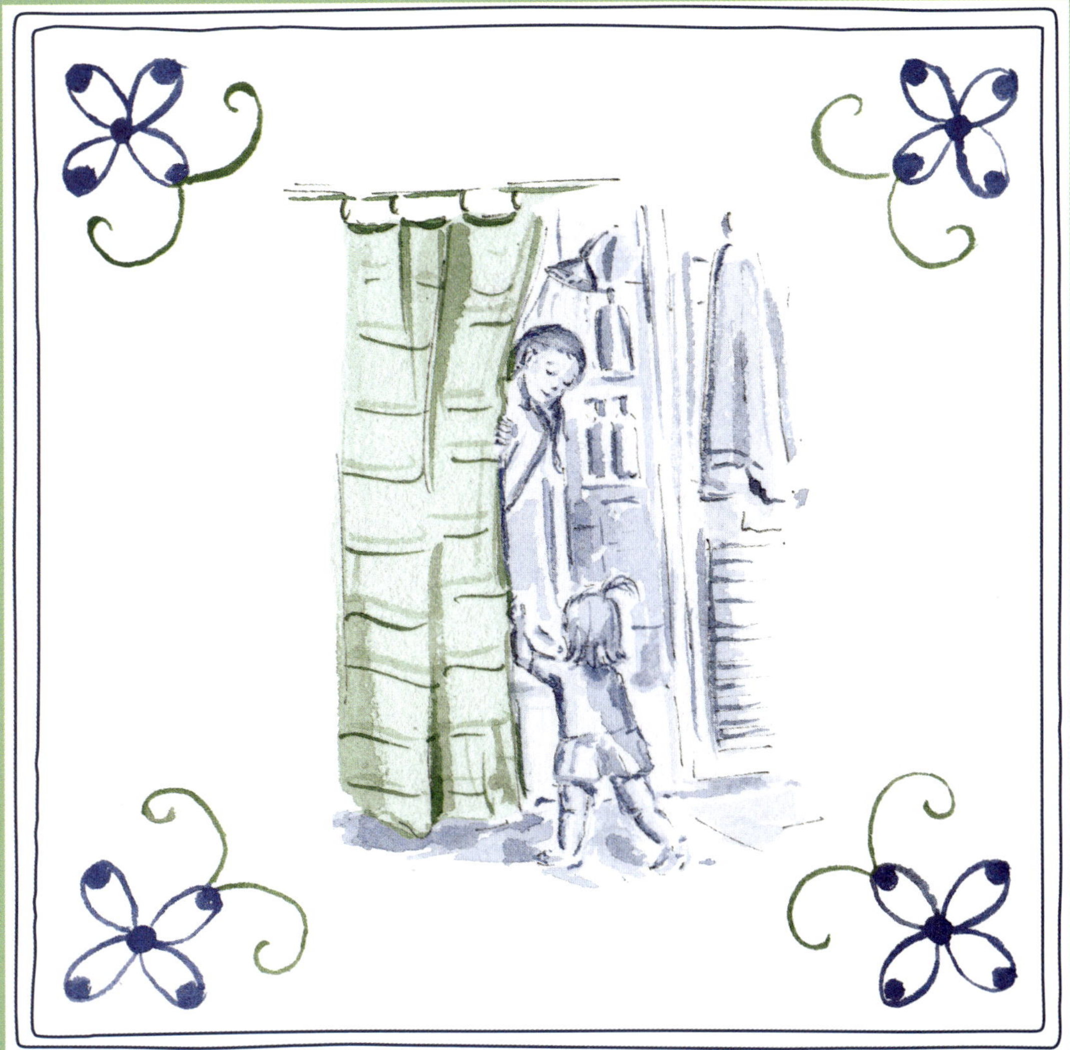

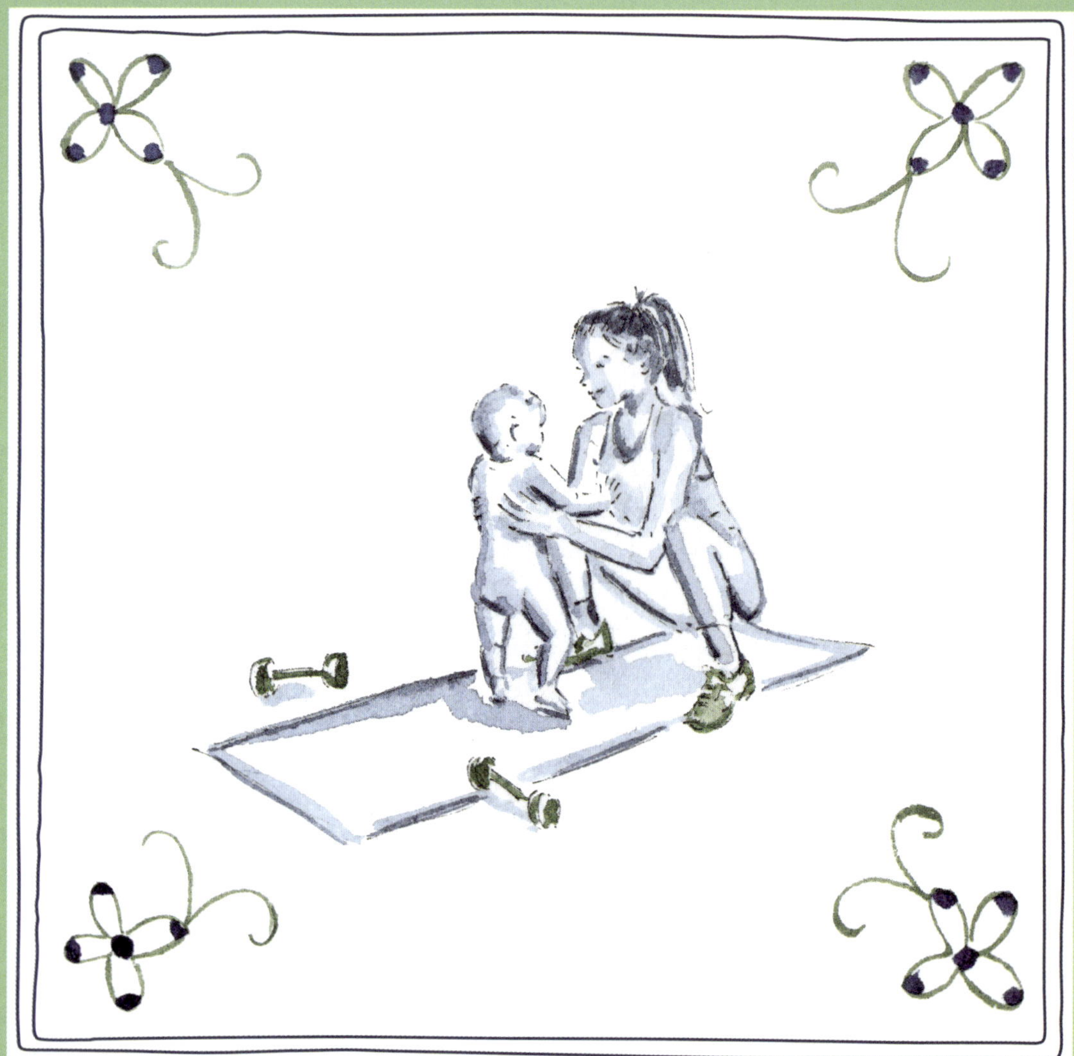

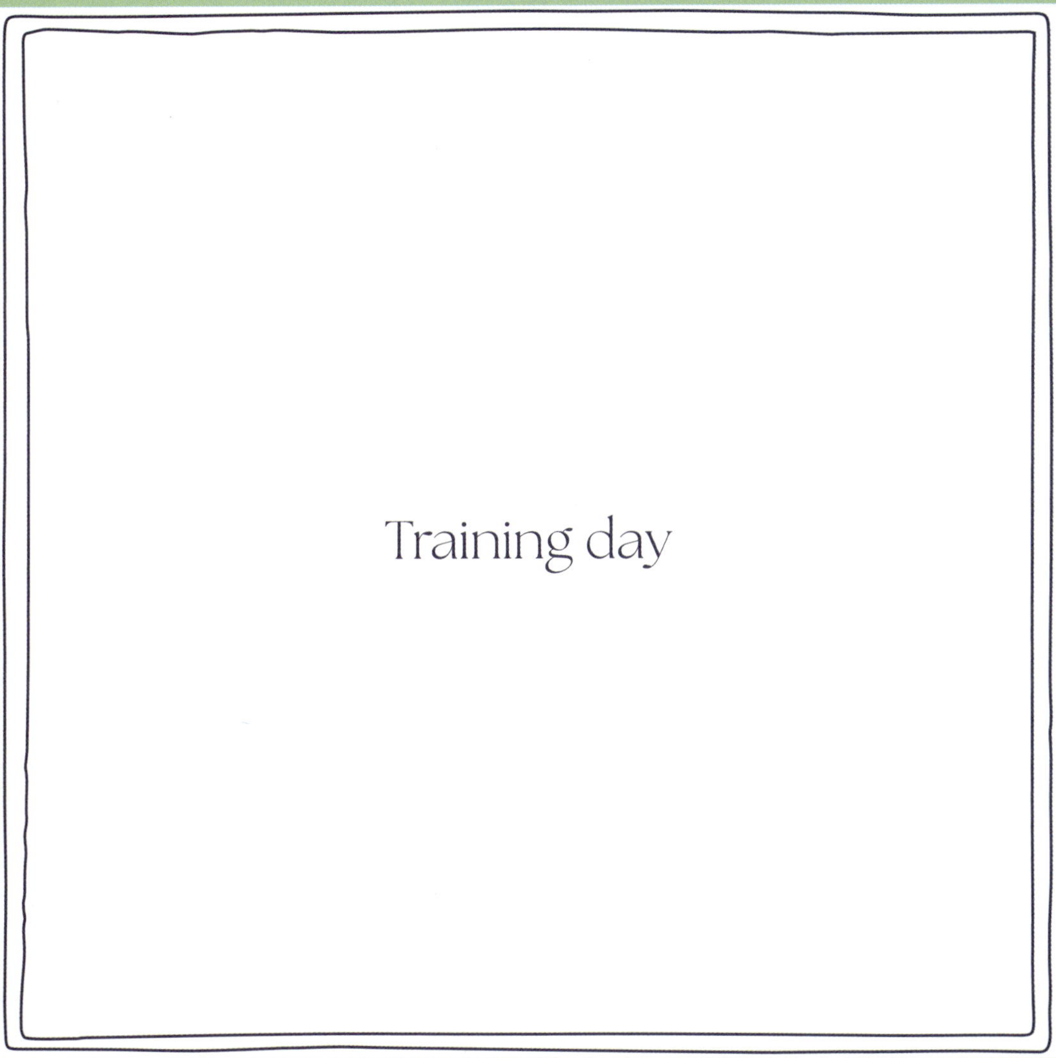

Training day

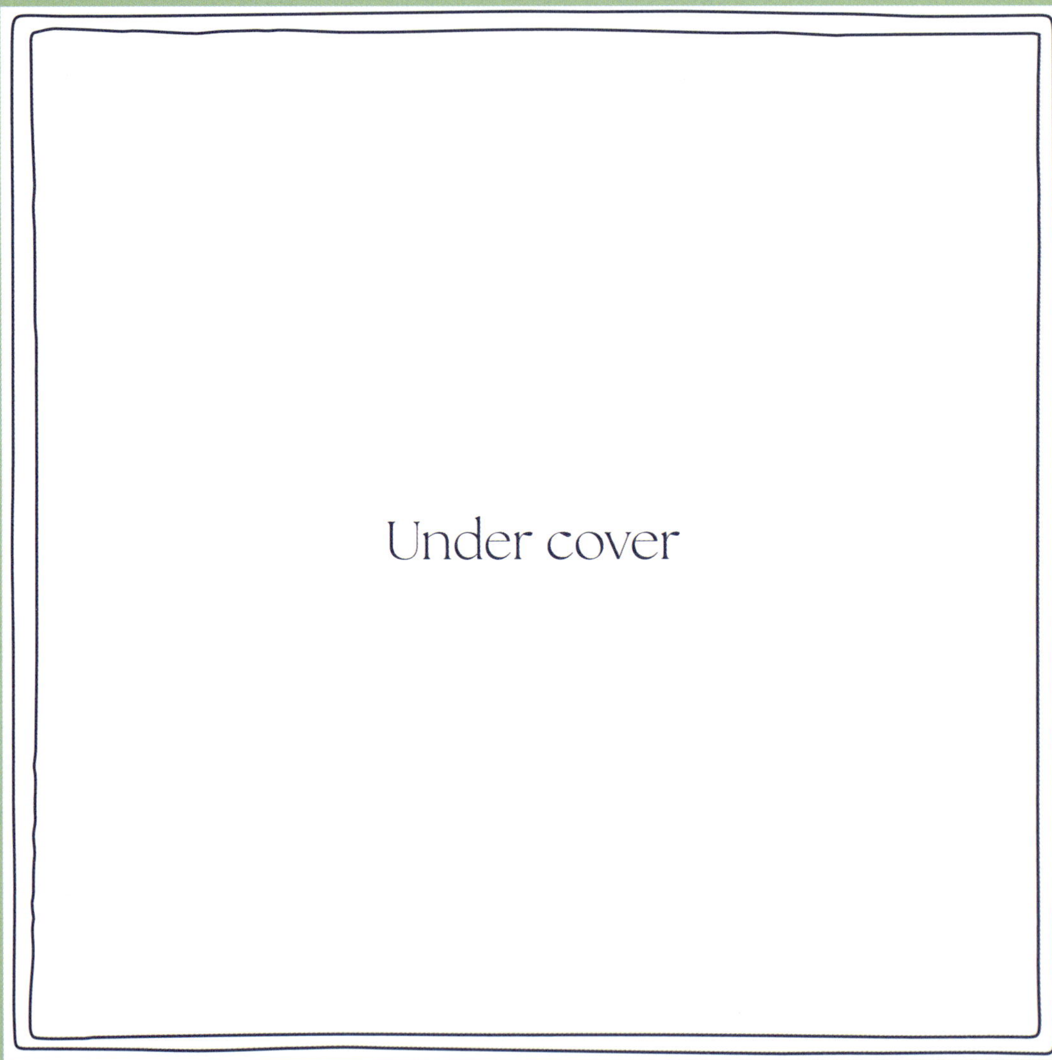

Under cover

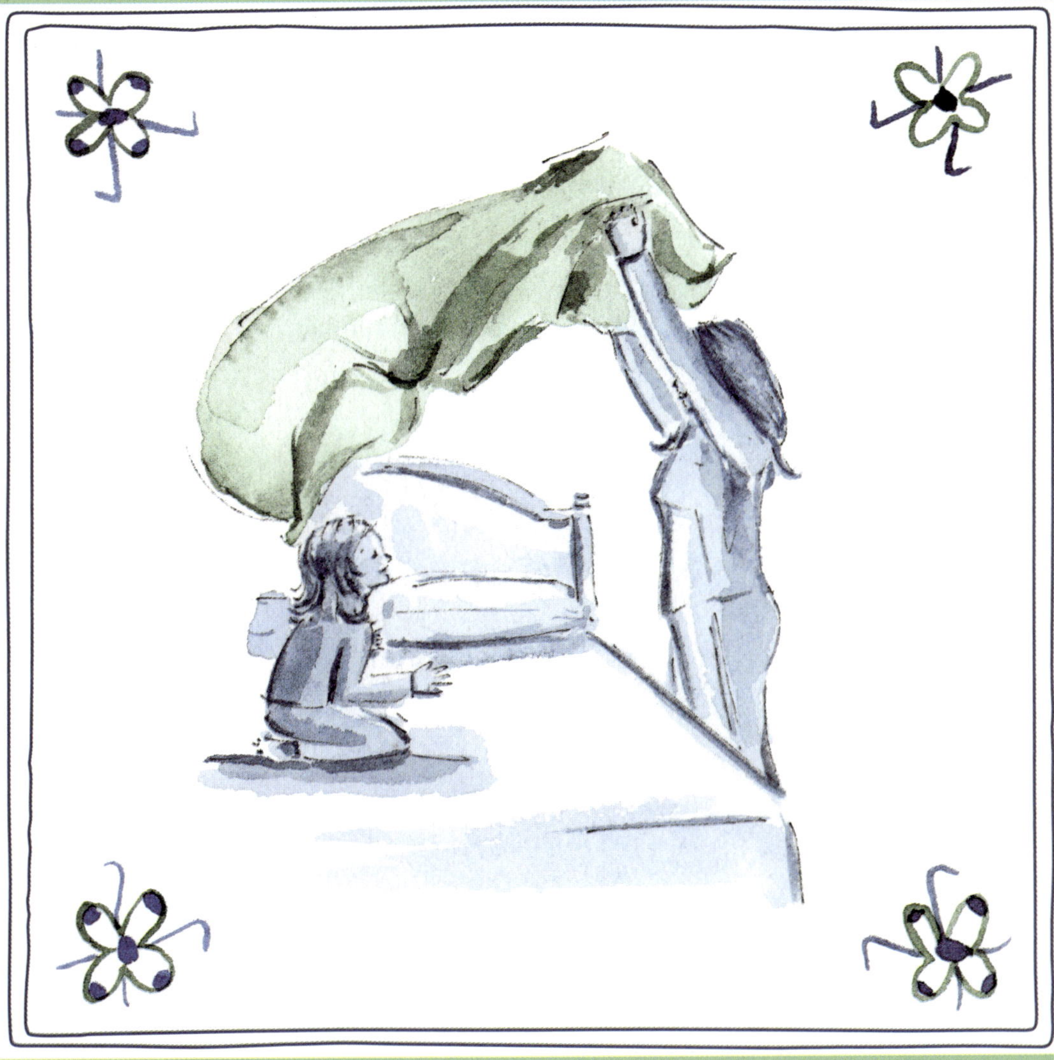

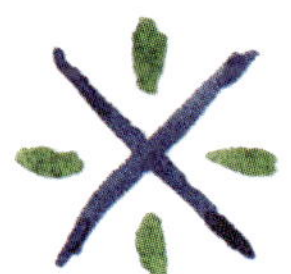
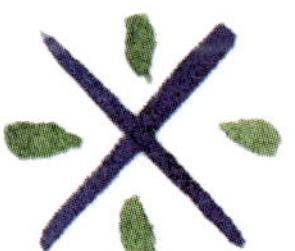
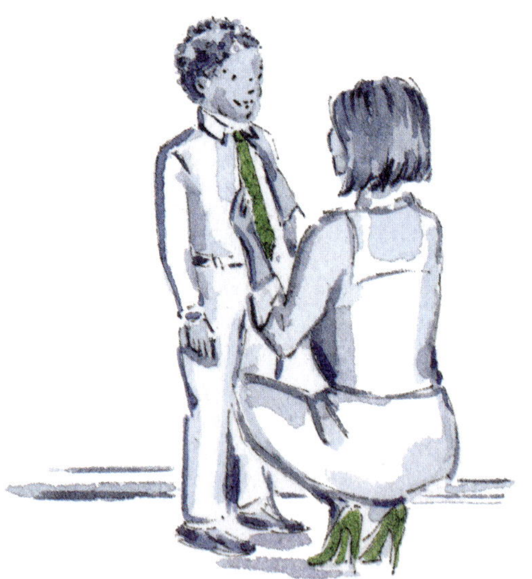
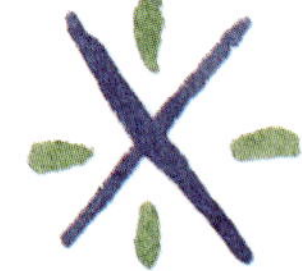
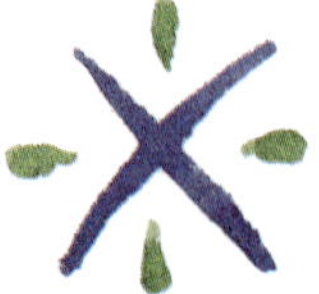

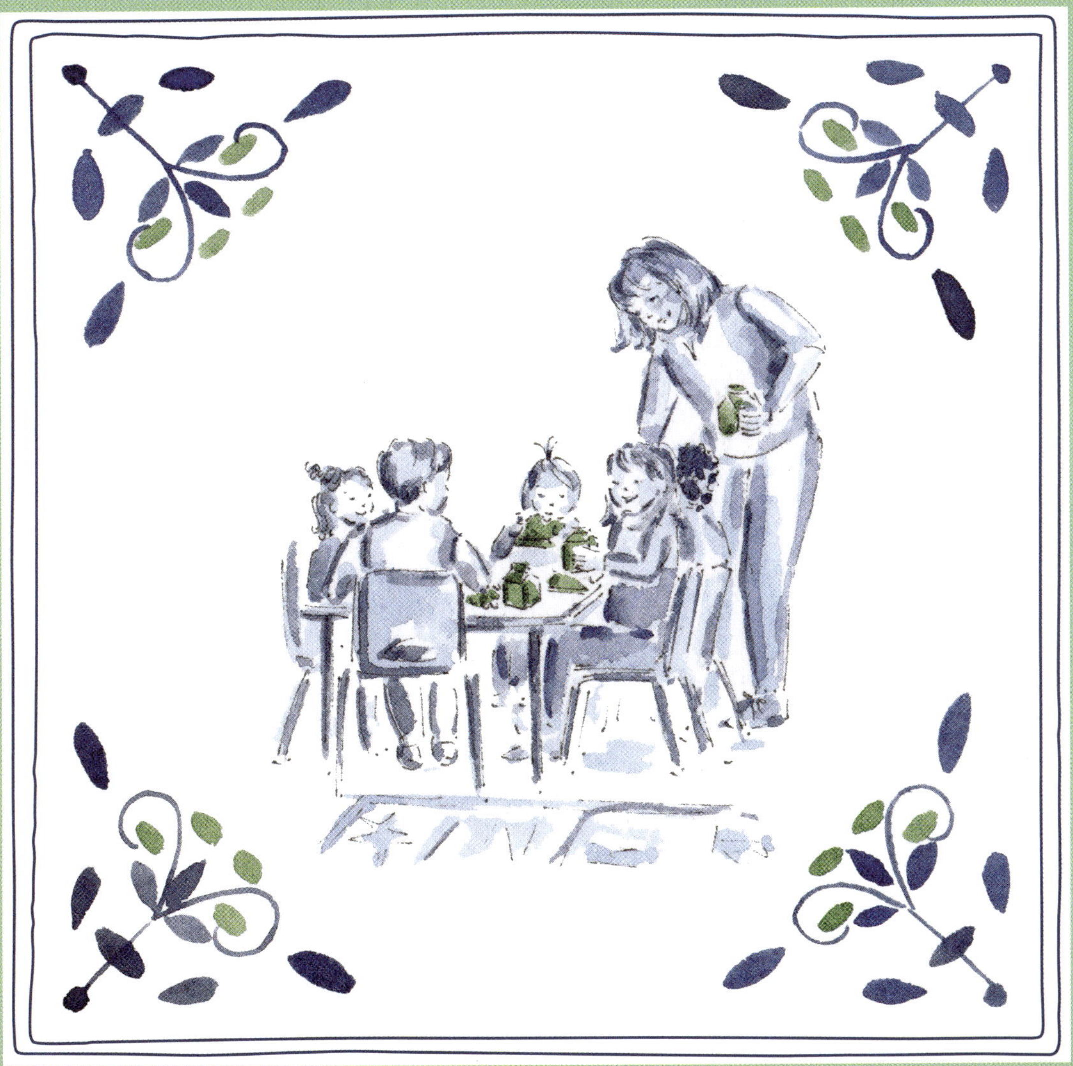

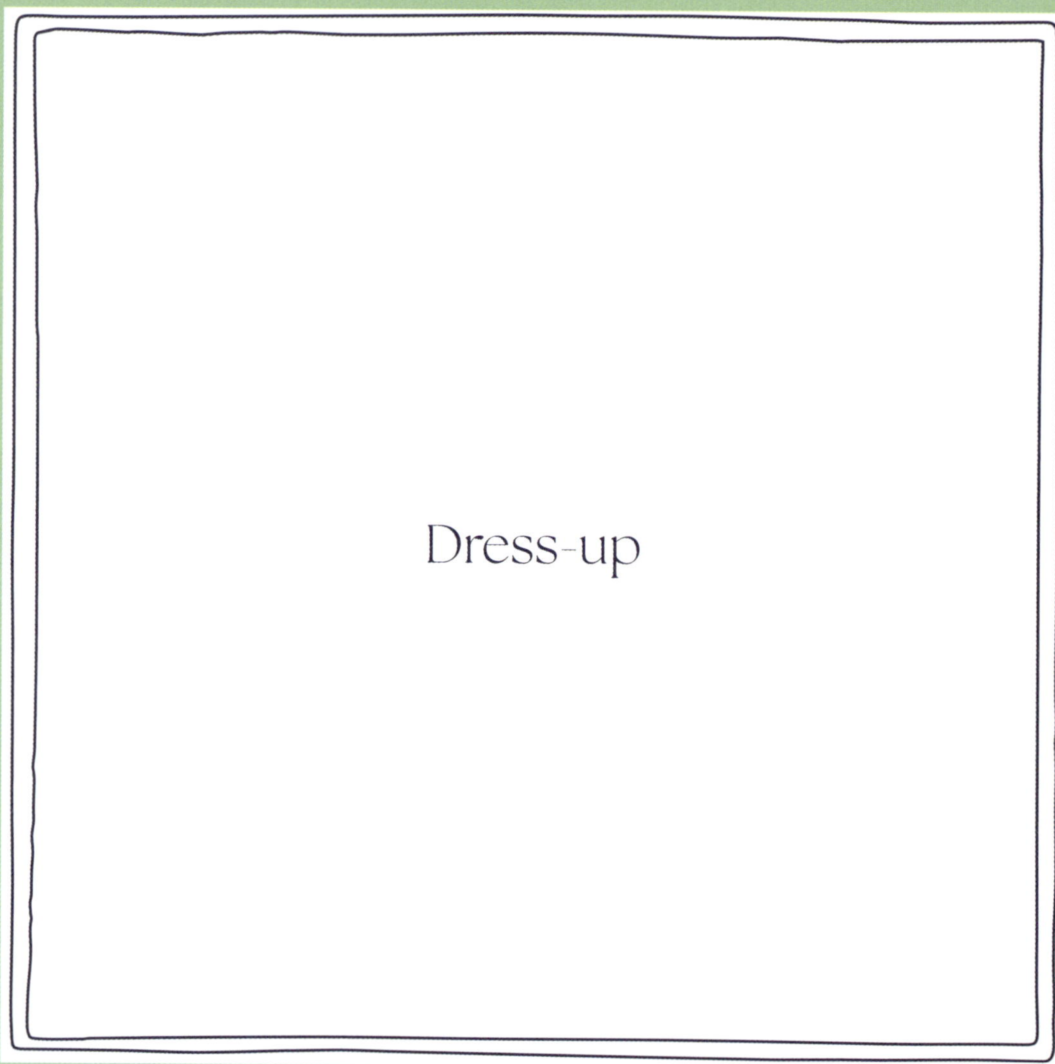

Dress-up

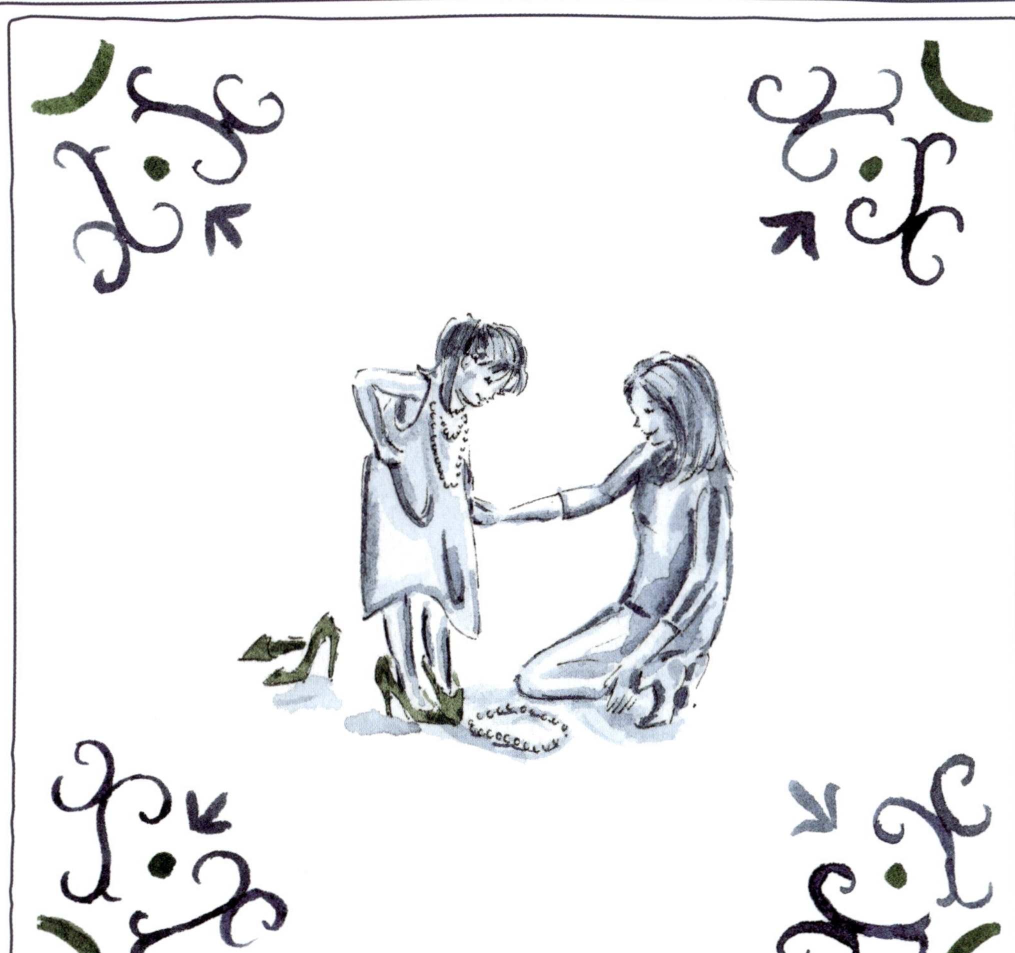

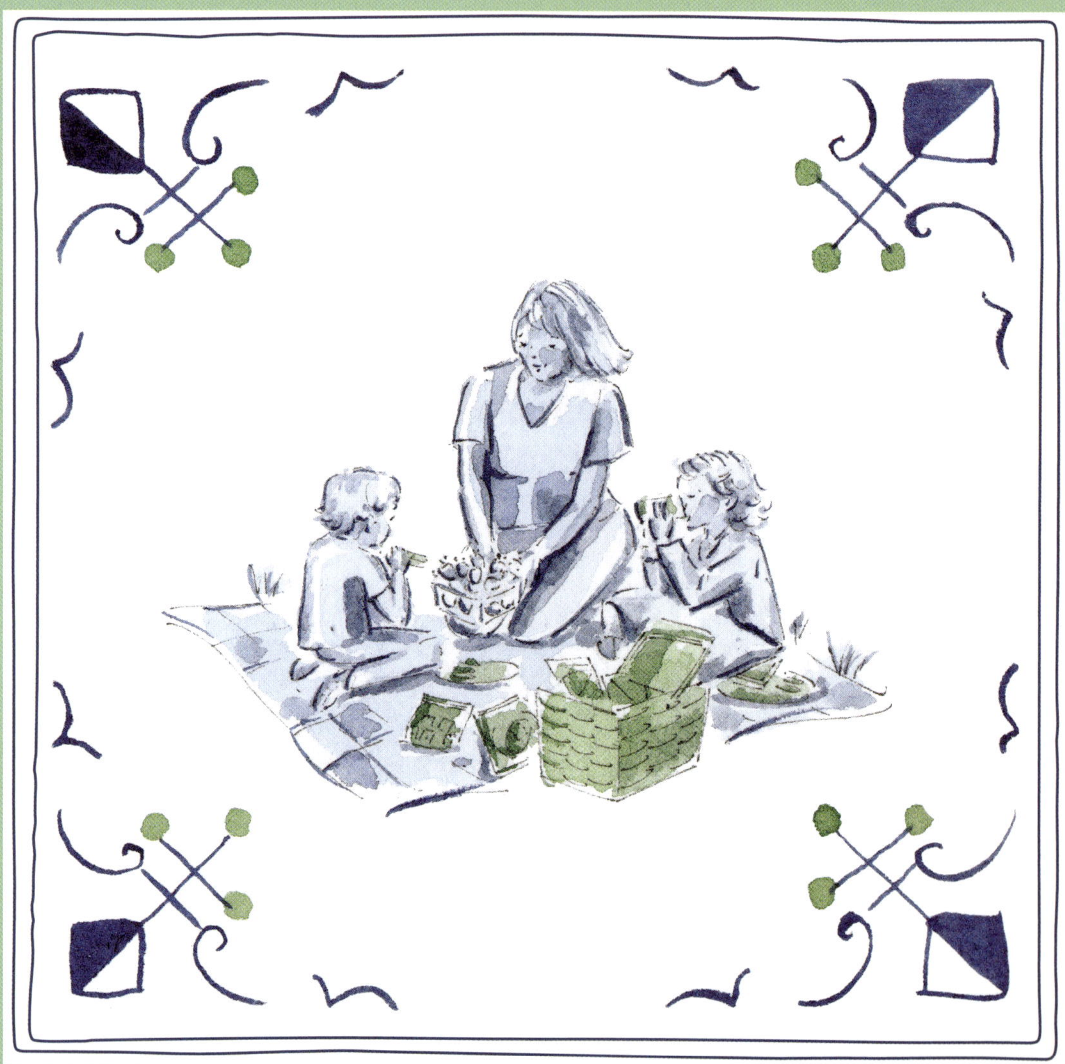

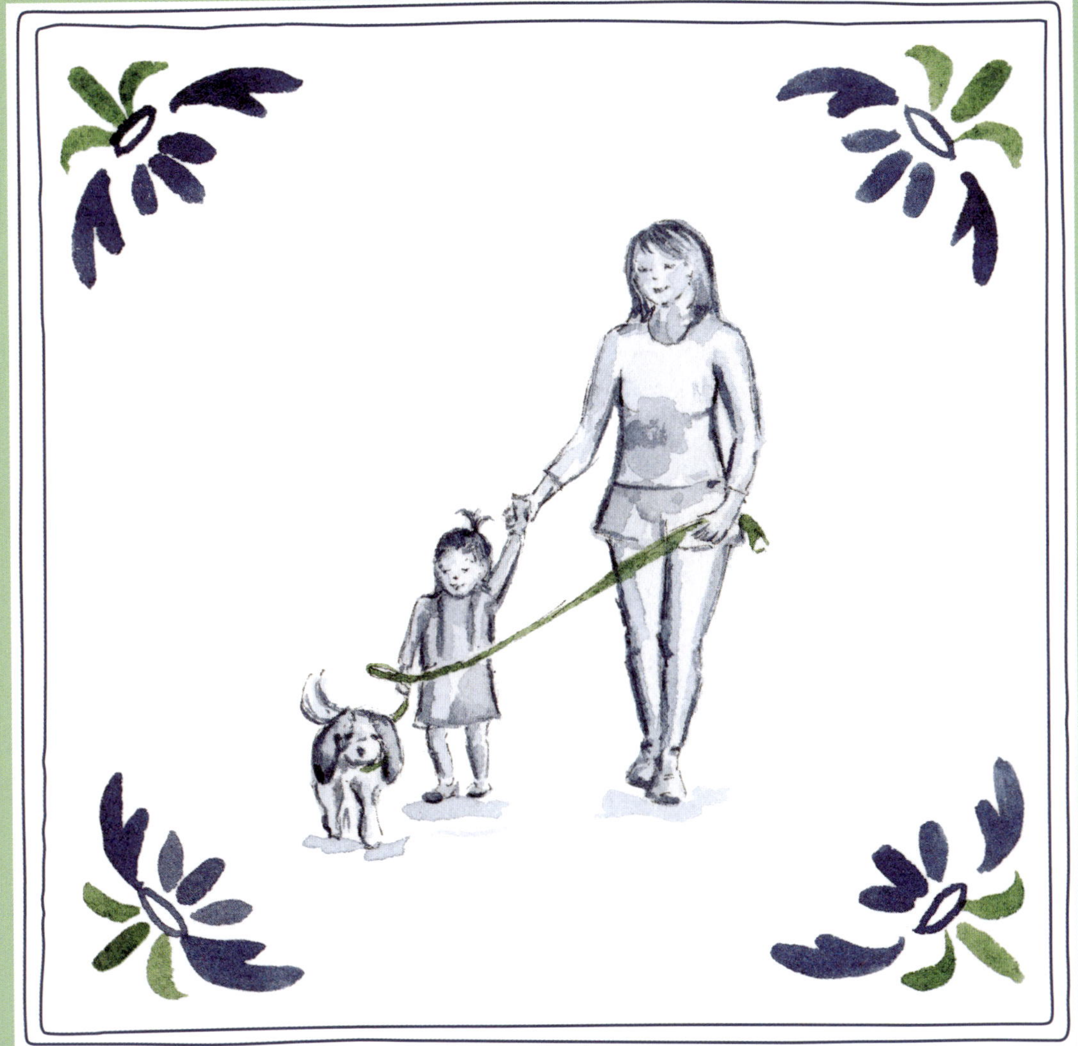

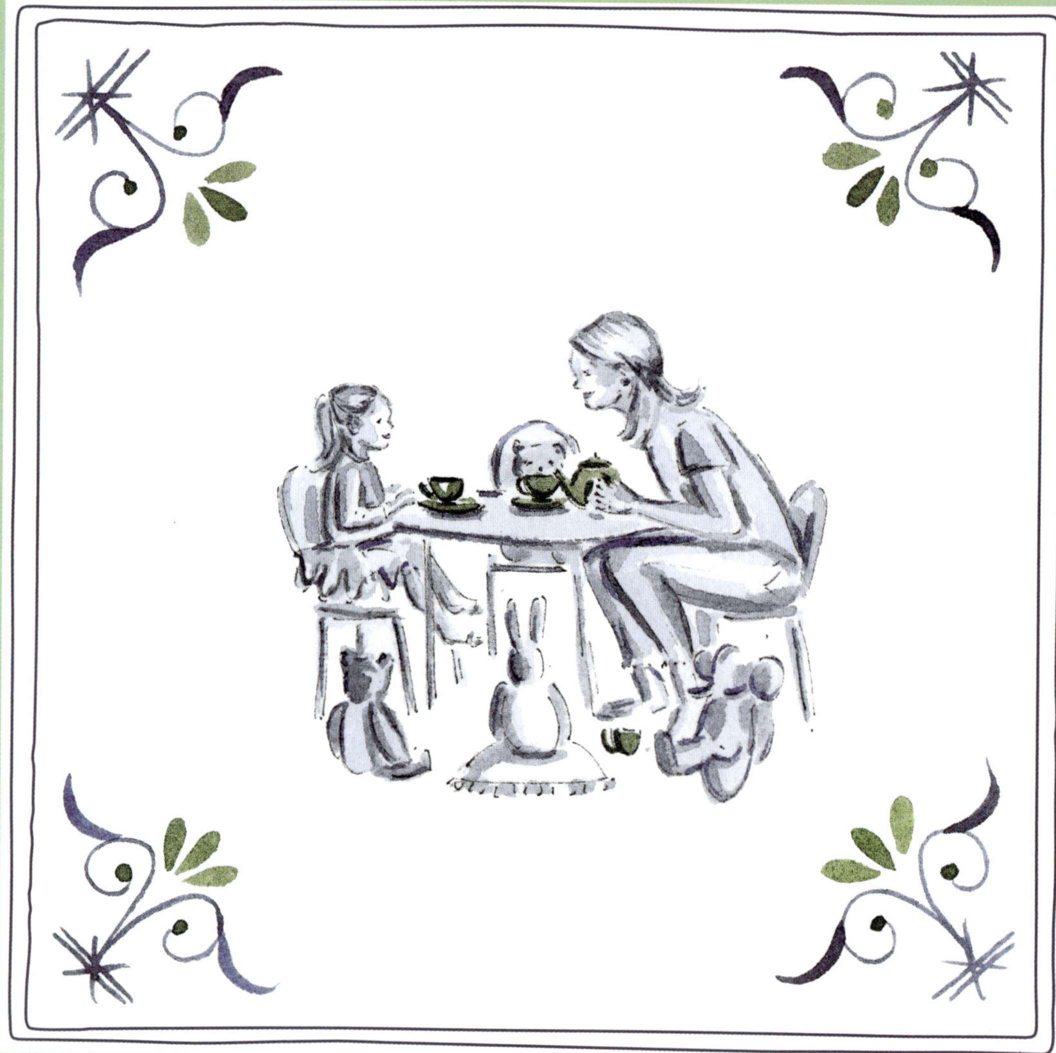

Afternoon tea

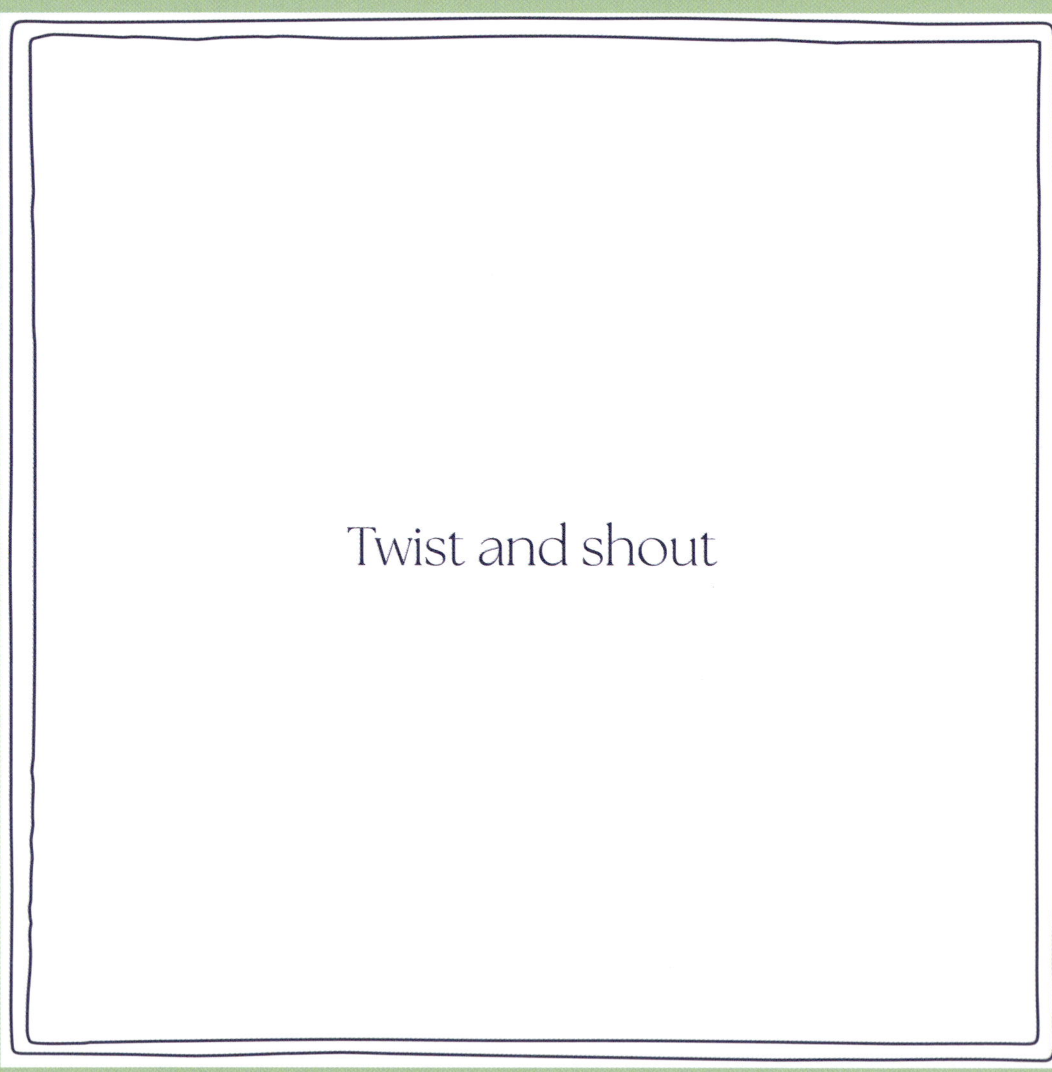

Twist and shout

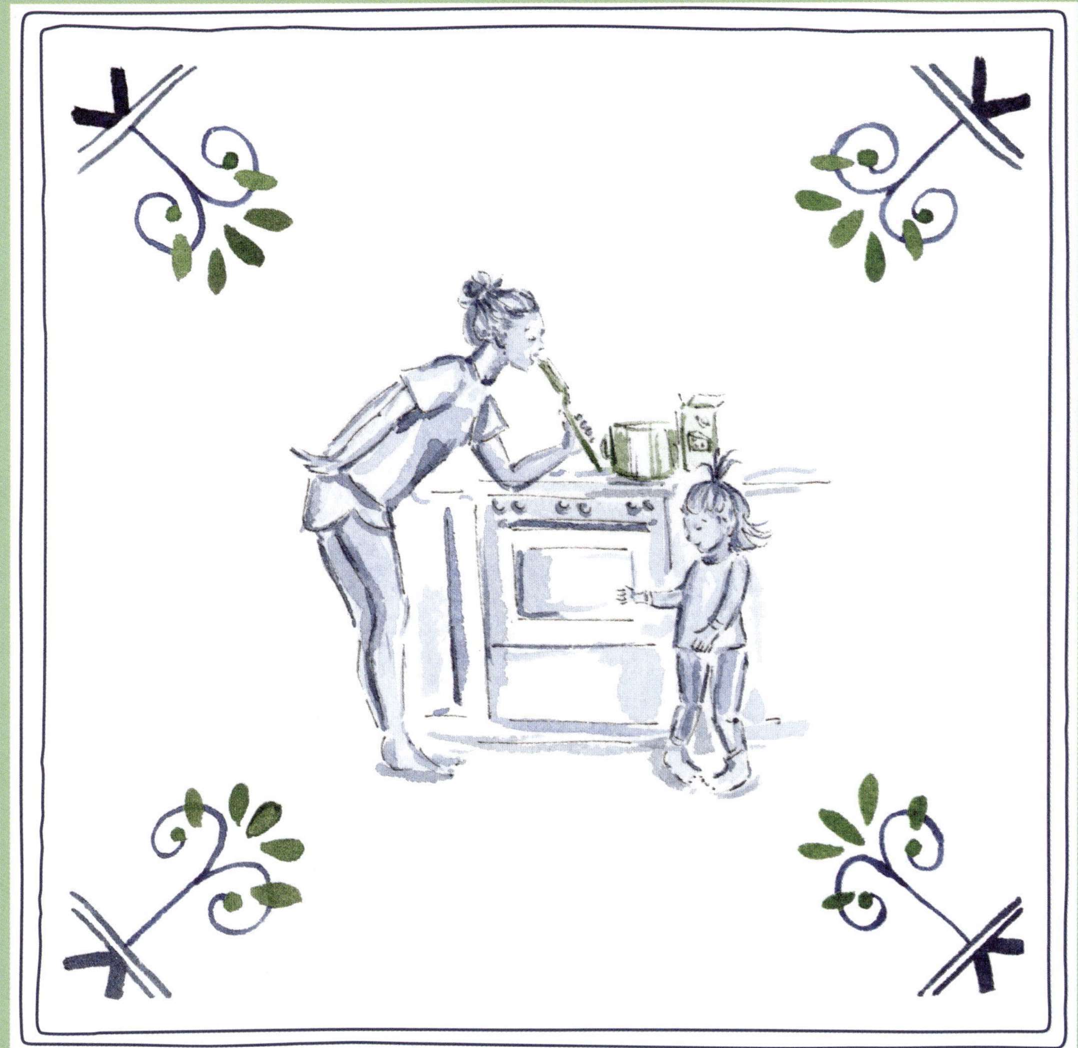

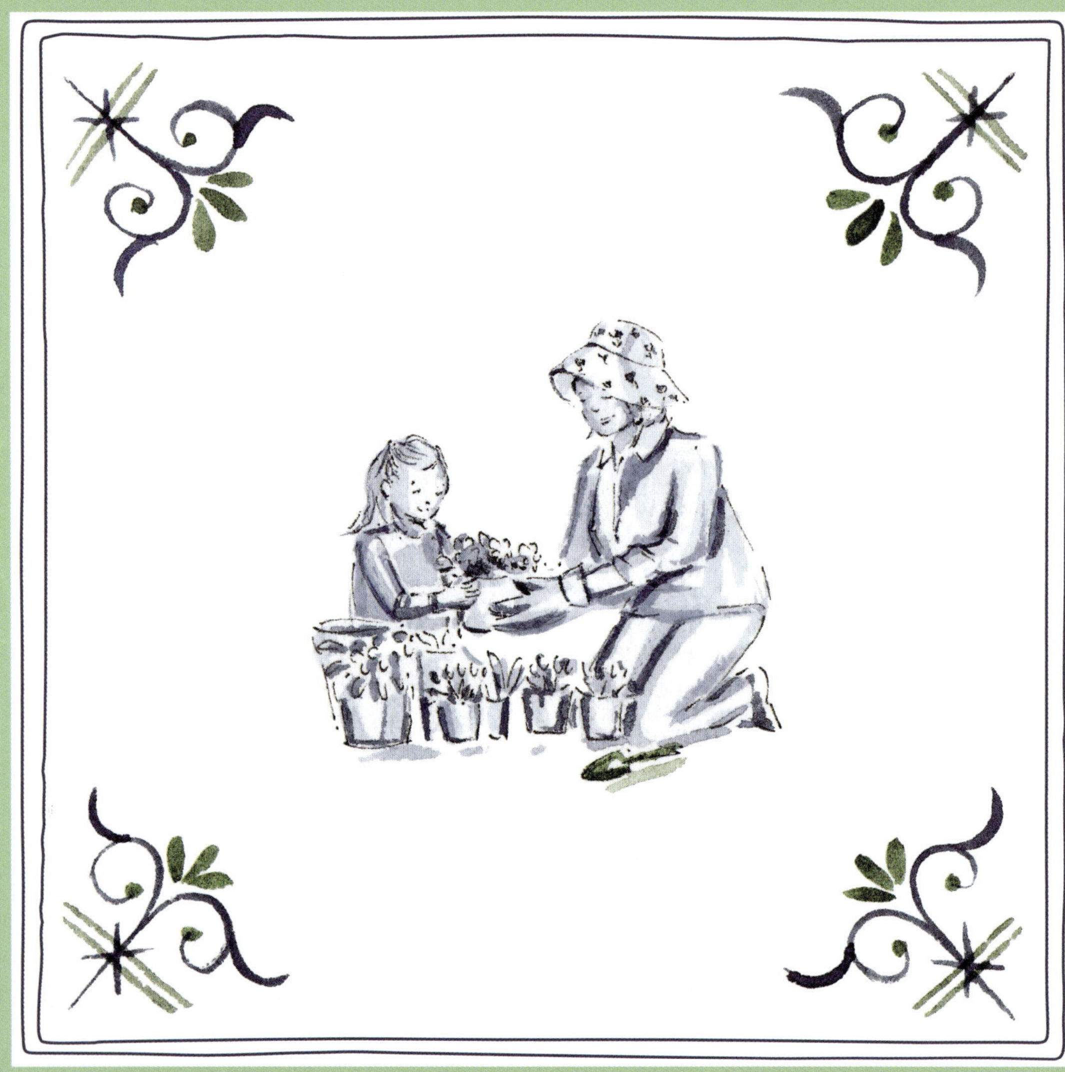

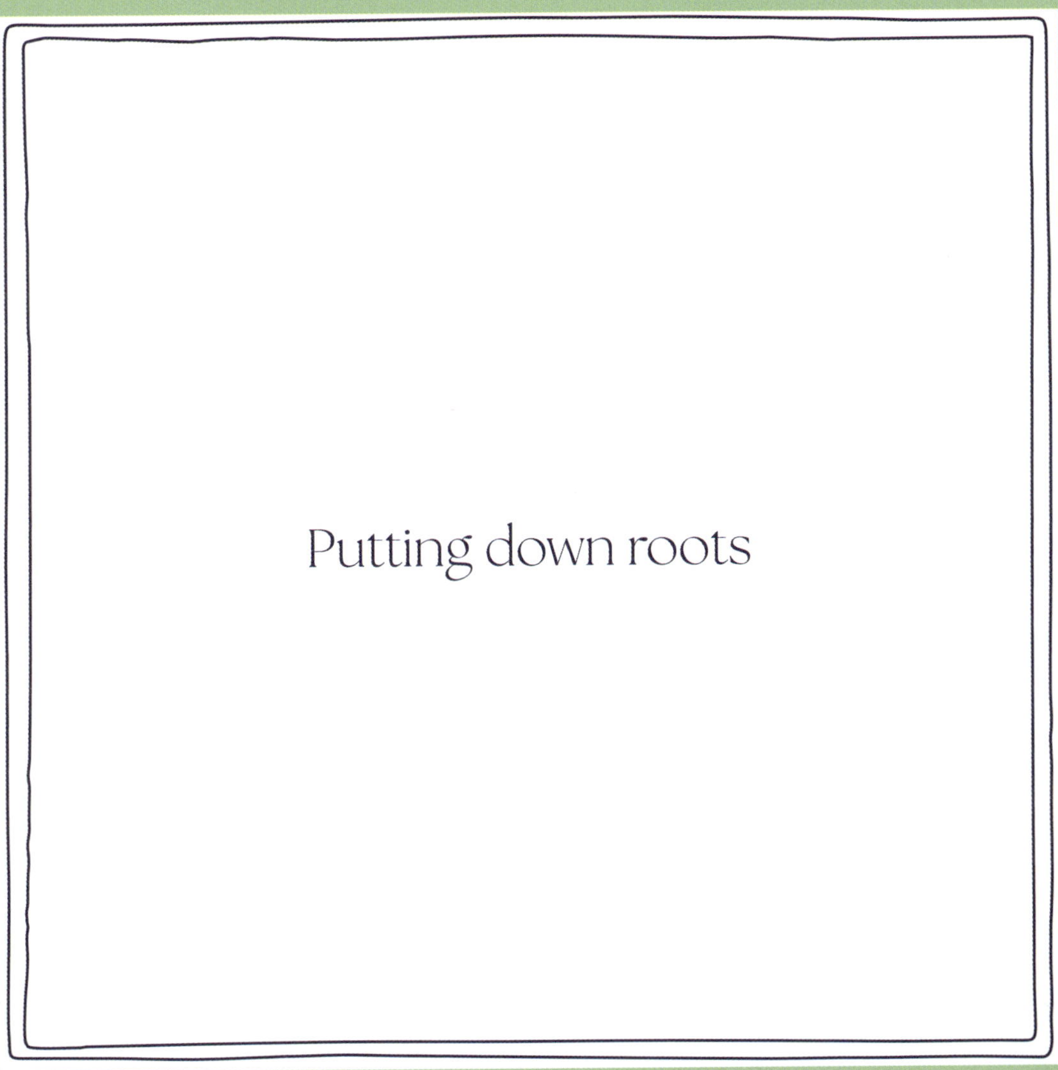

Putting down roots

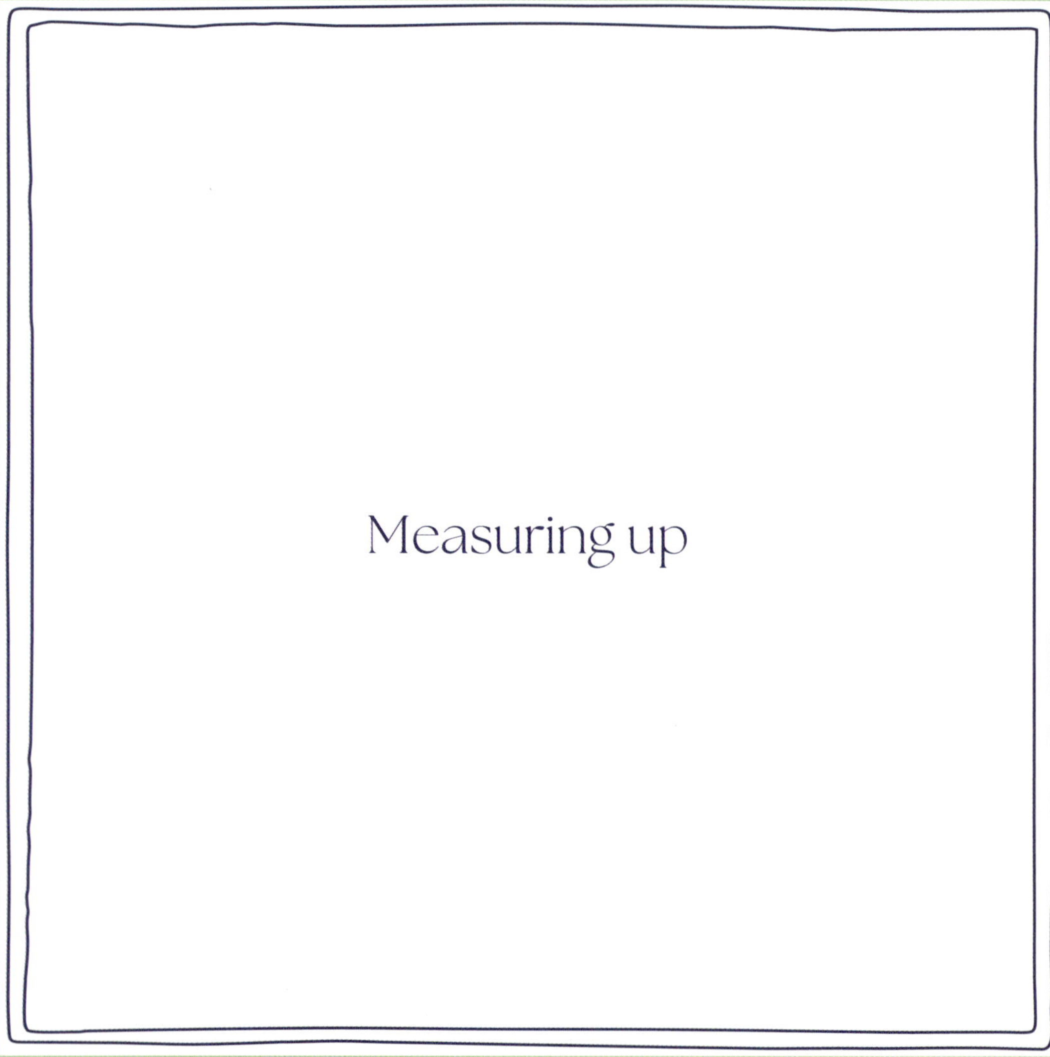

Measuring up

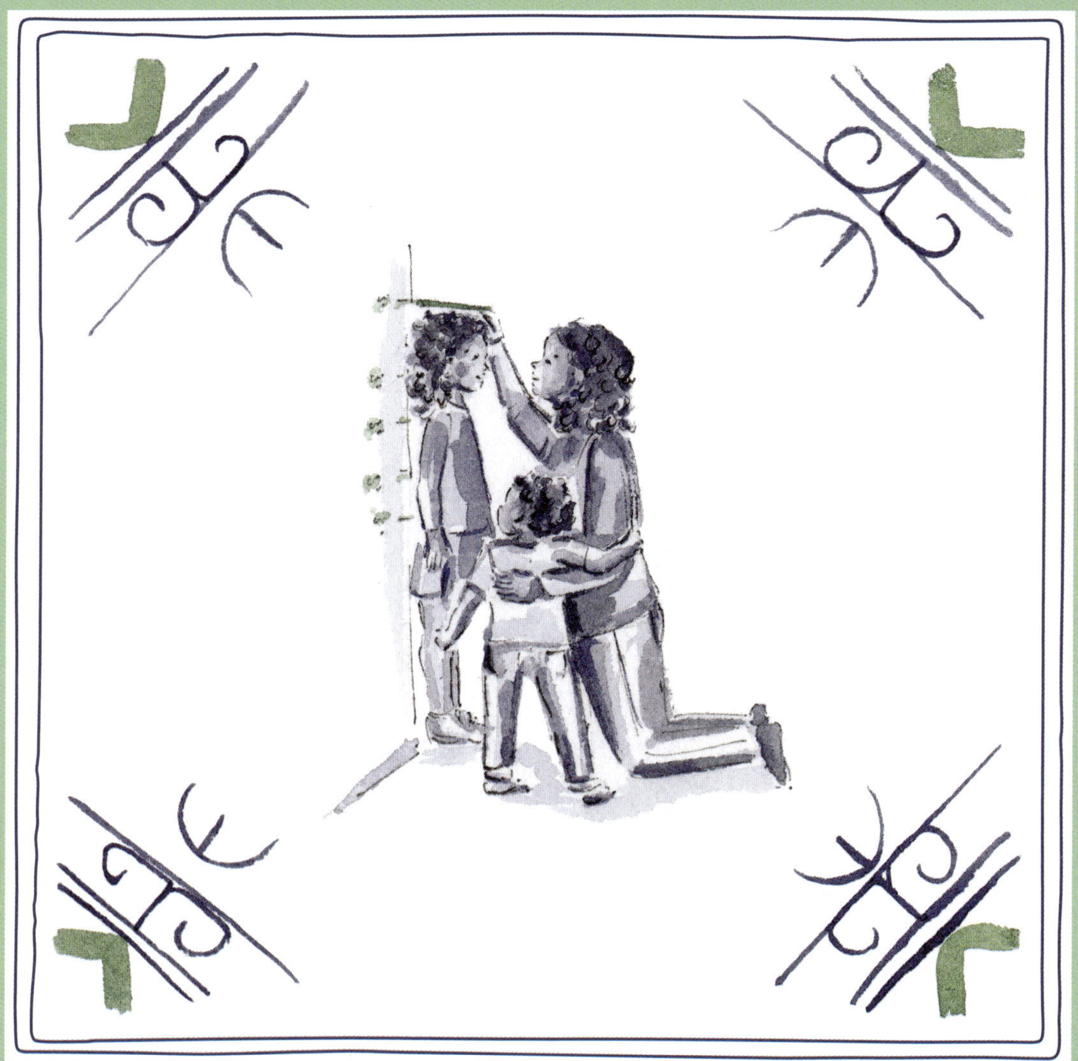

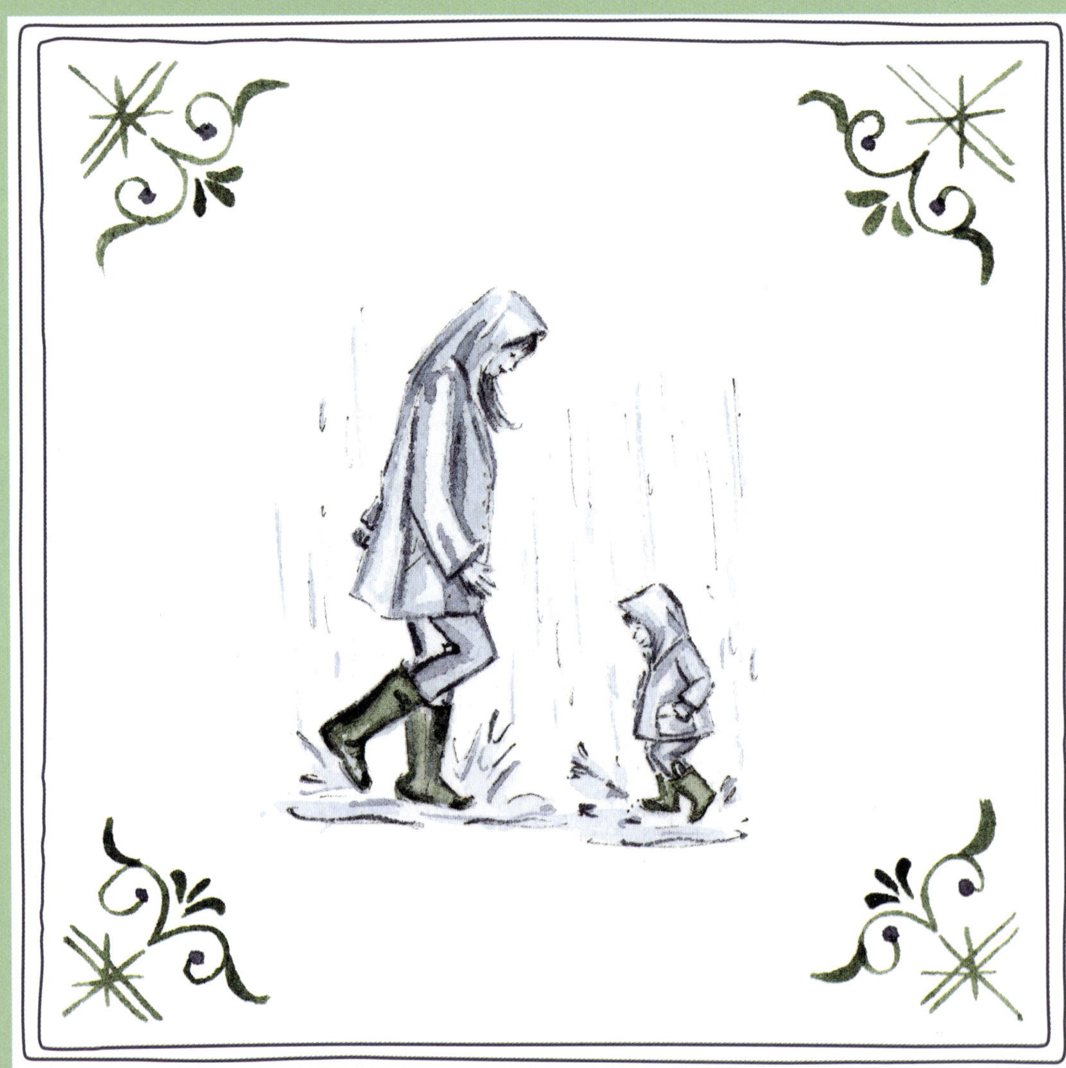

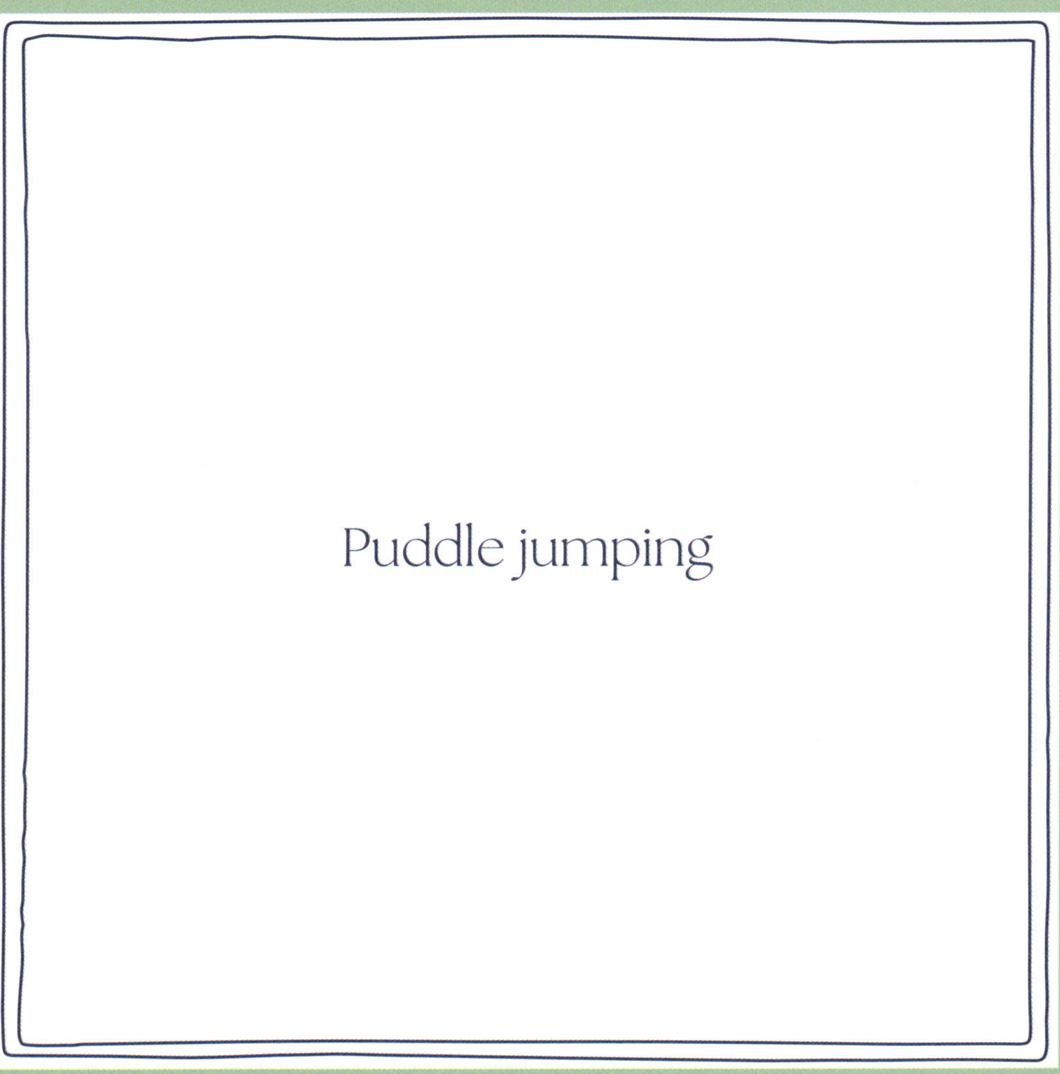

Puddle jumping

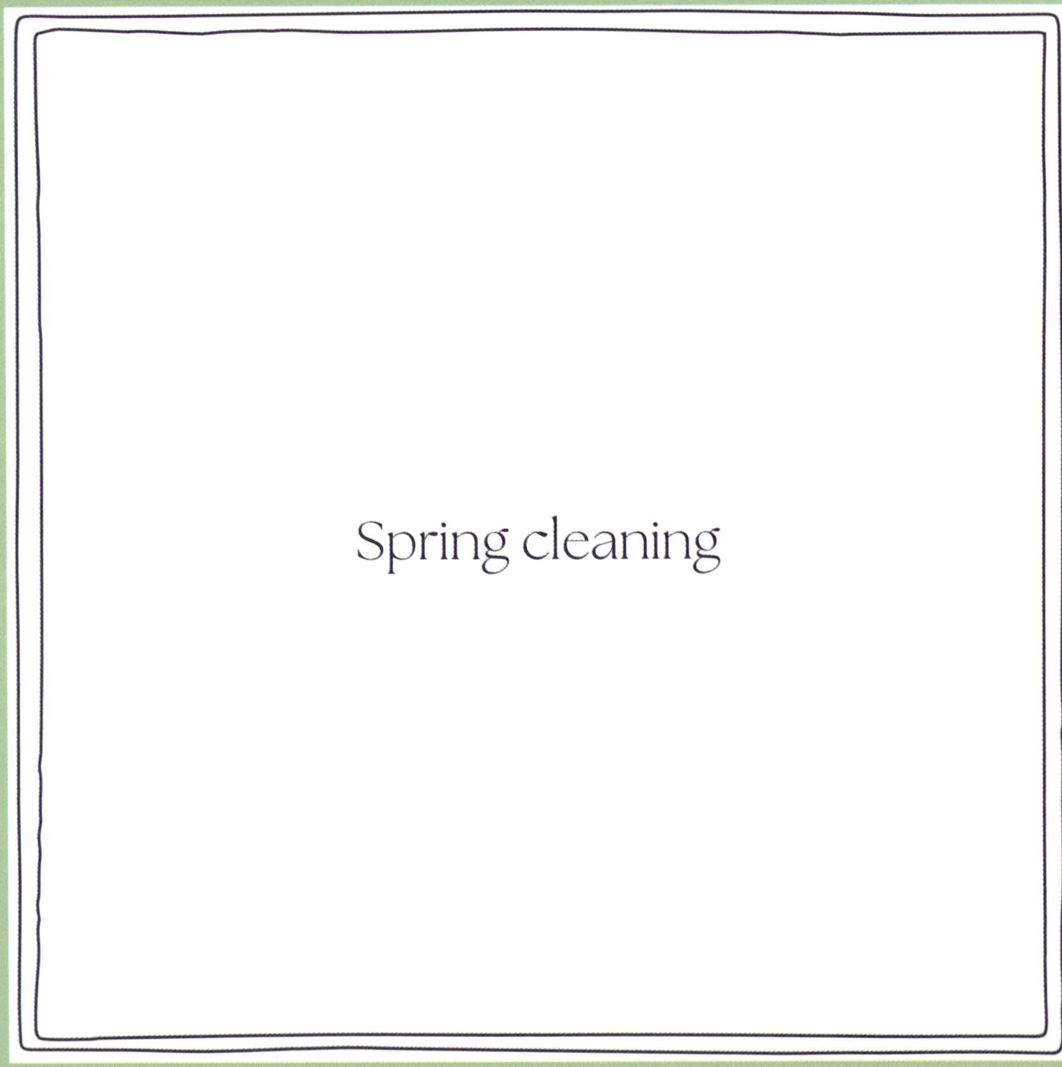

Spring cleaning

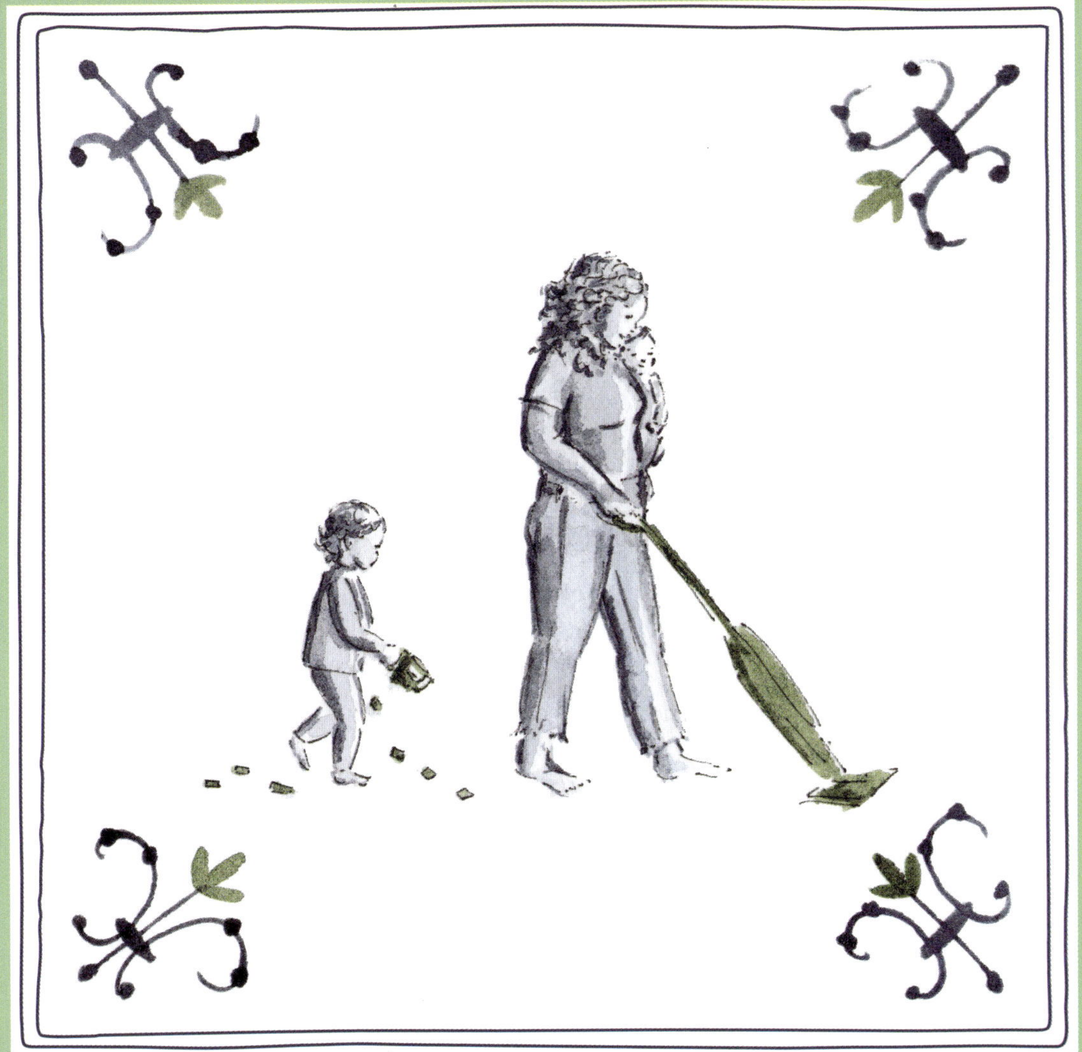

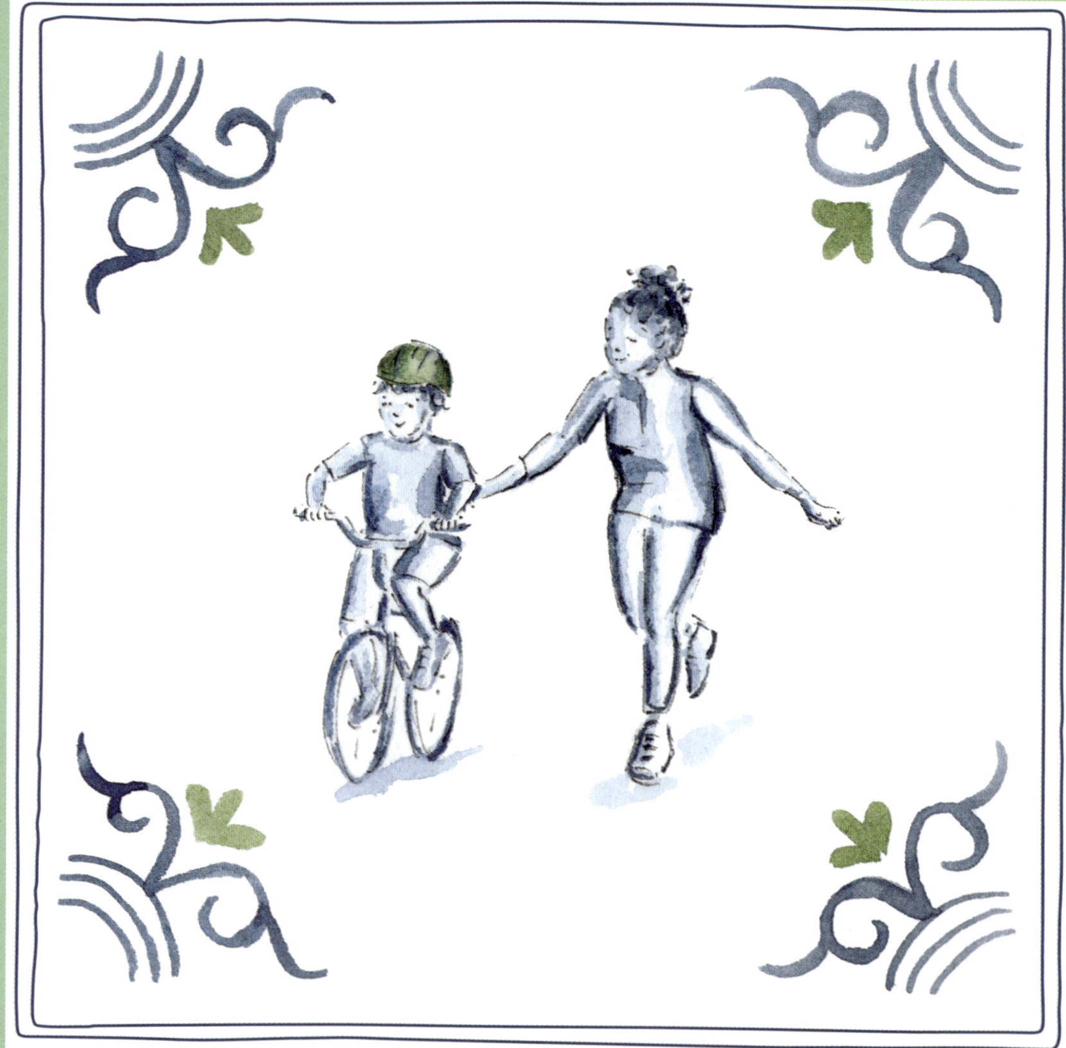

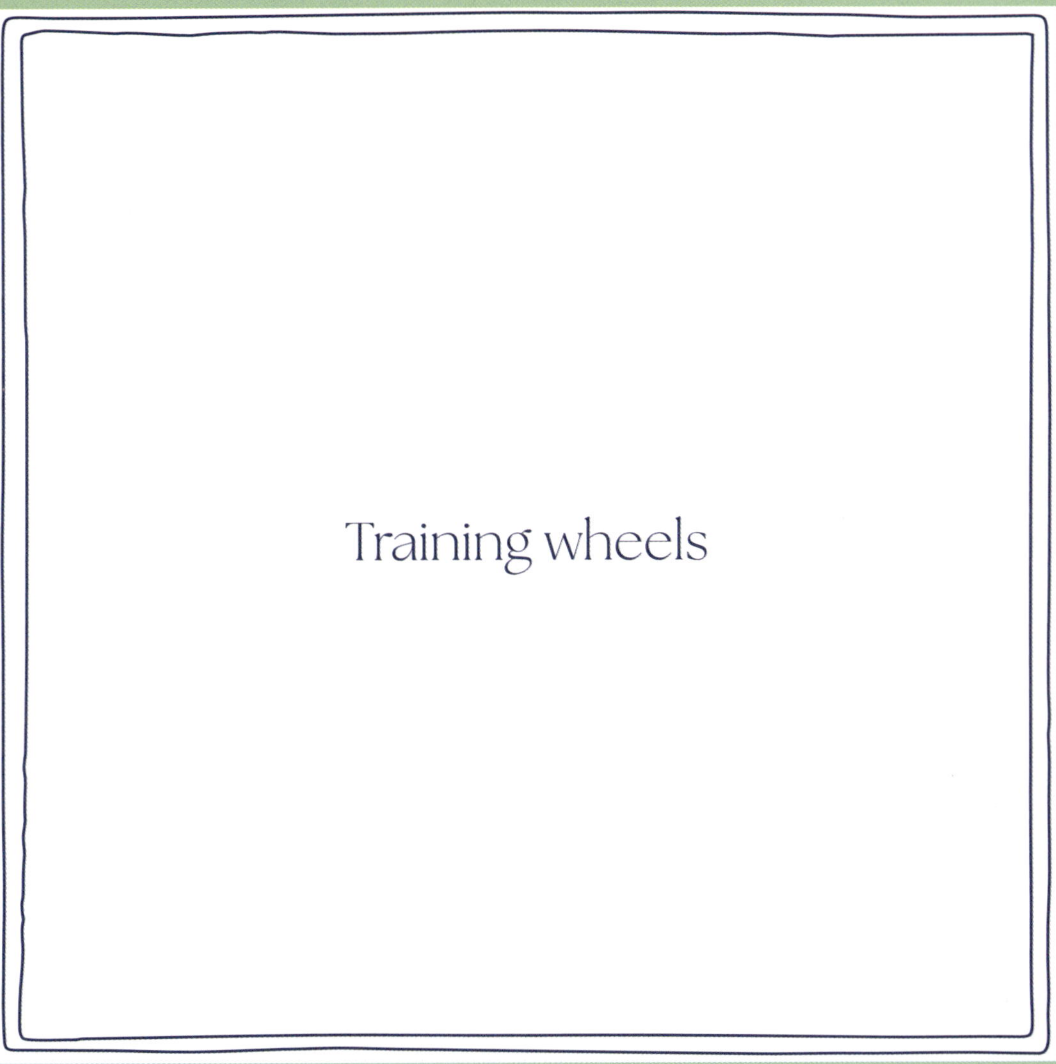

Training wheels

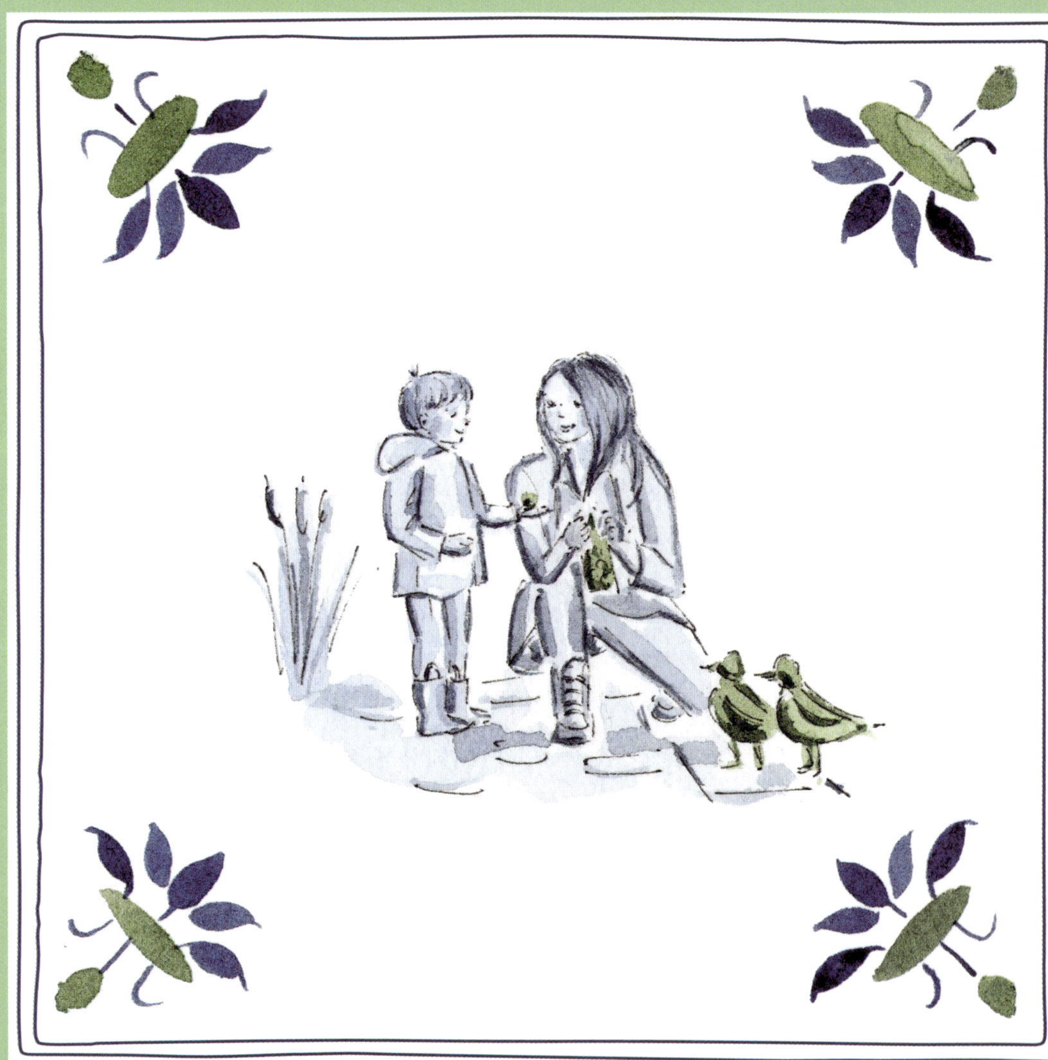

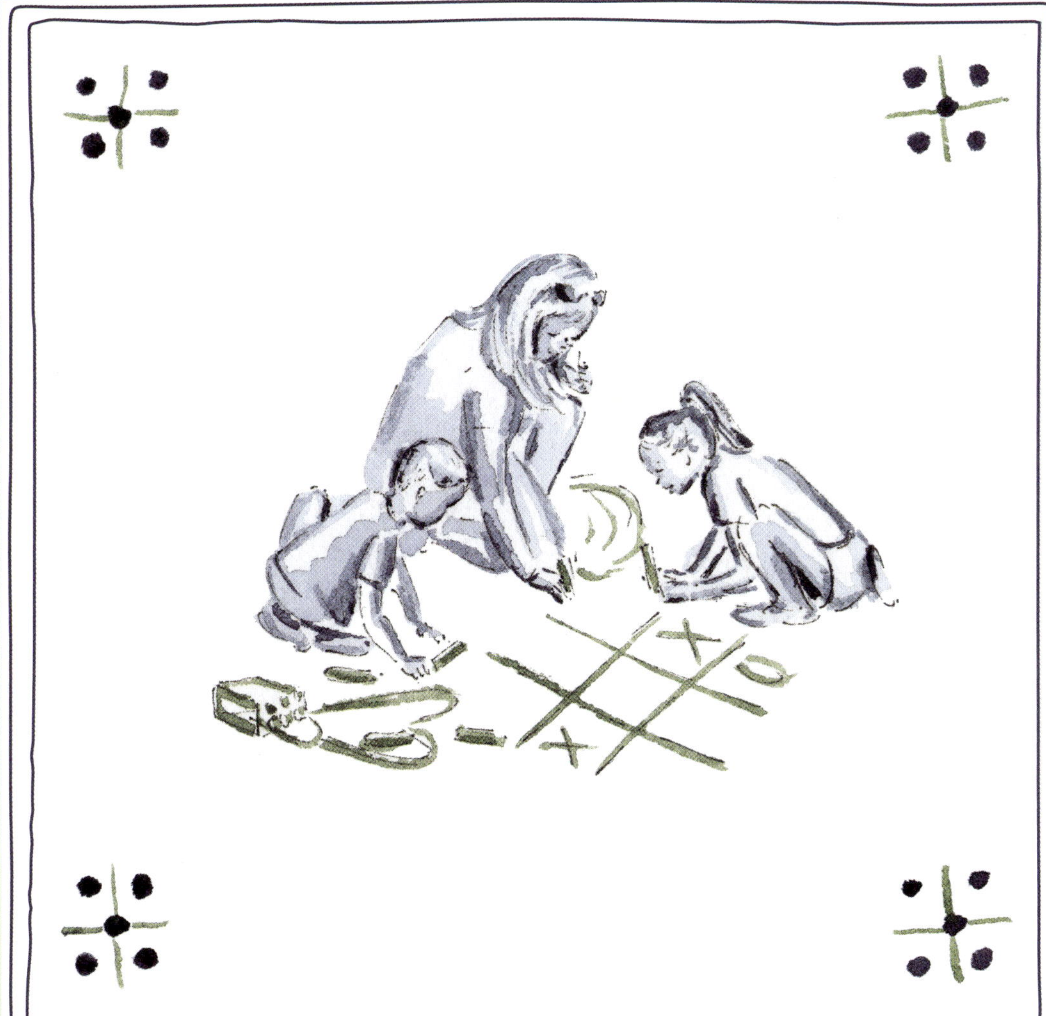
X
O
X

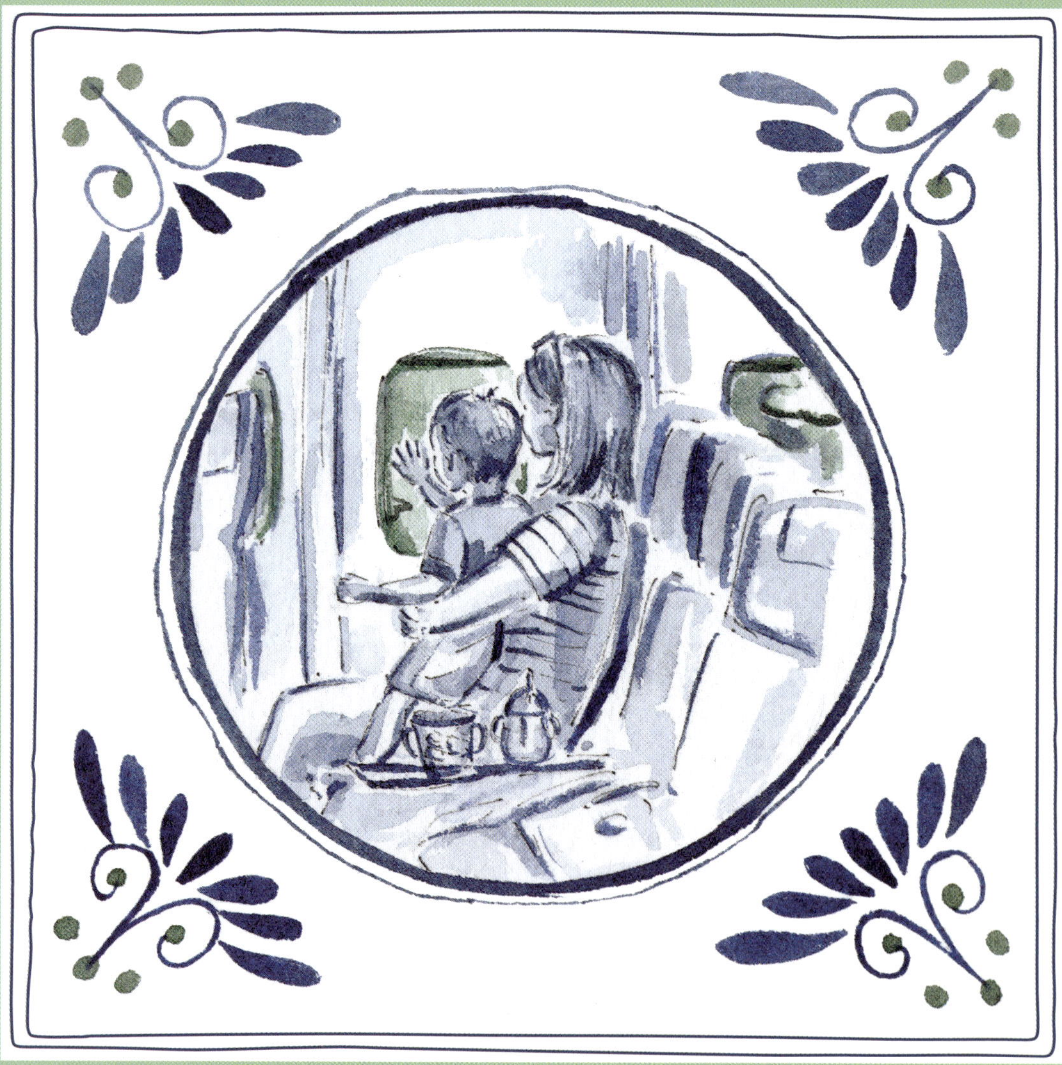

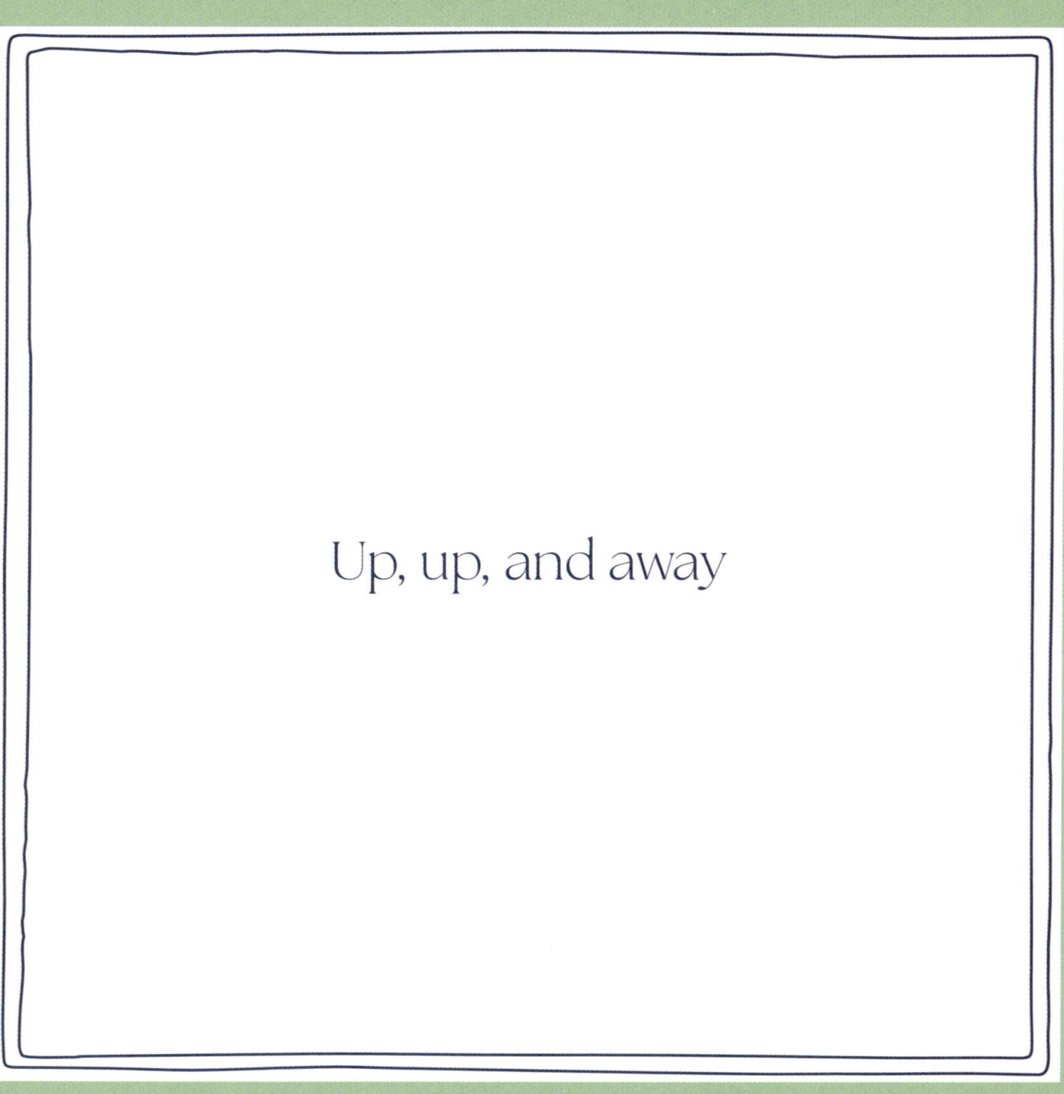
Up, up, and away

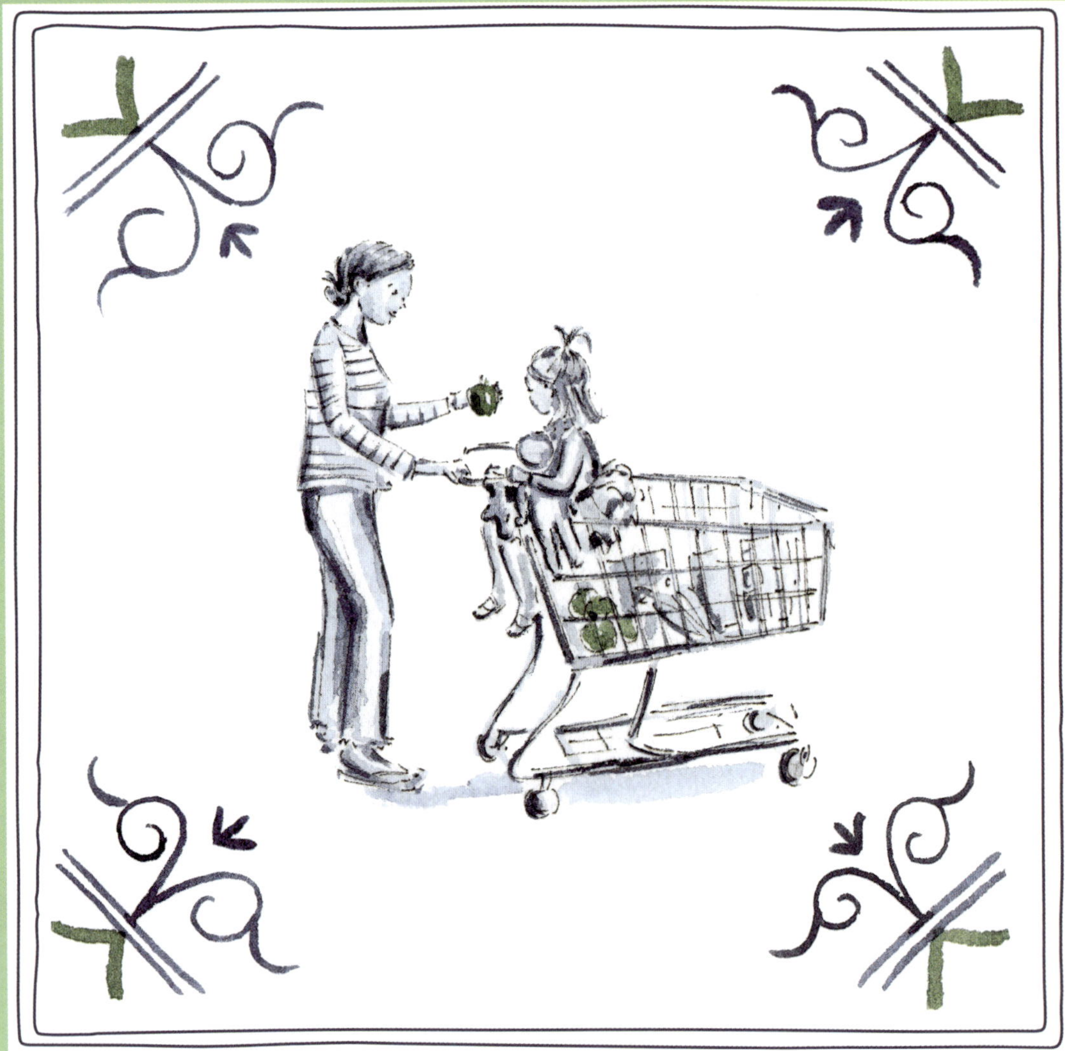

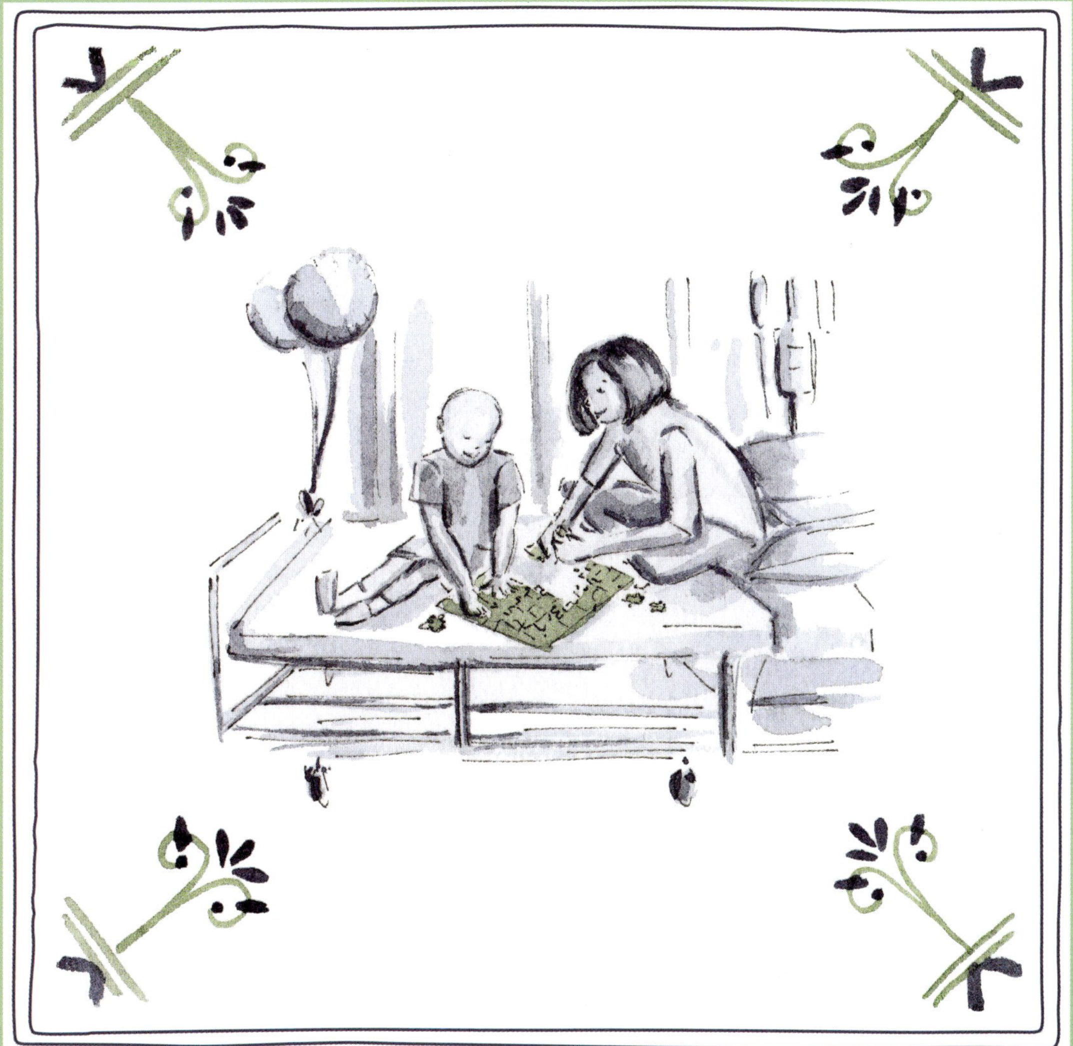

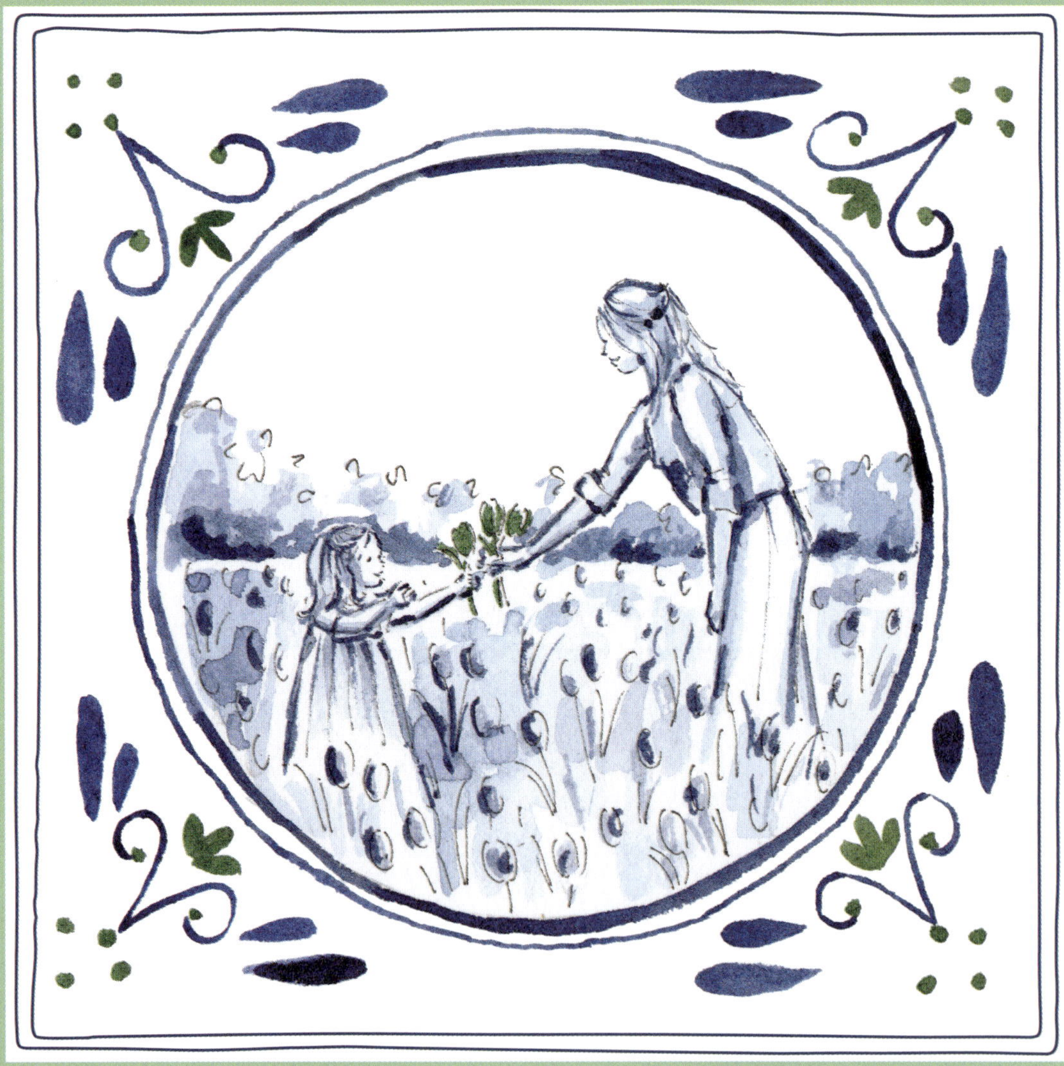

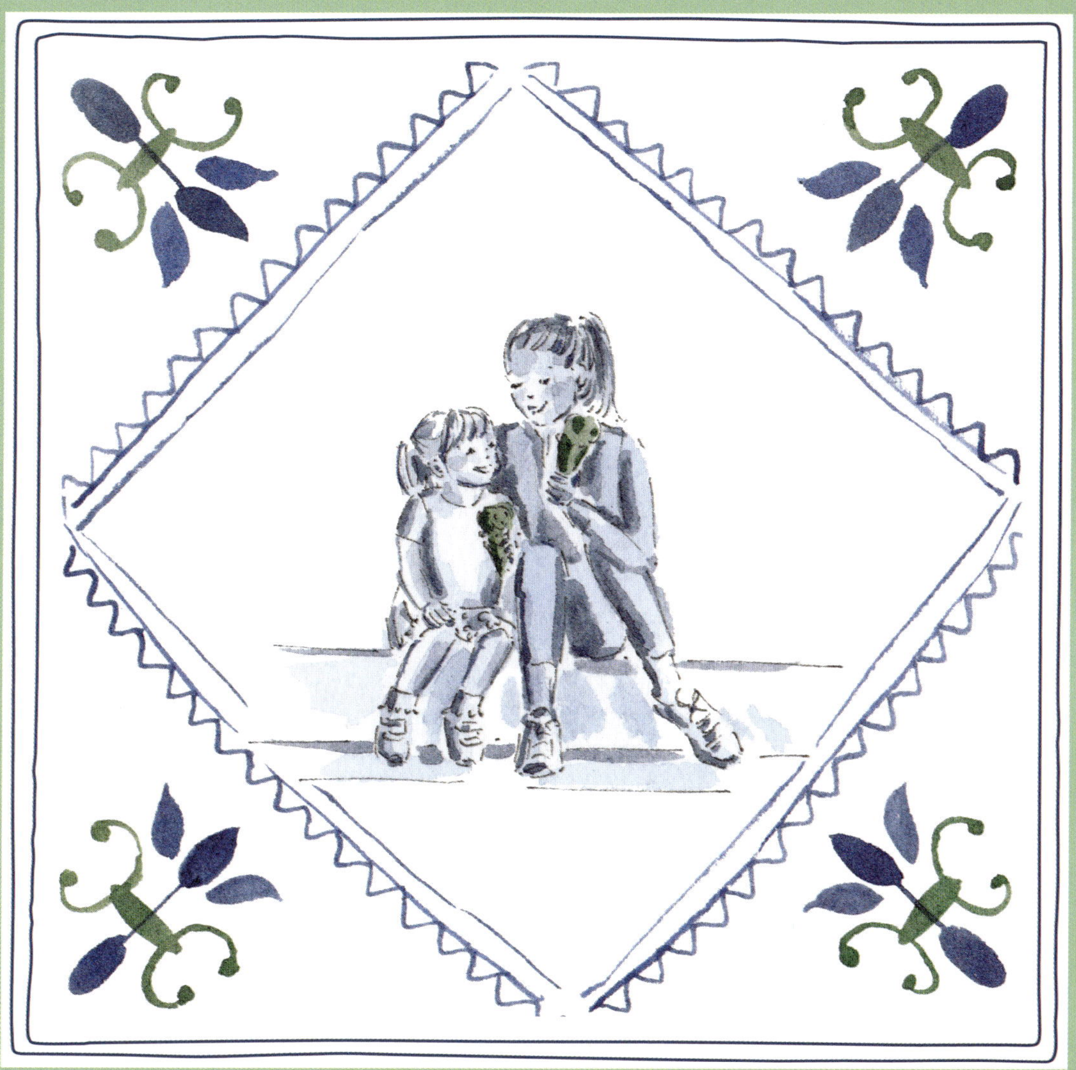

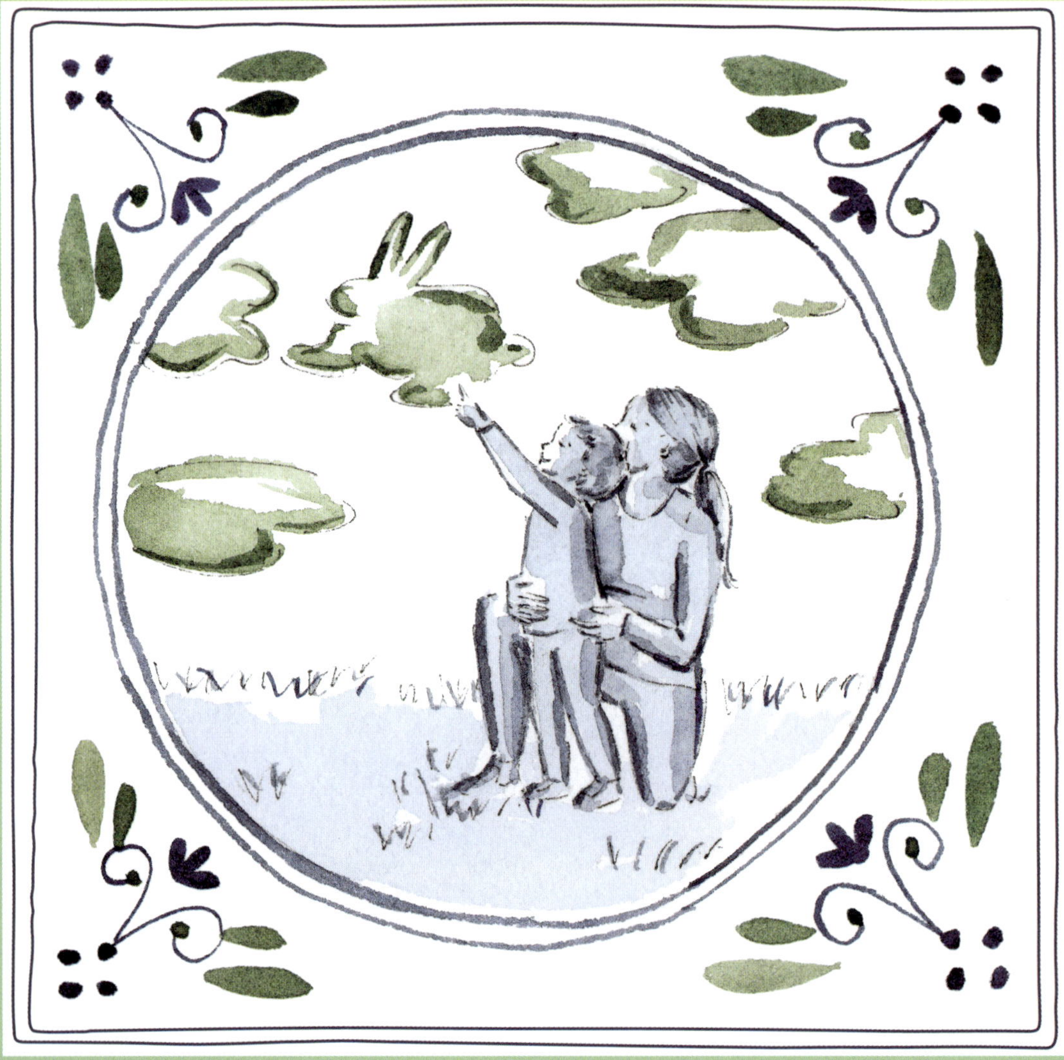

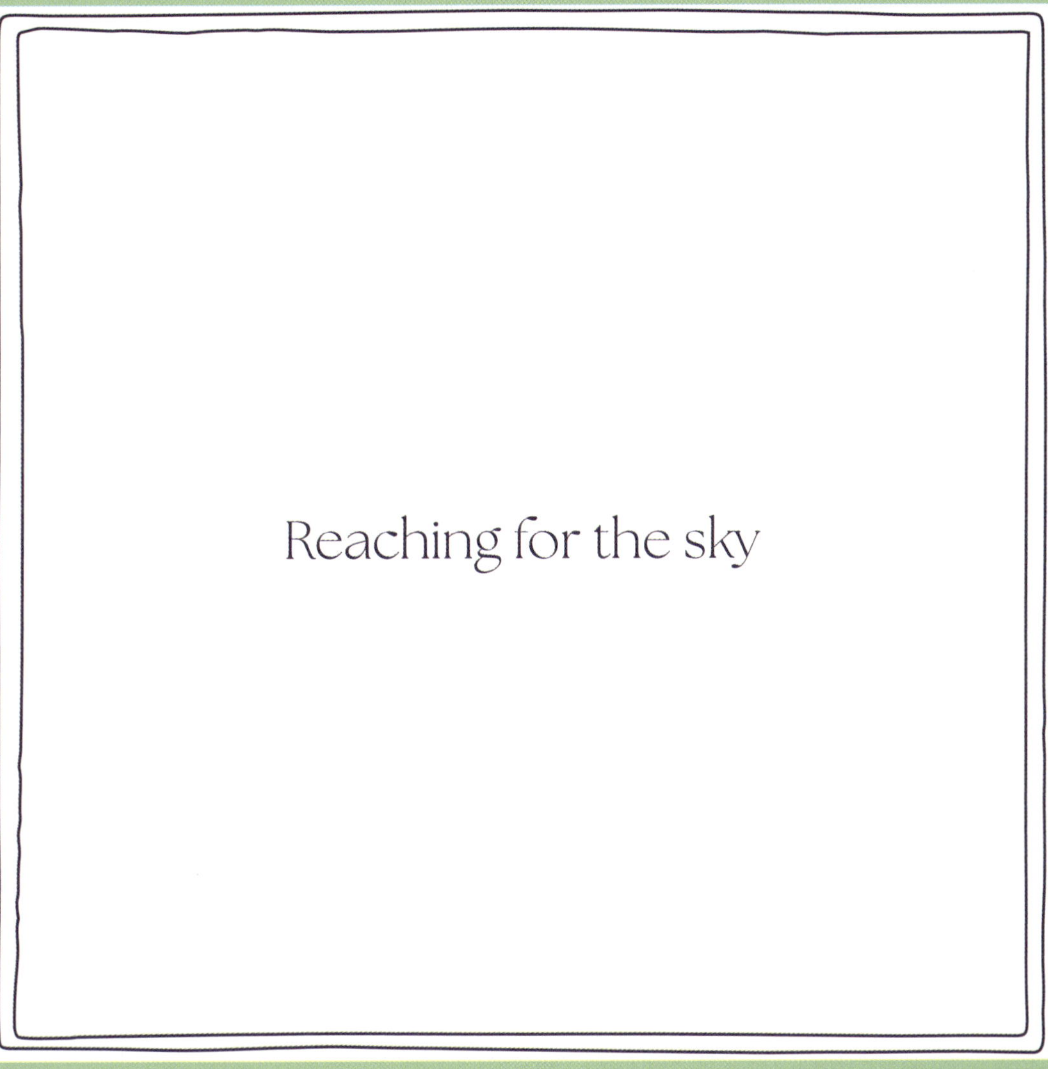

Reaching for the sky

Bejeweled

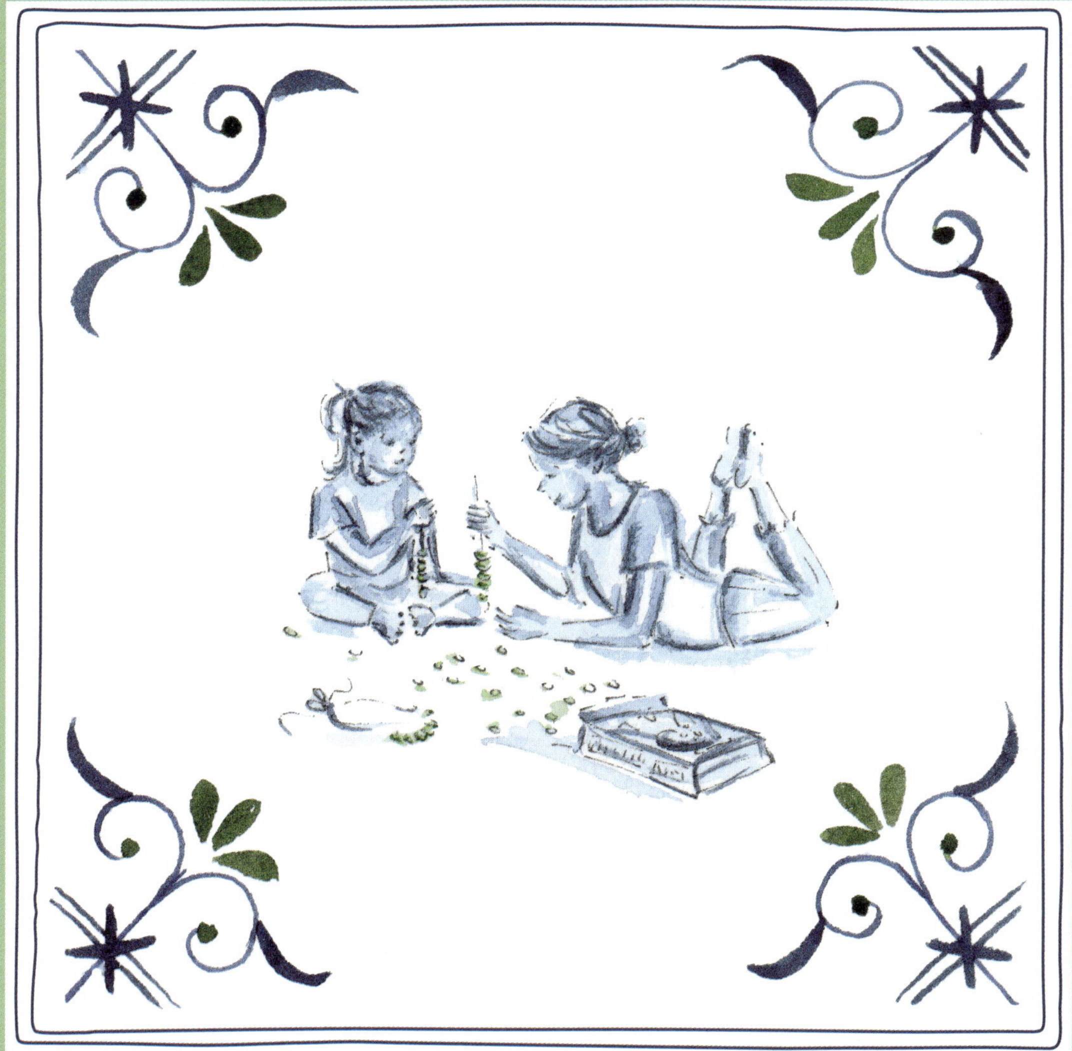

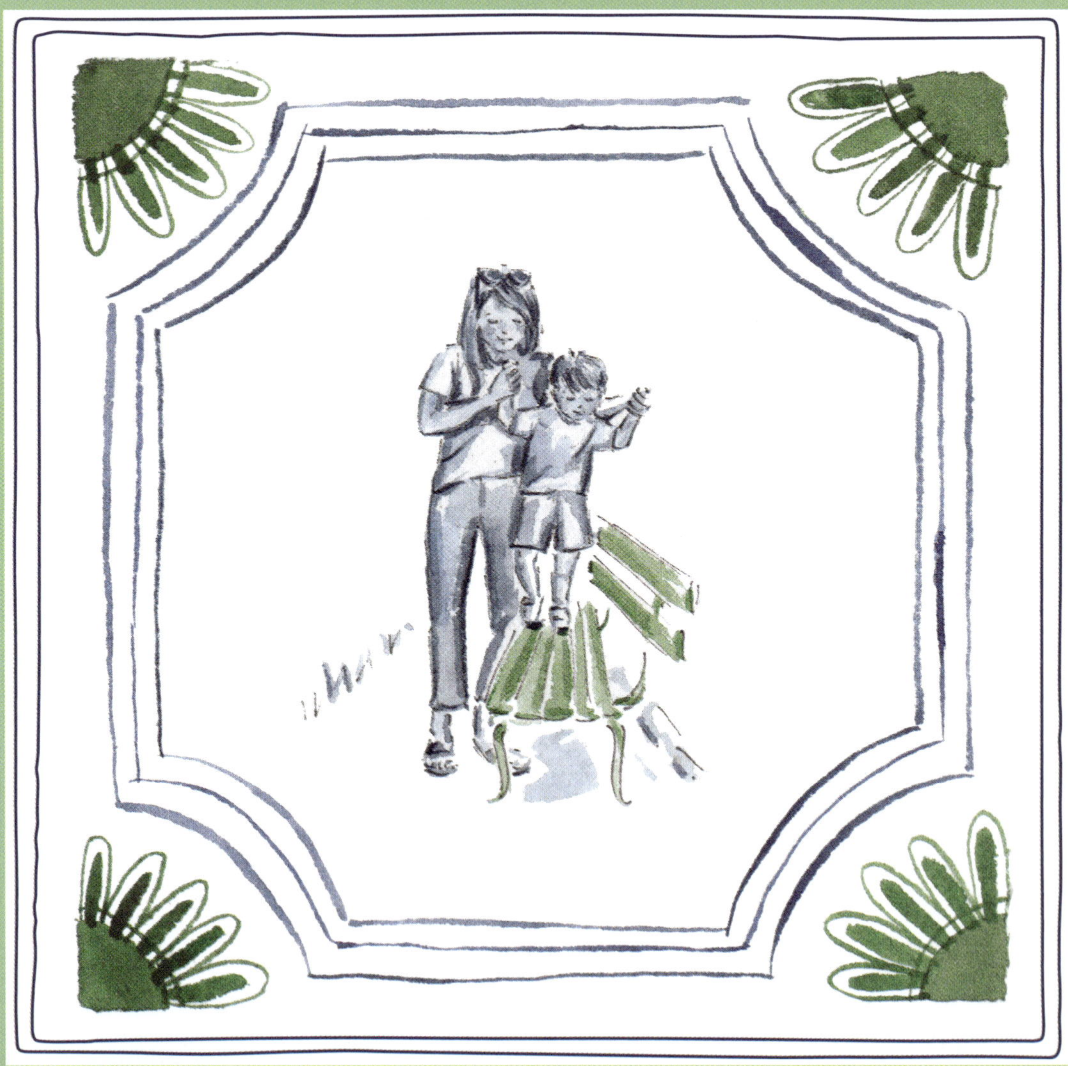

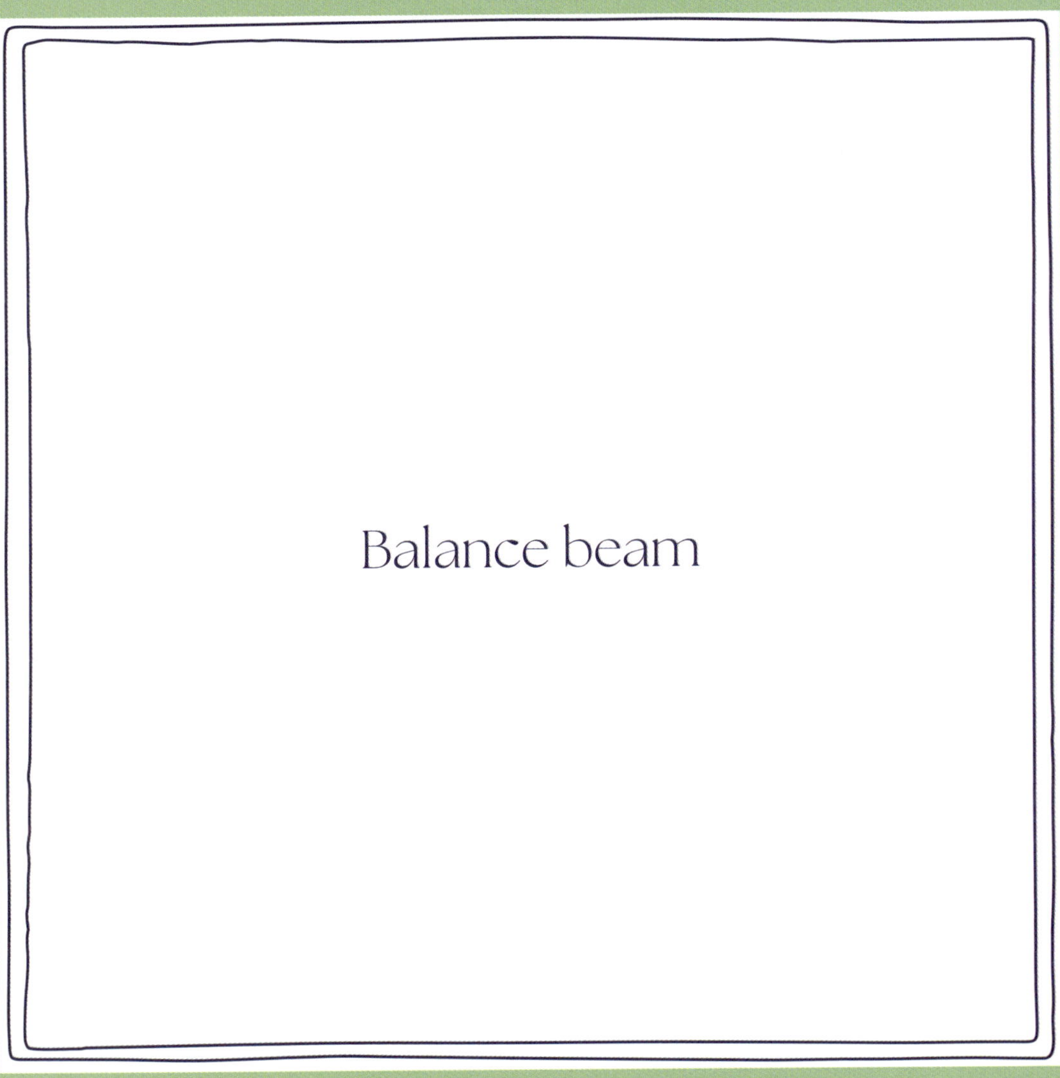

Balance beam

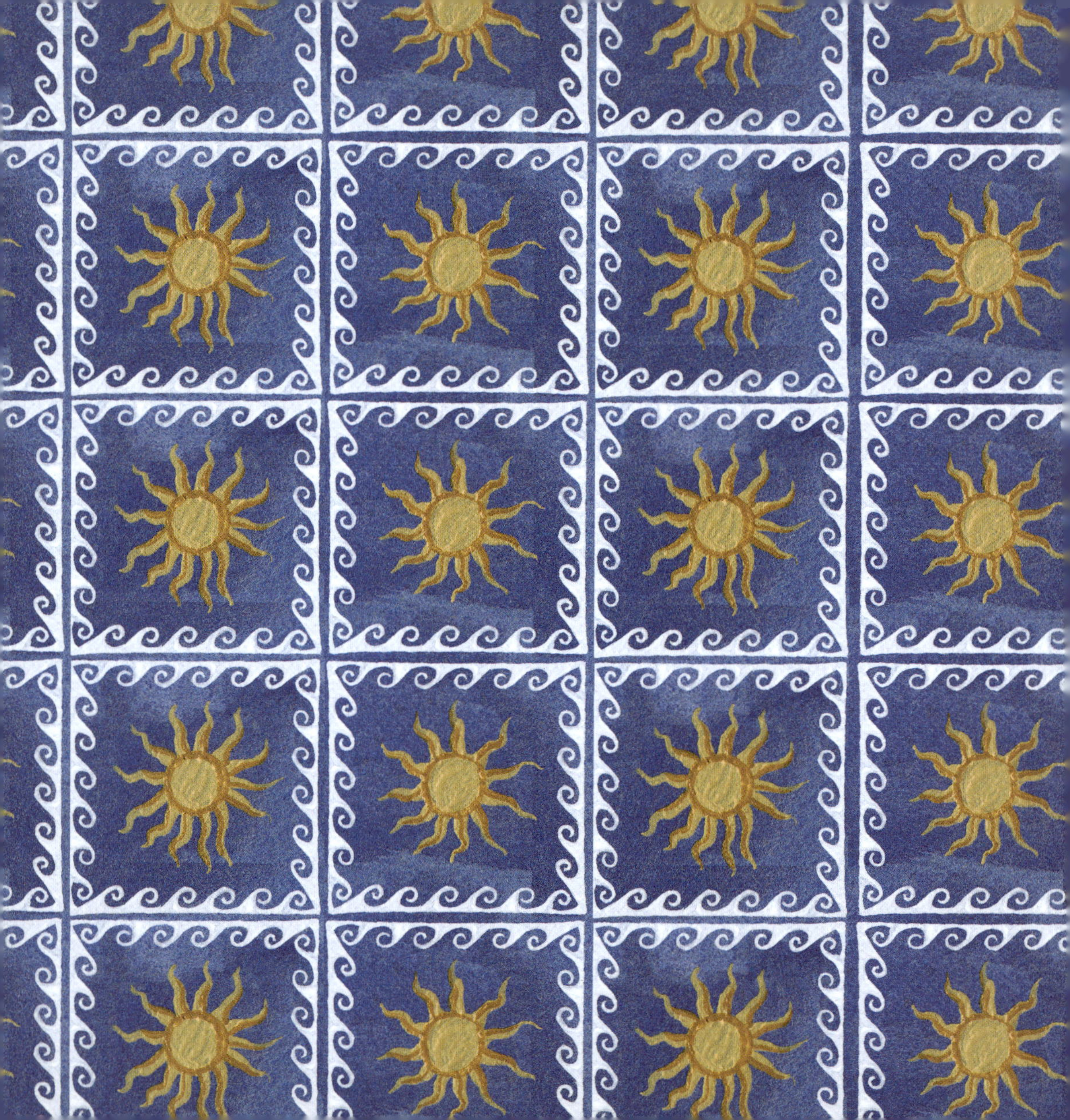

summer

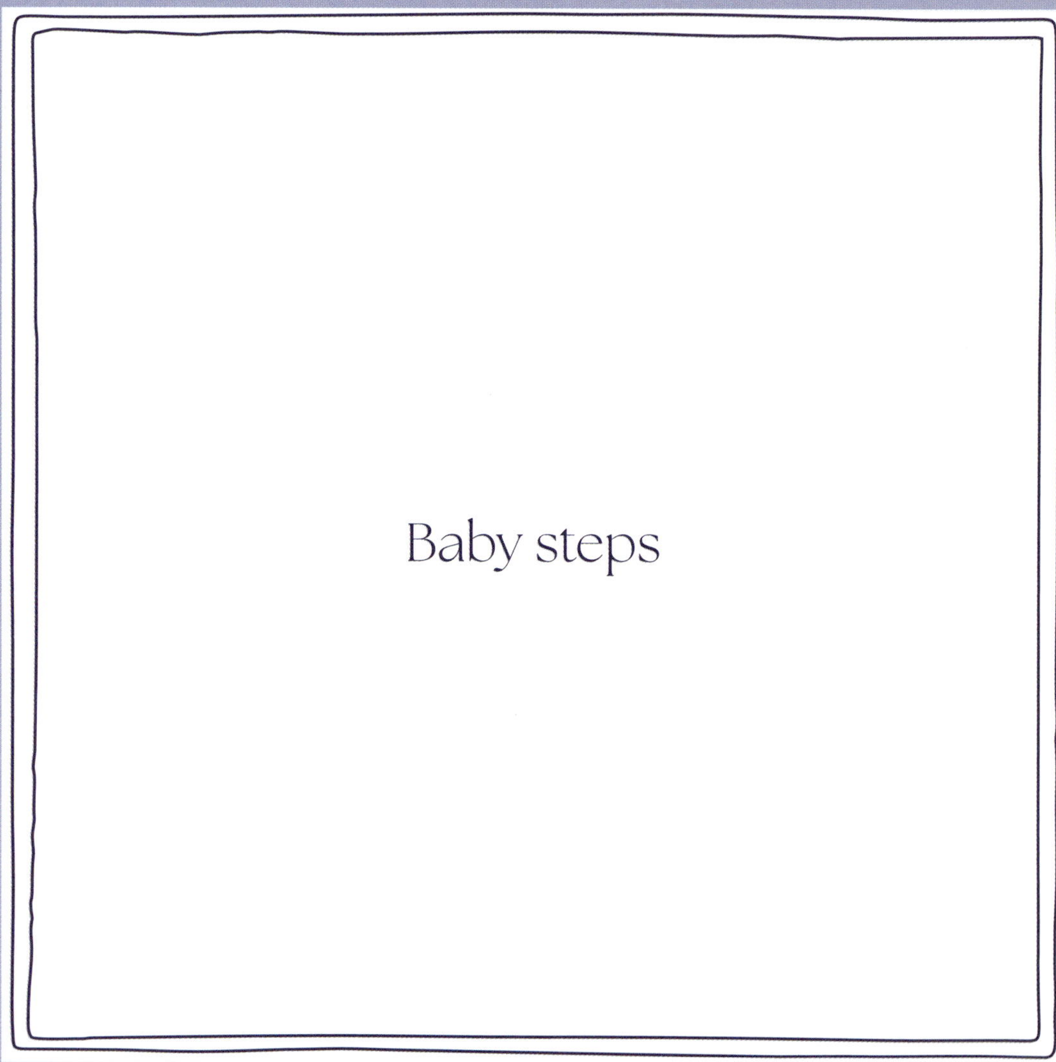

Baby steps

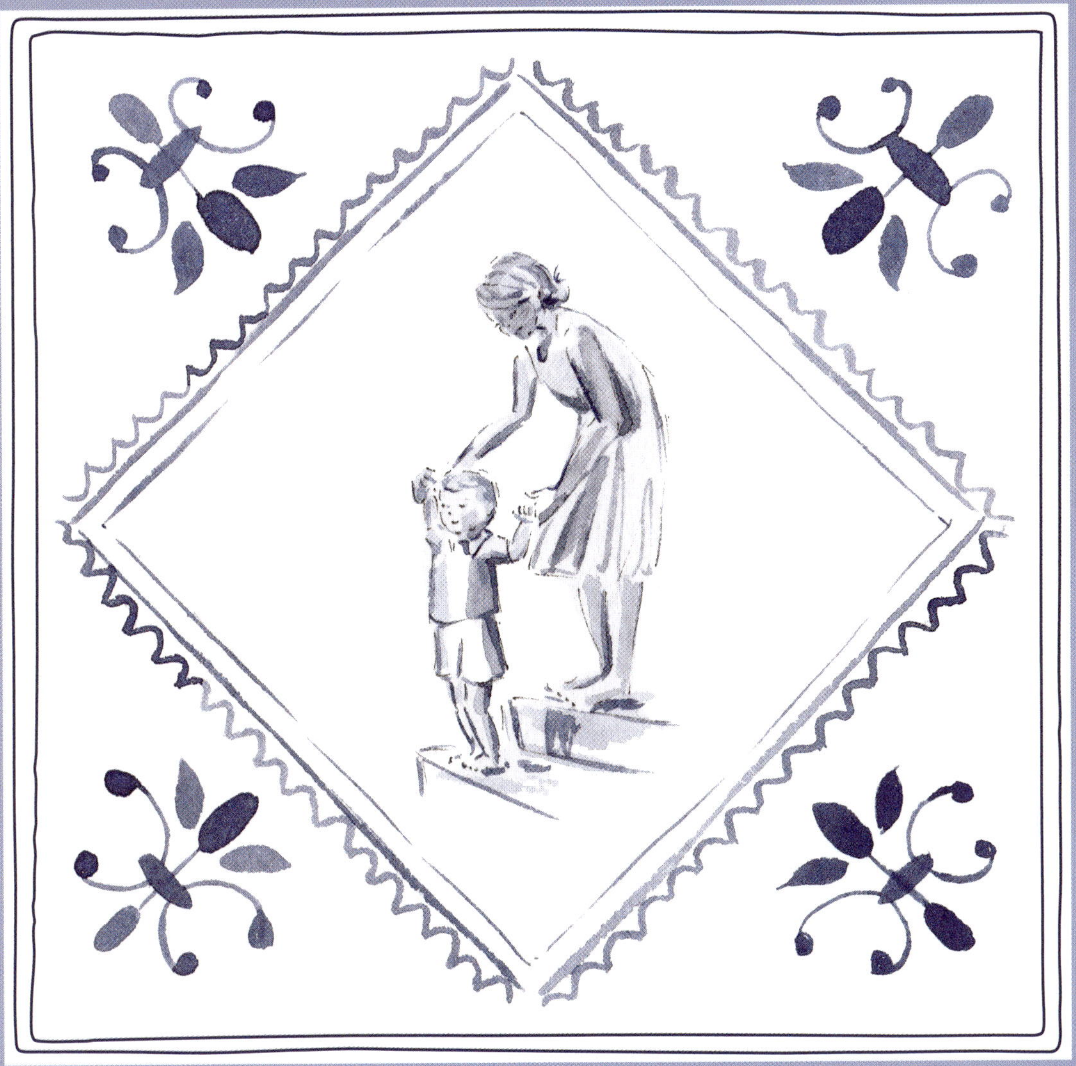

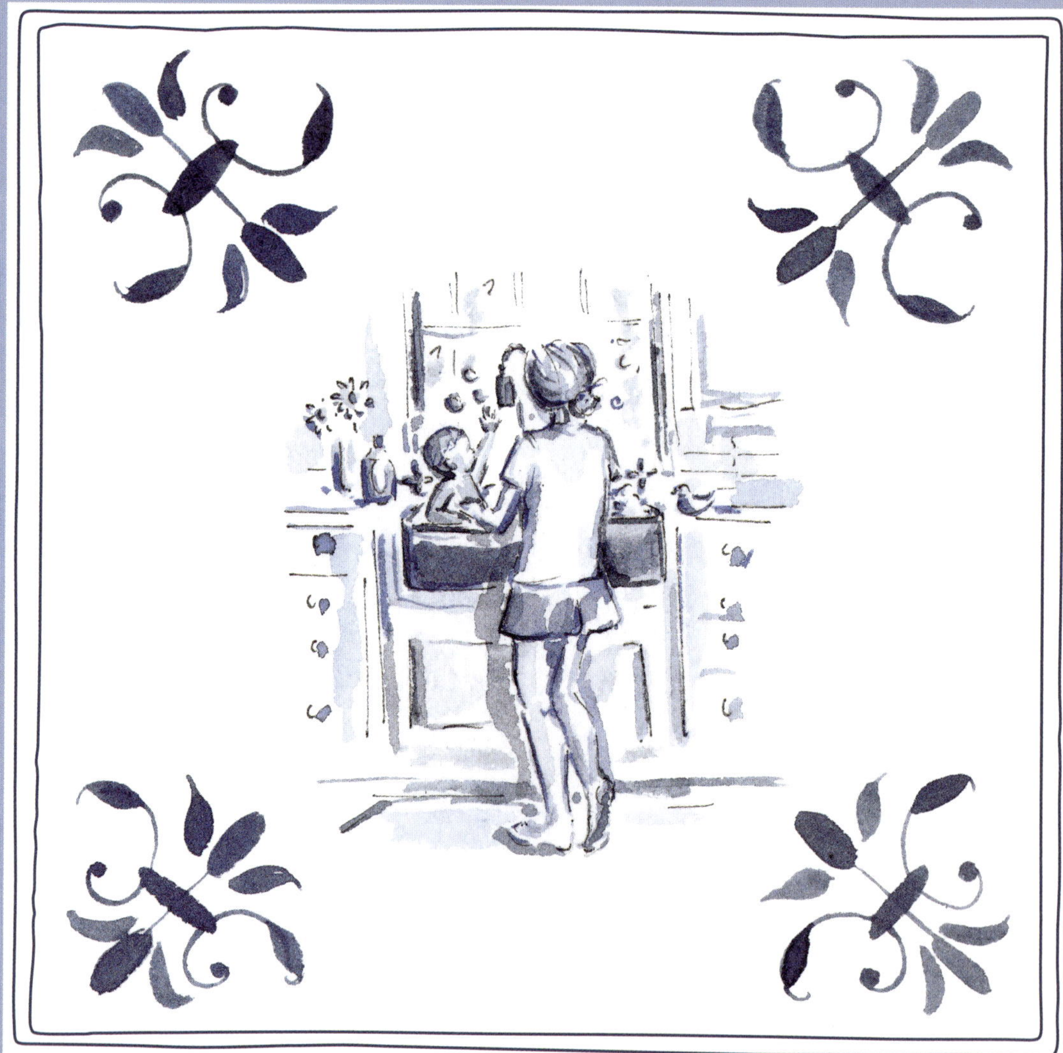

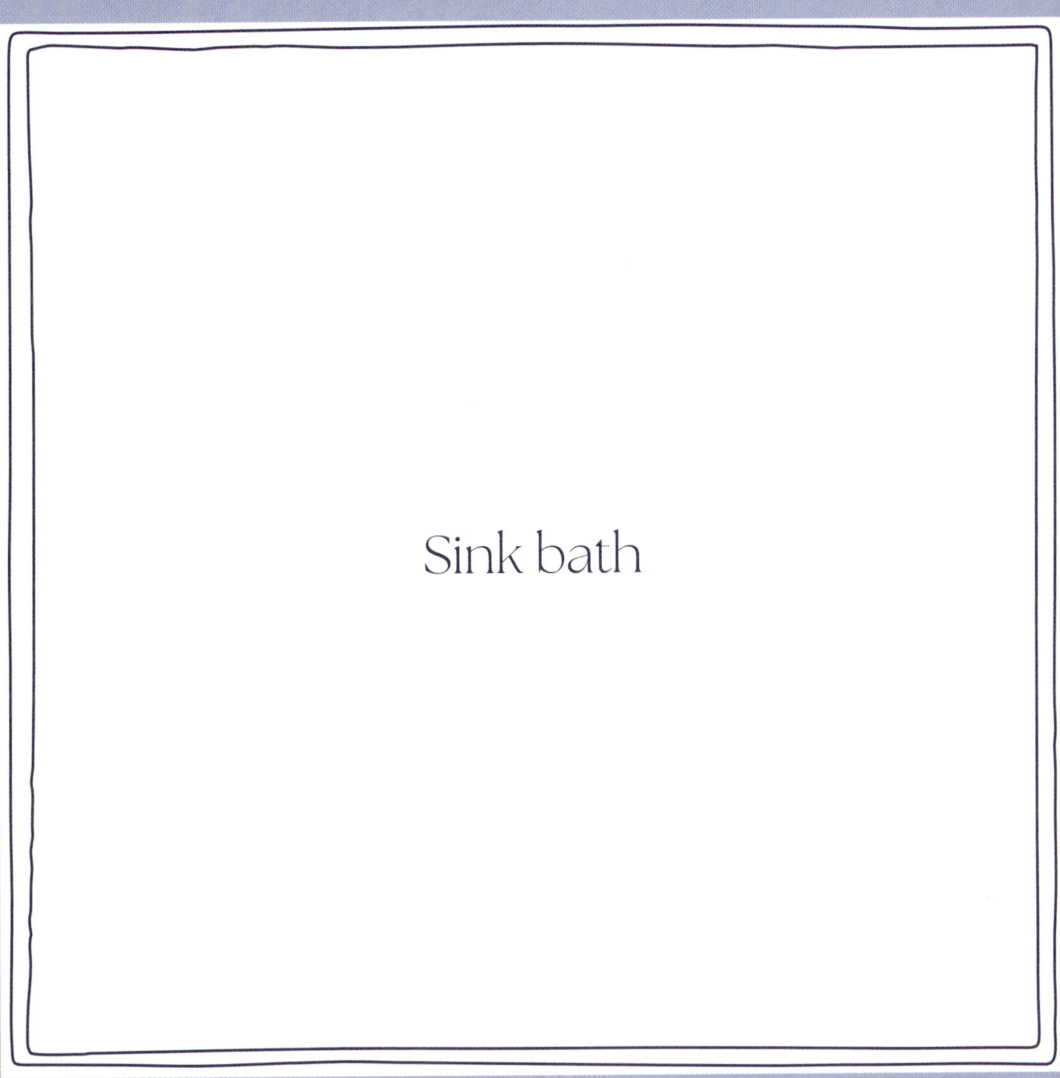

Sink bath

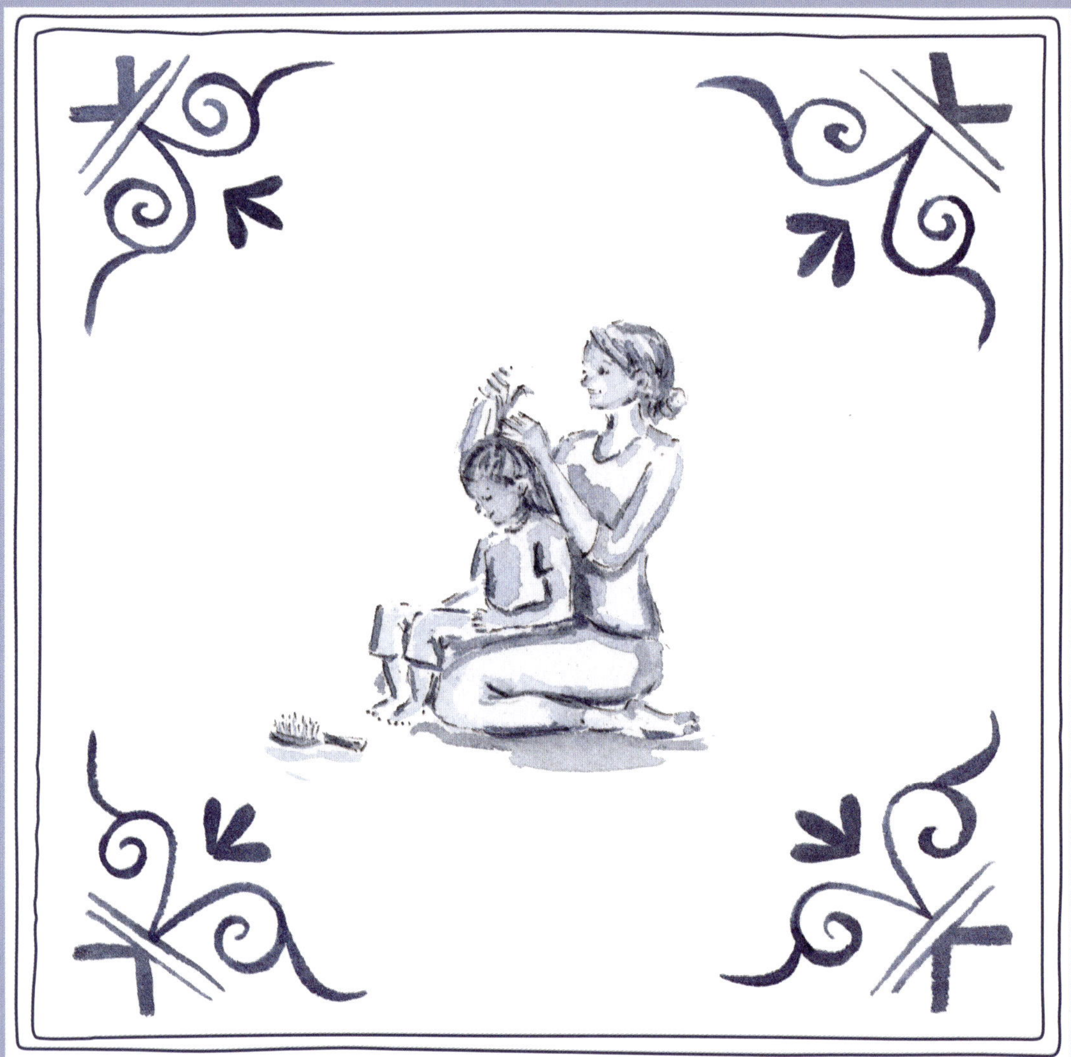

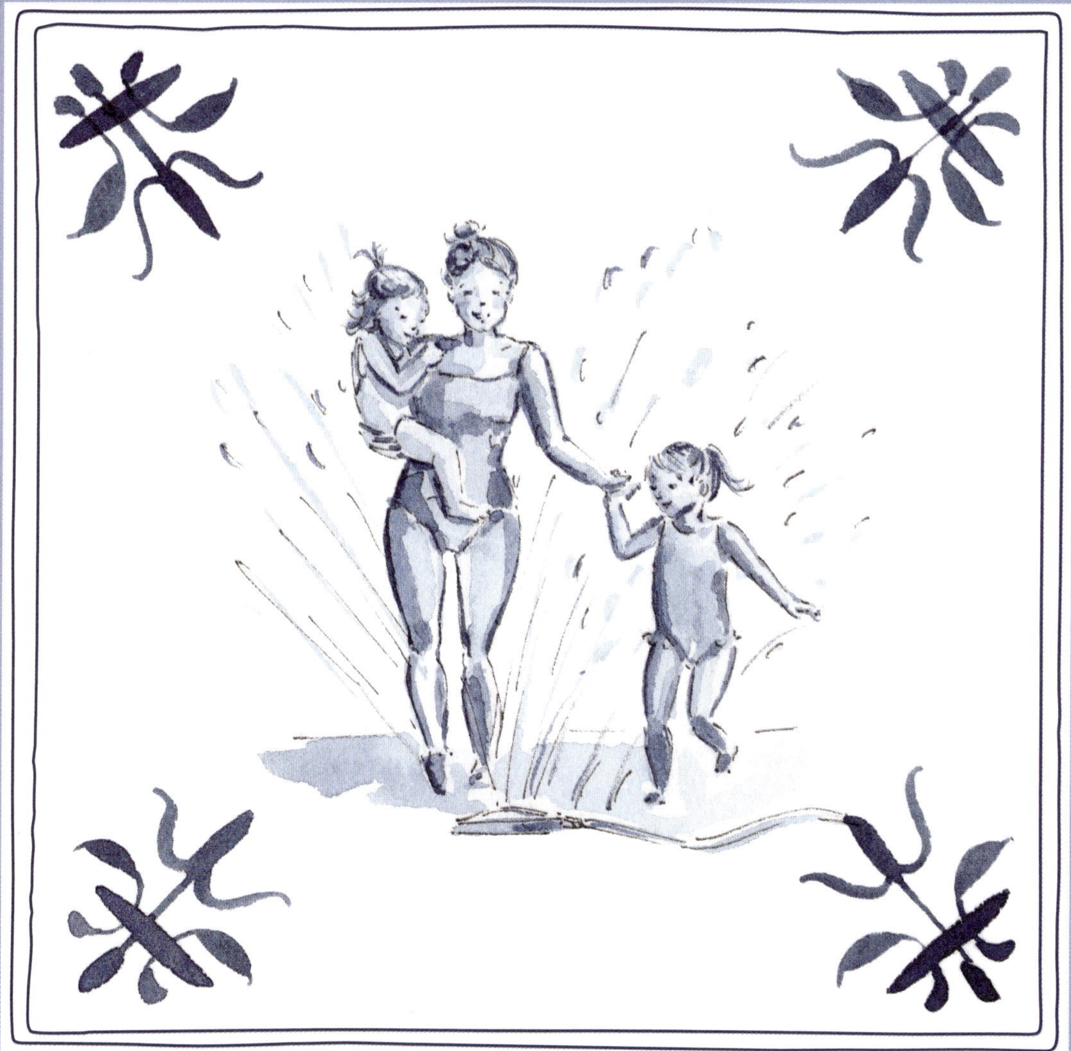

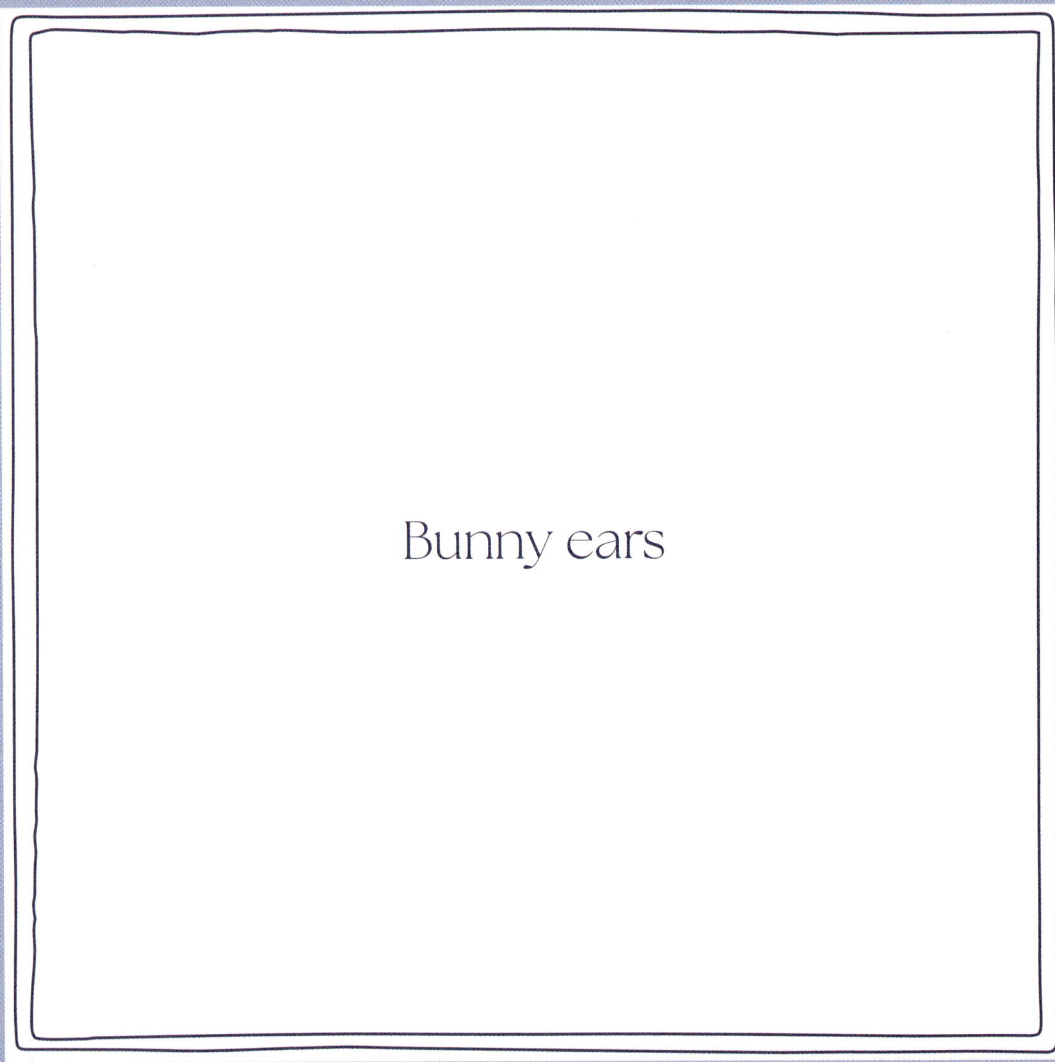

Bunny ears

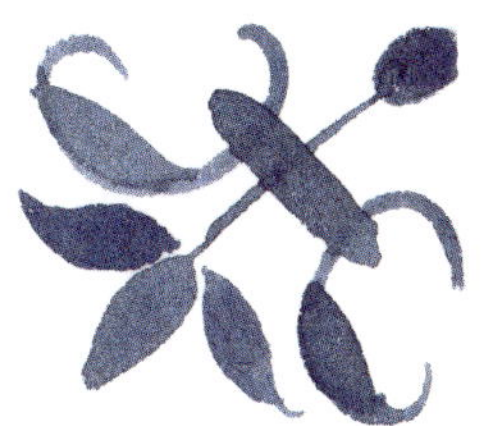
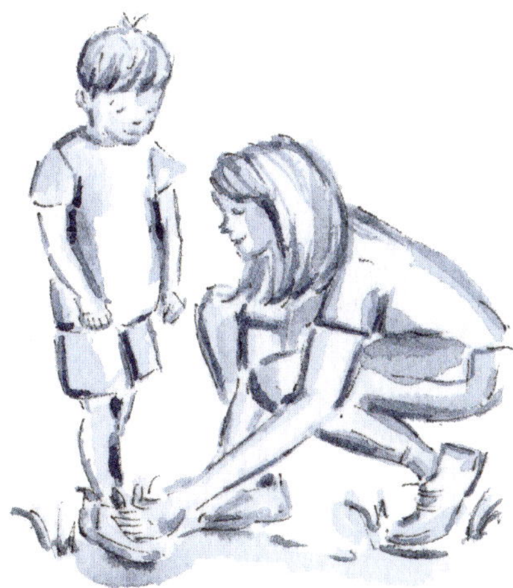
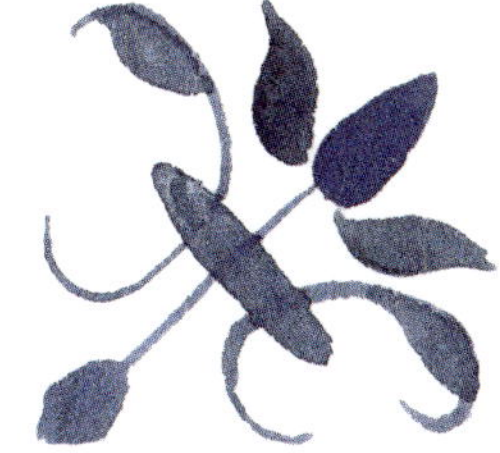

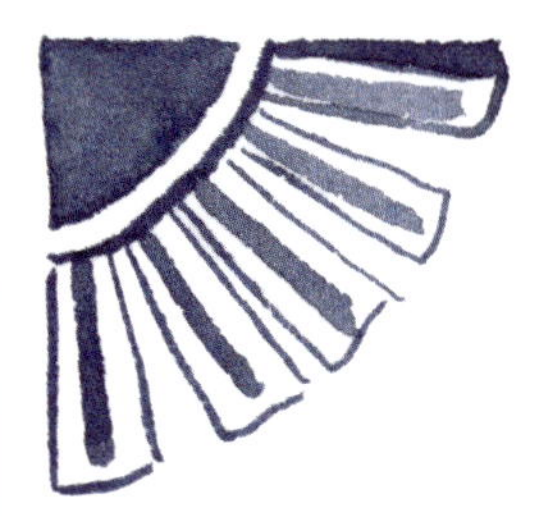
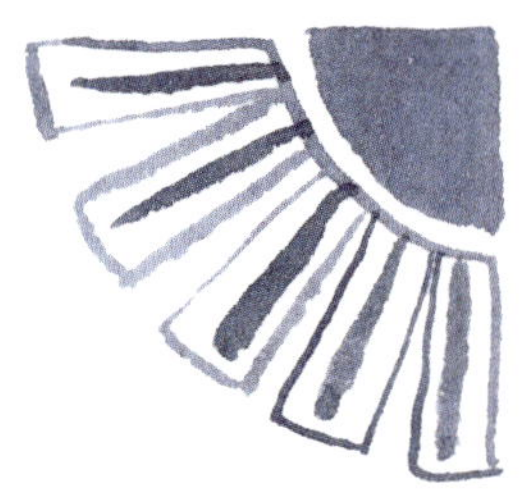
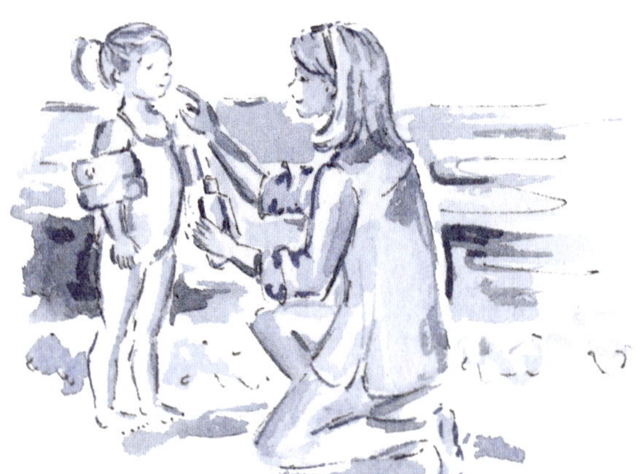
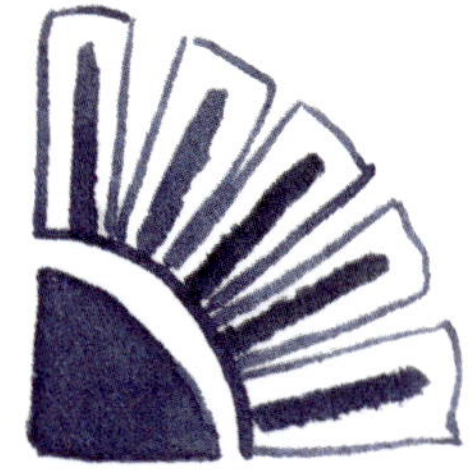
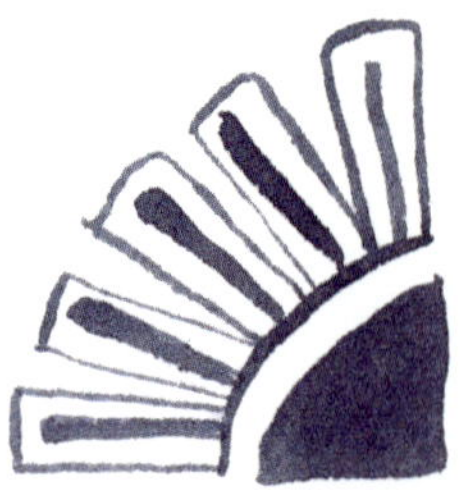

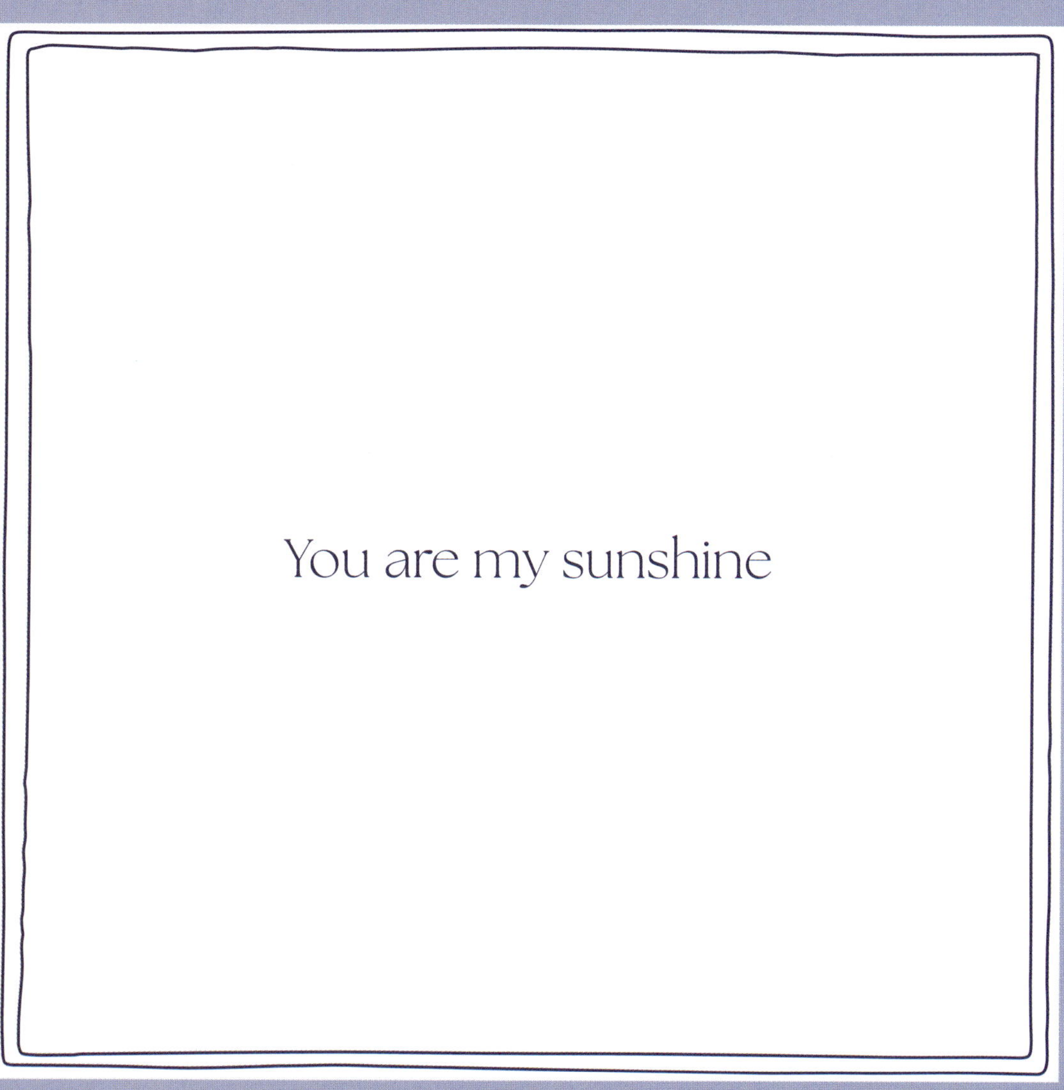
You are my sunshine

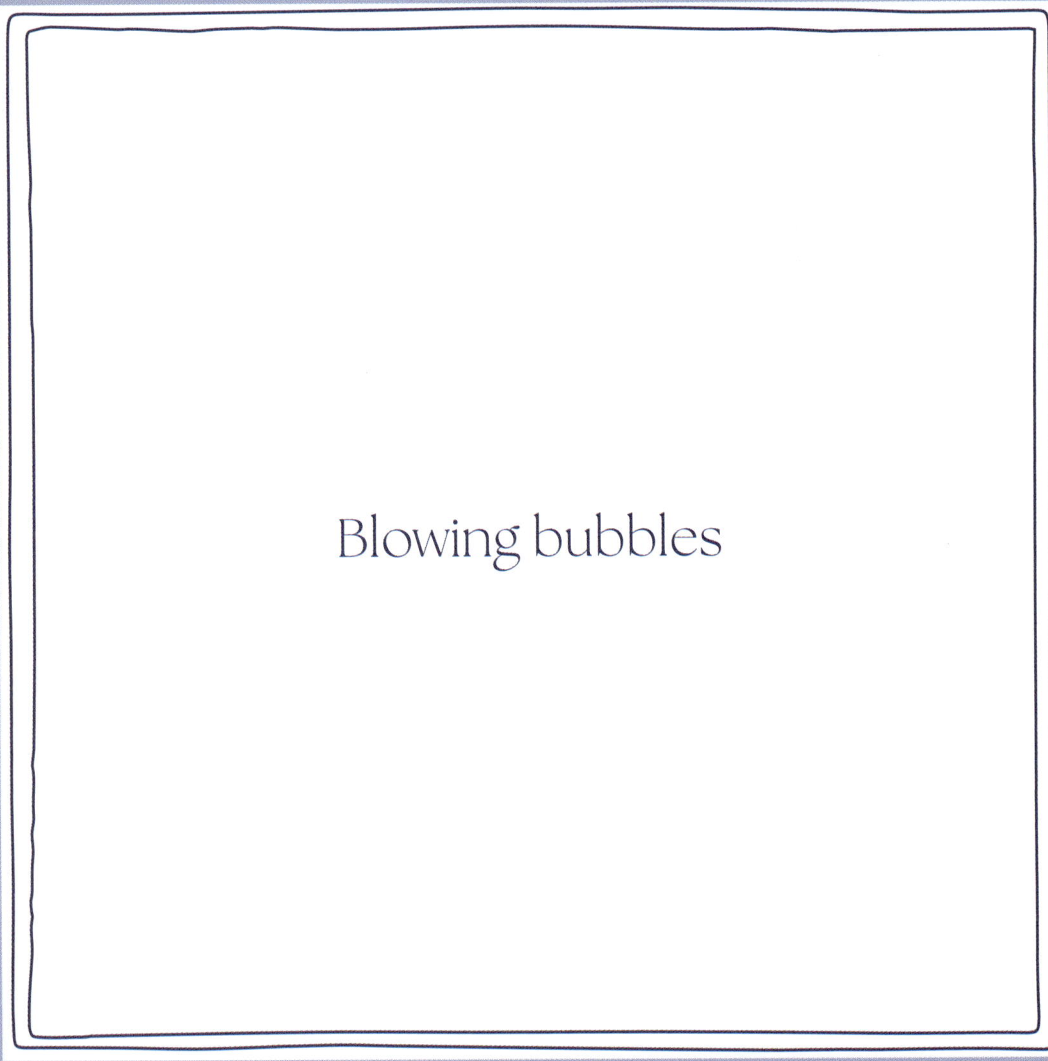

Blowing bubbles

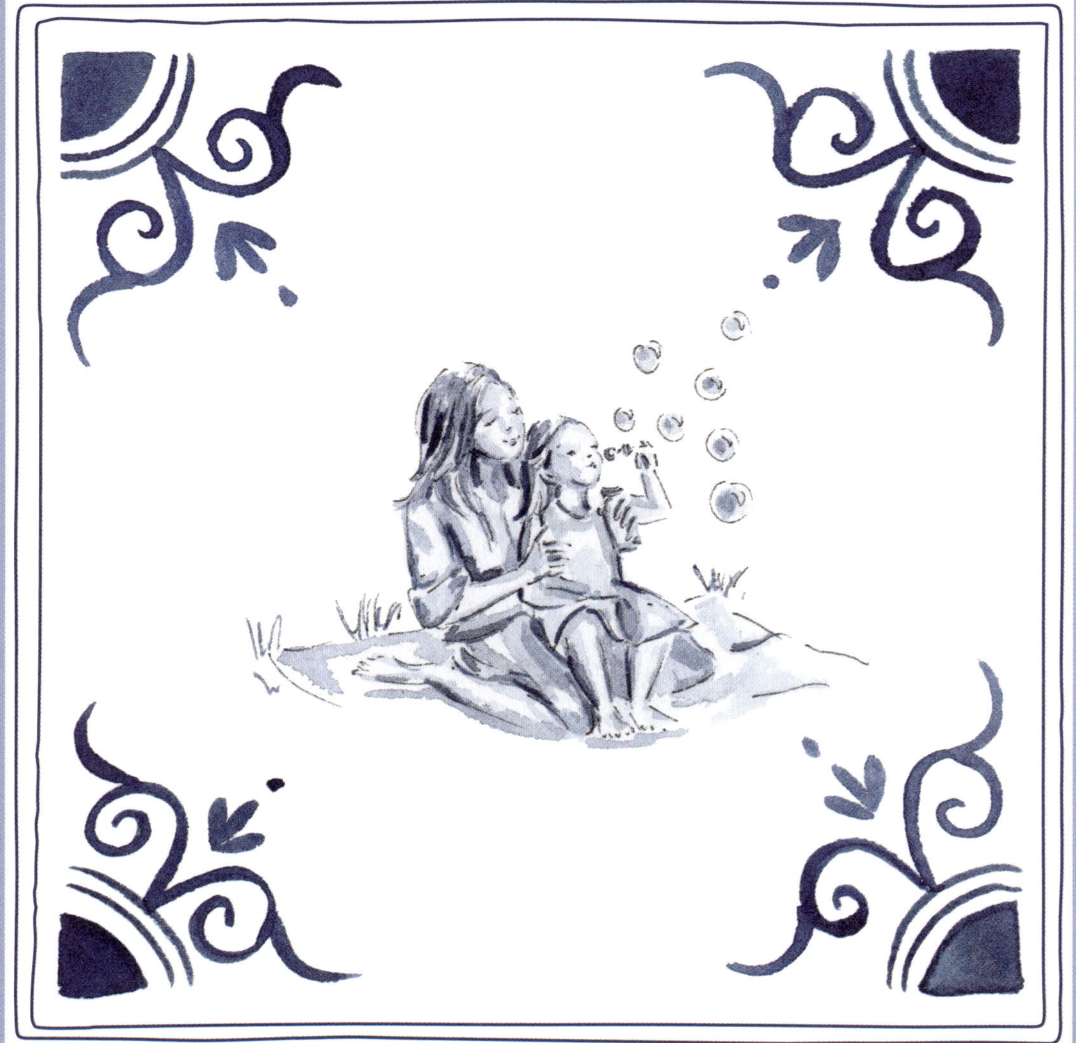

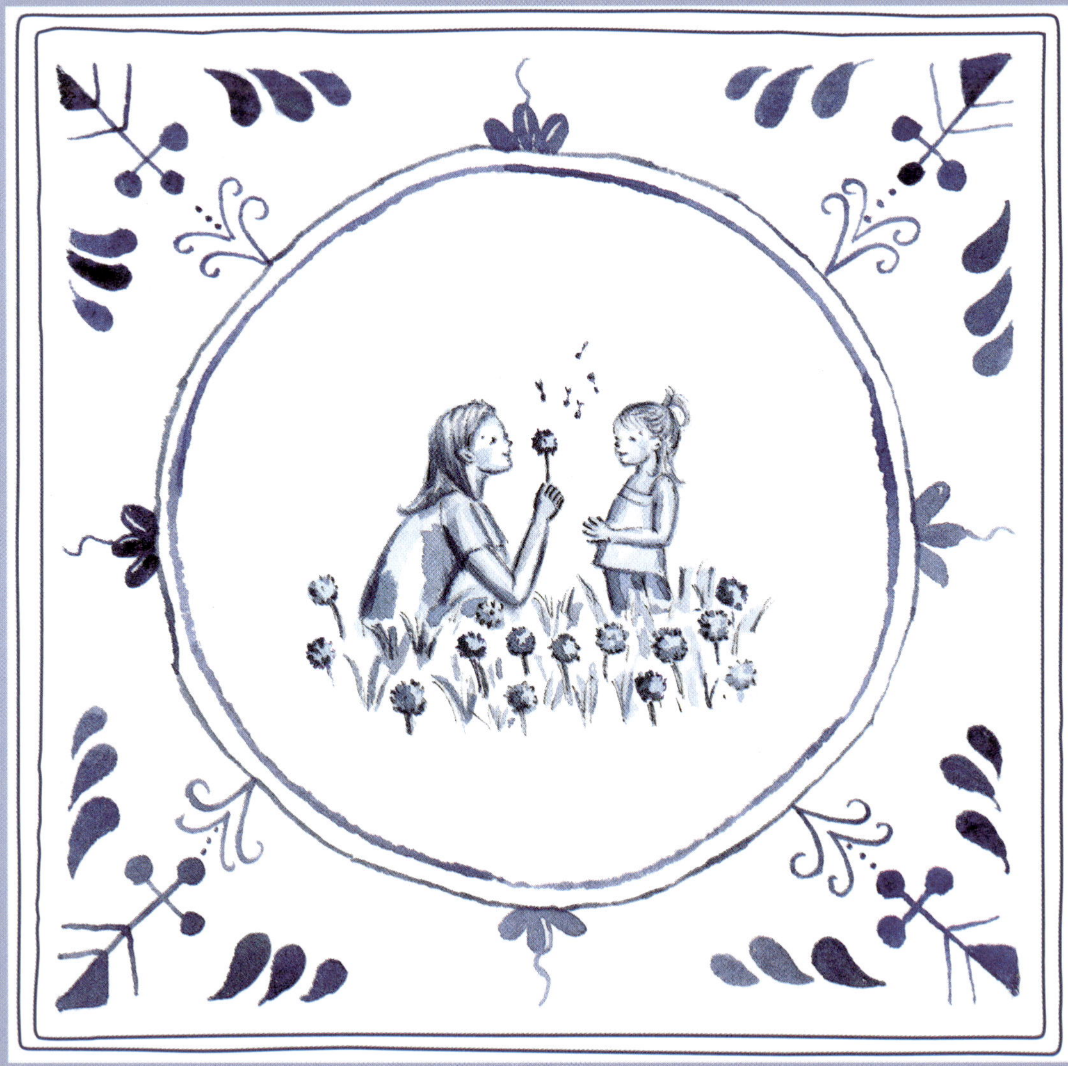

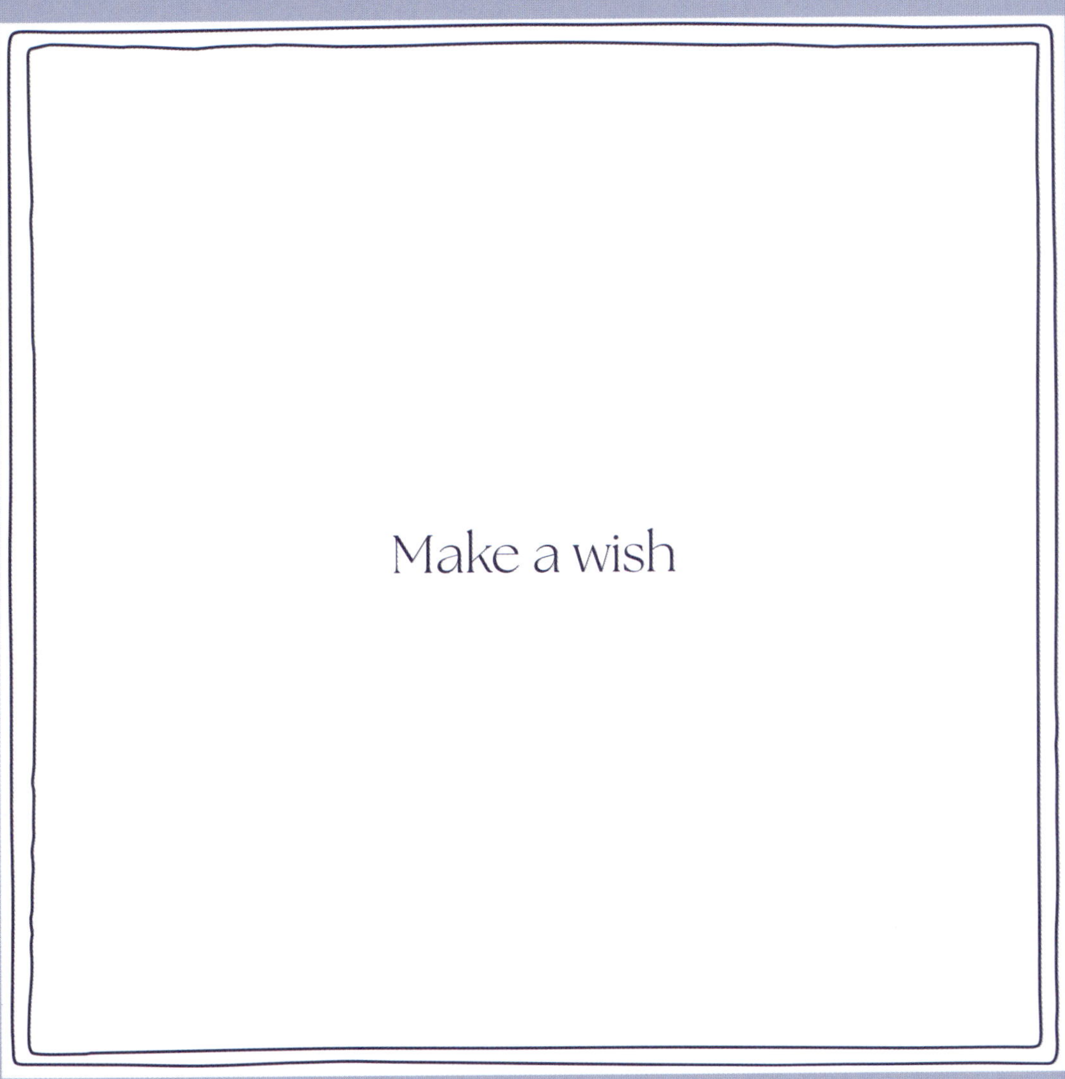

Make a wish

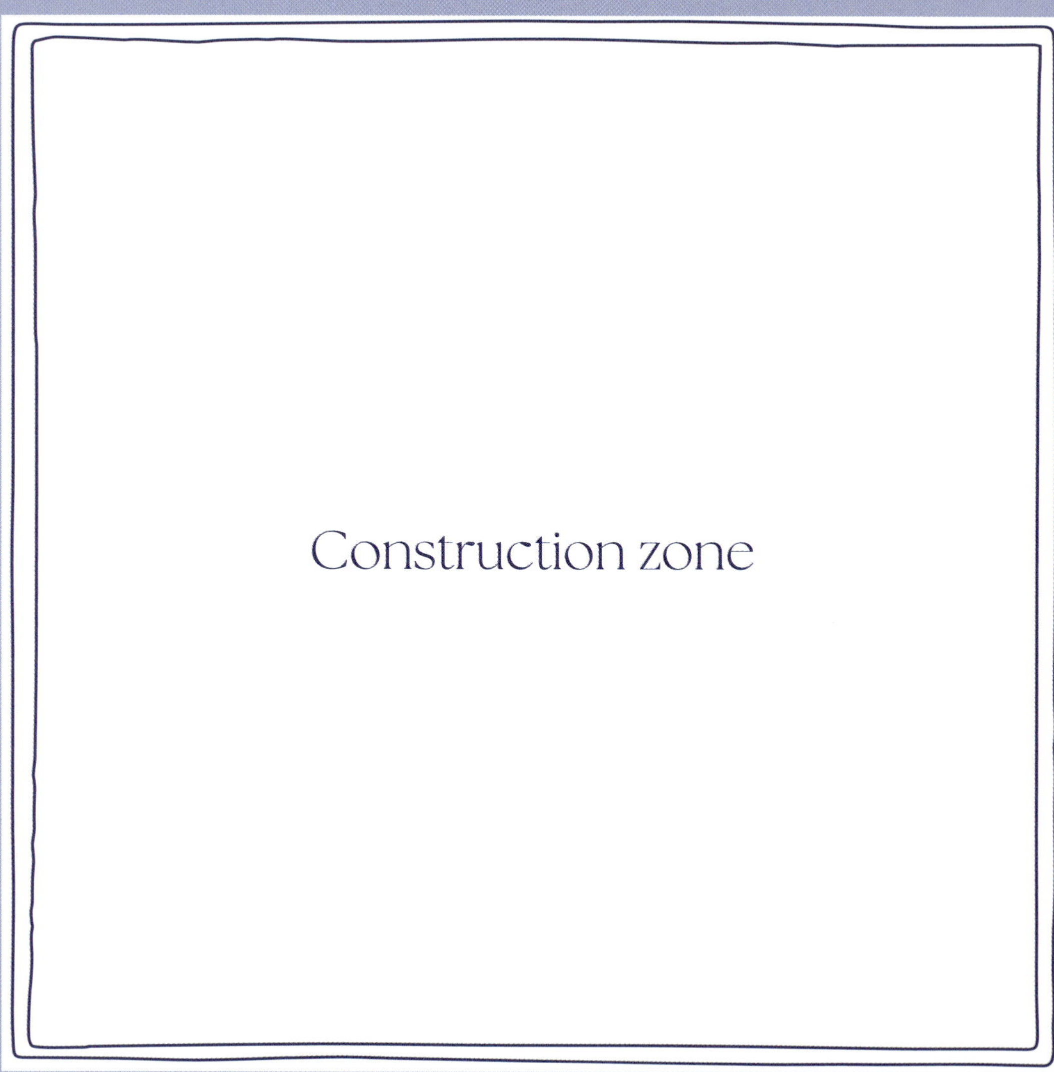

Construction zone

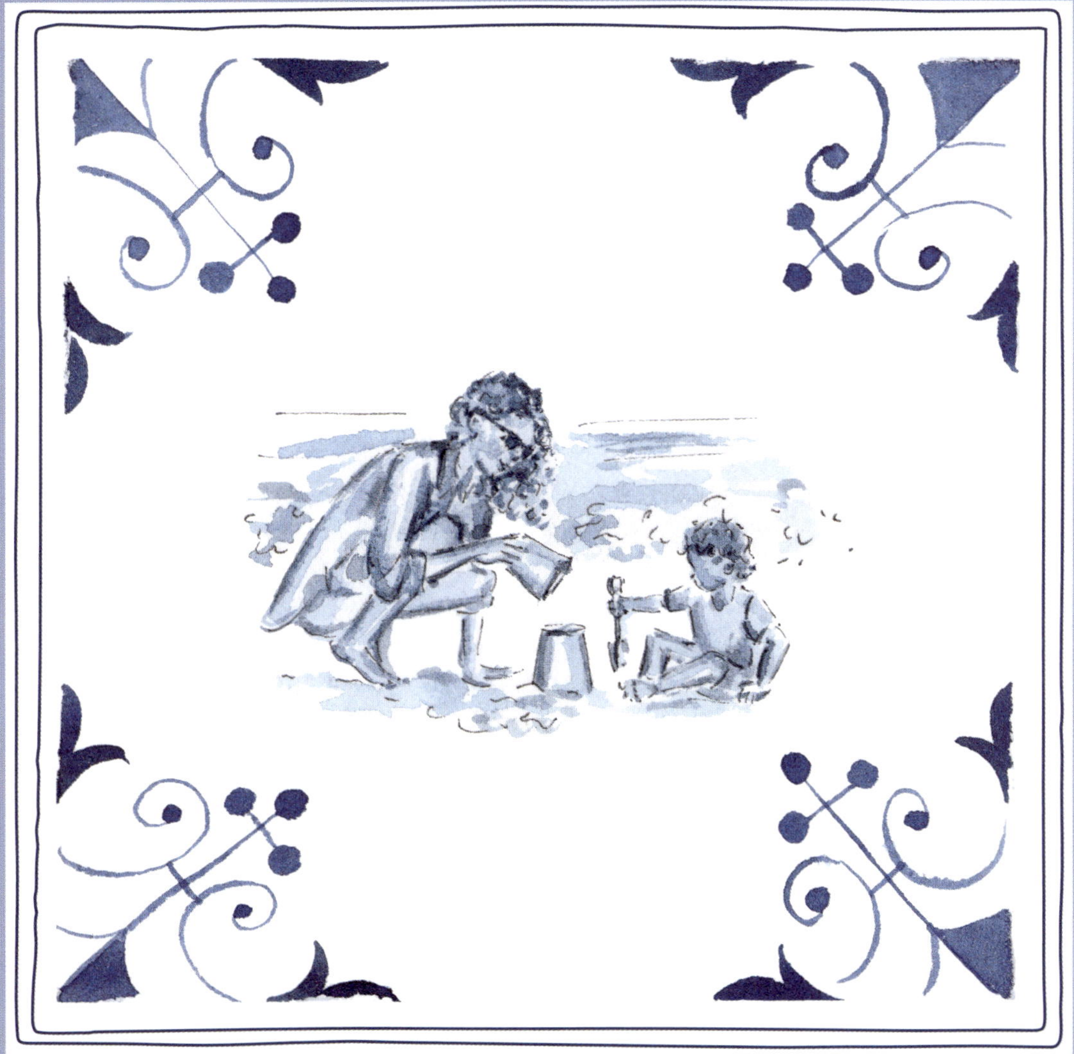

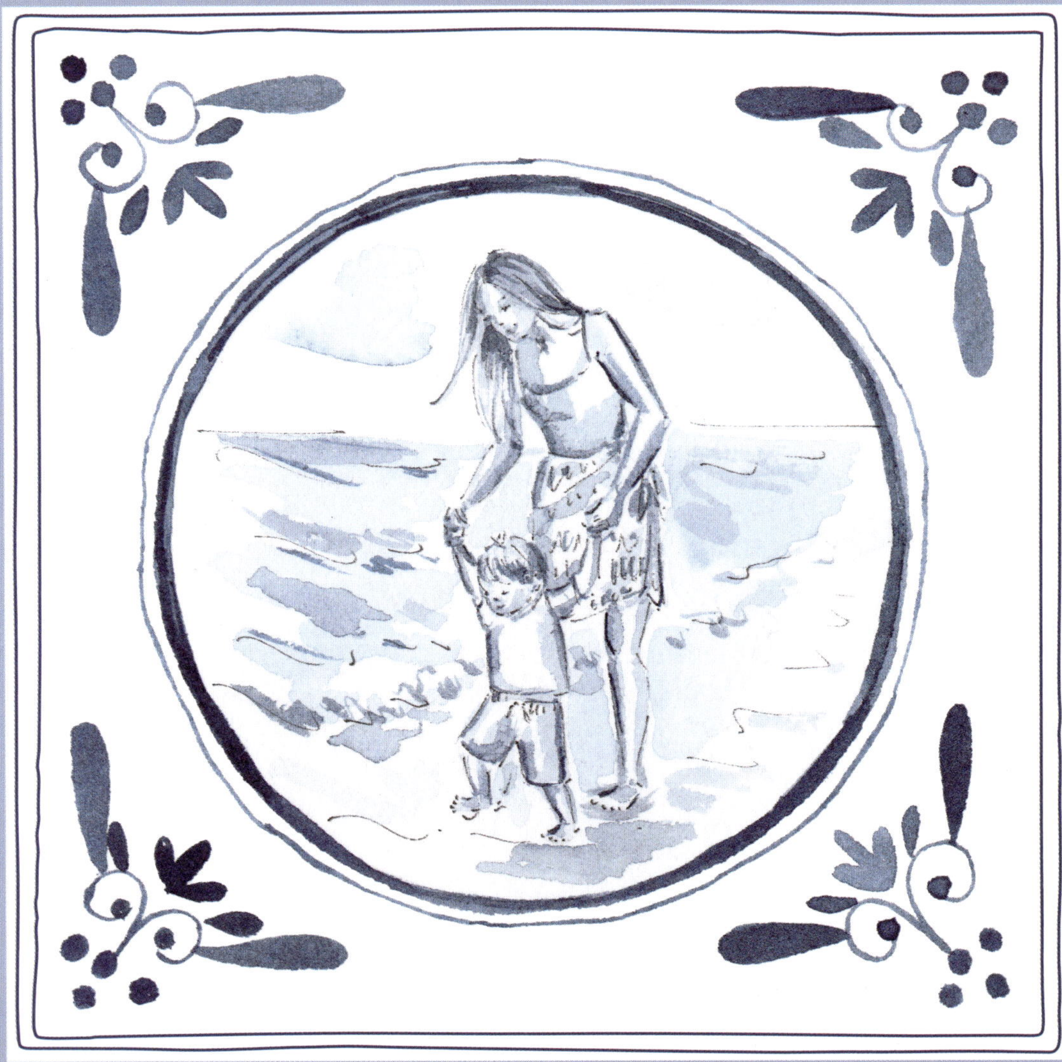

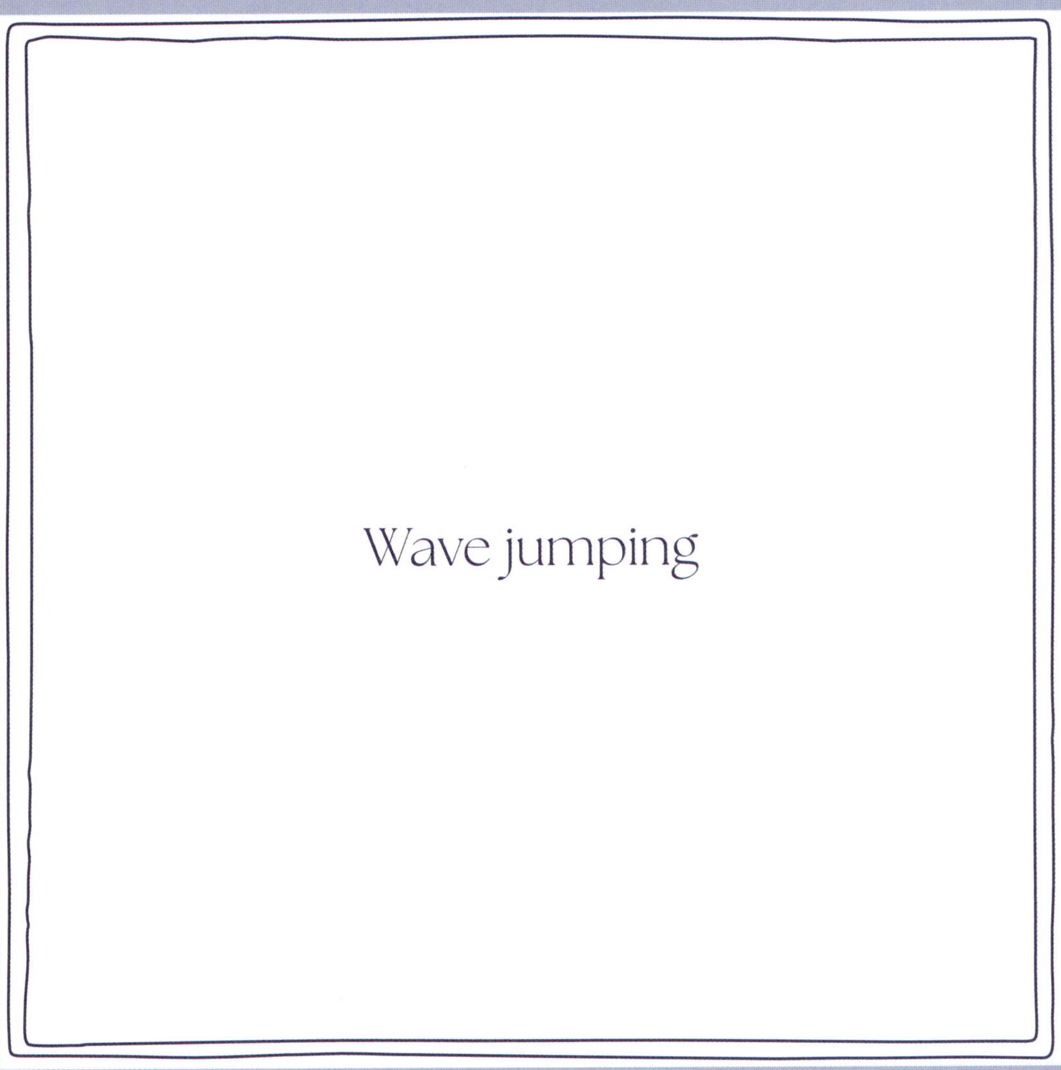

Wave jumping

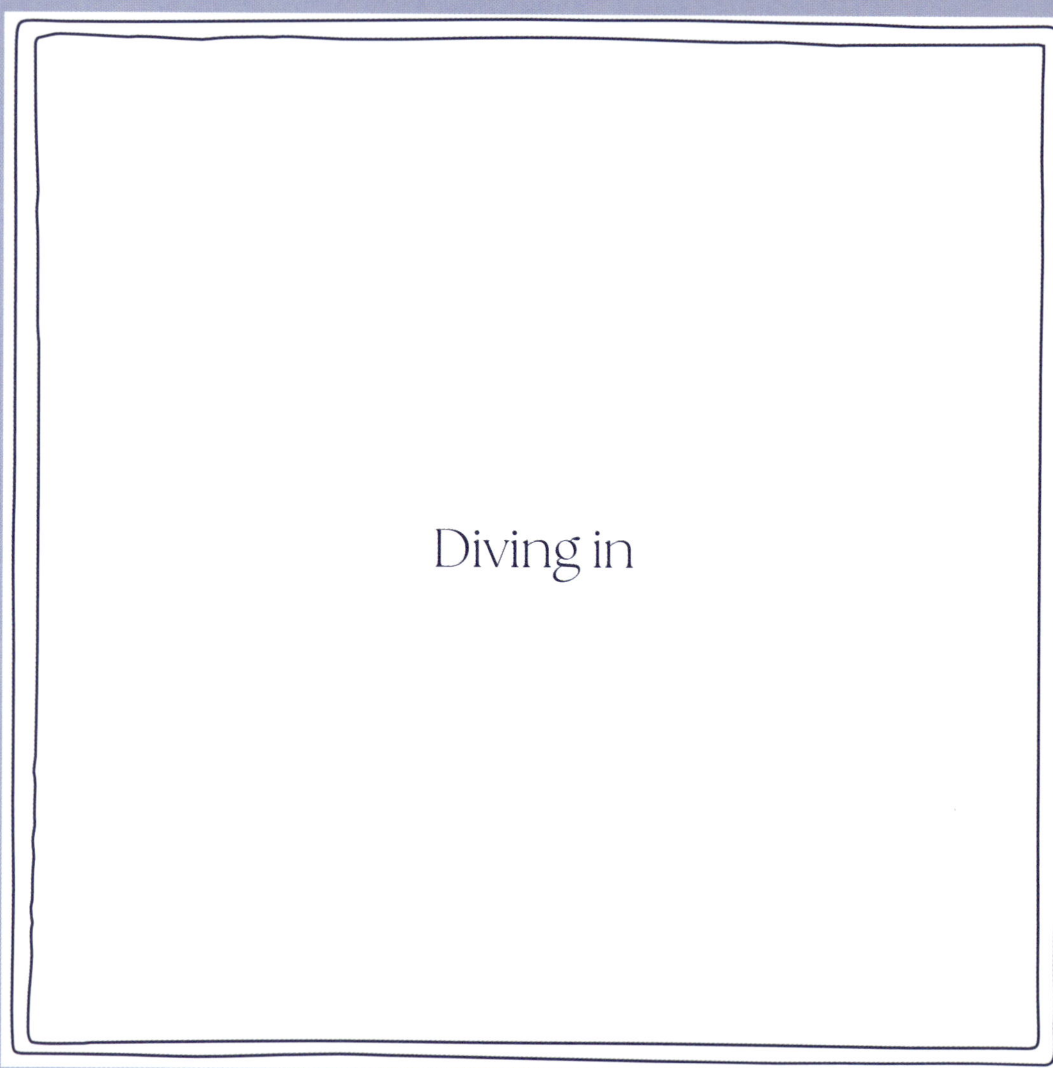

Diving in

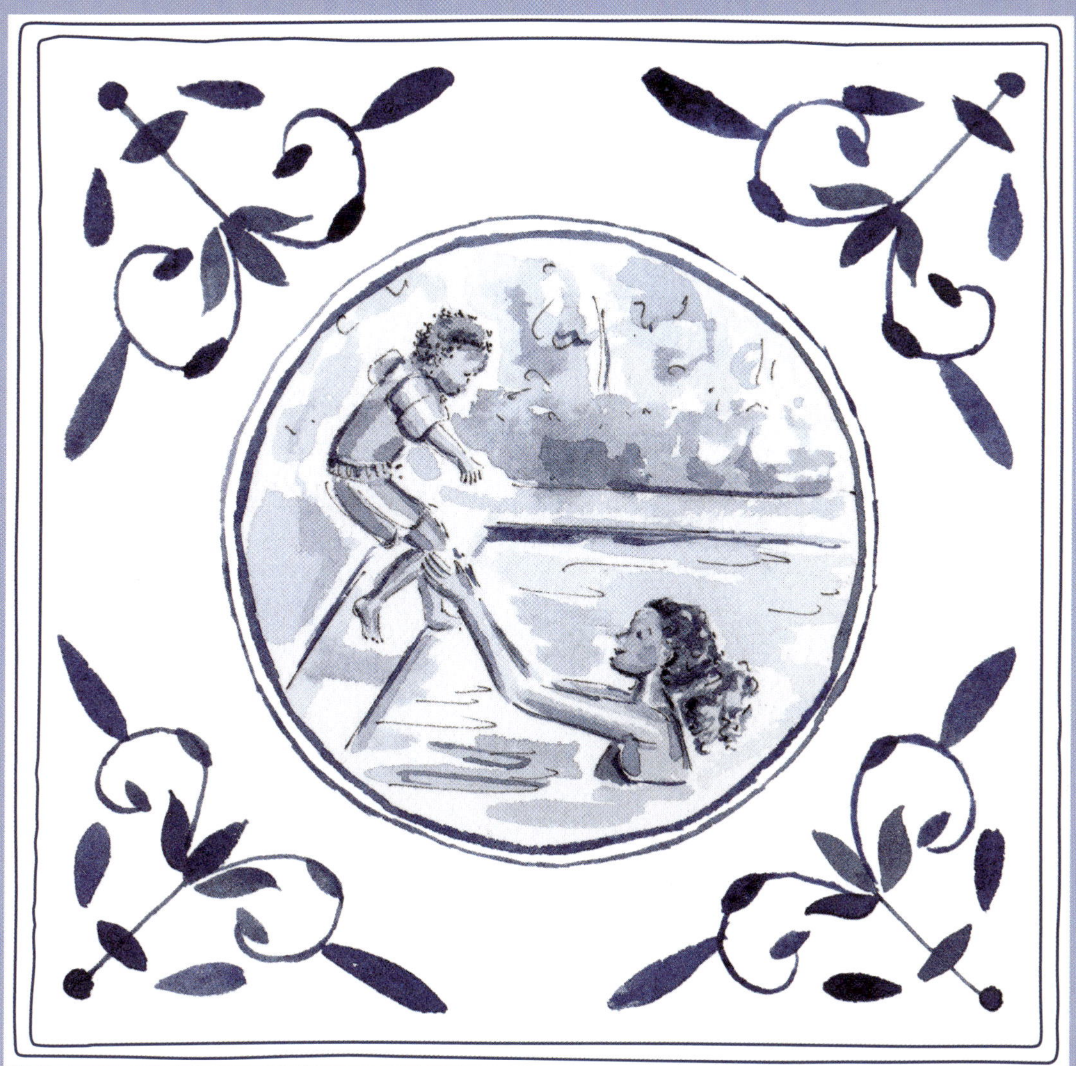

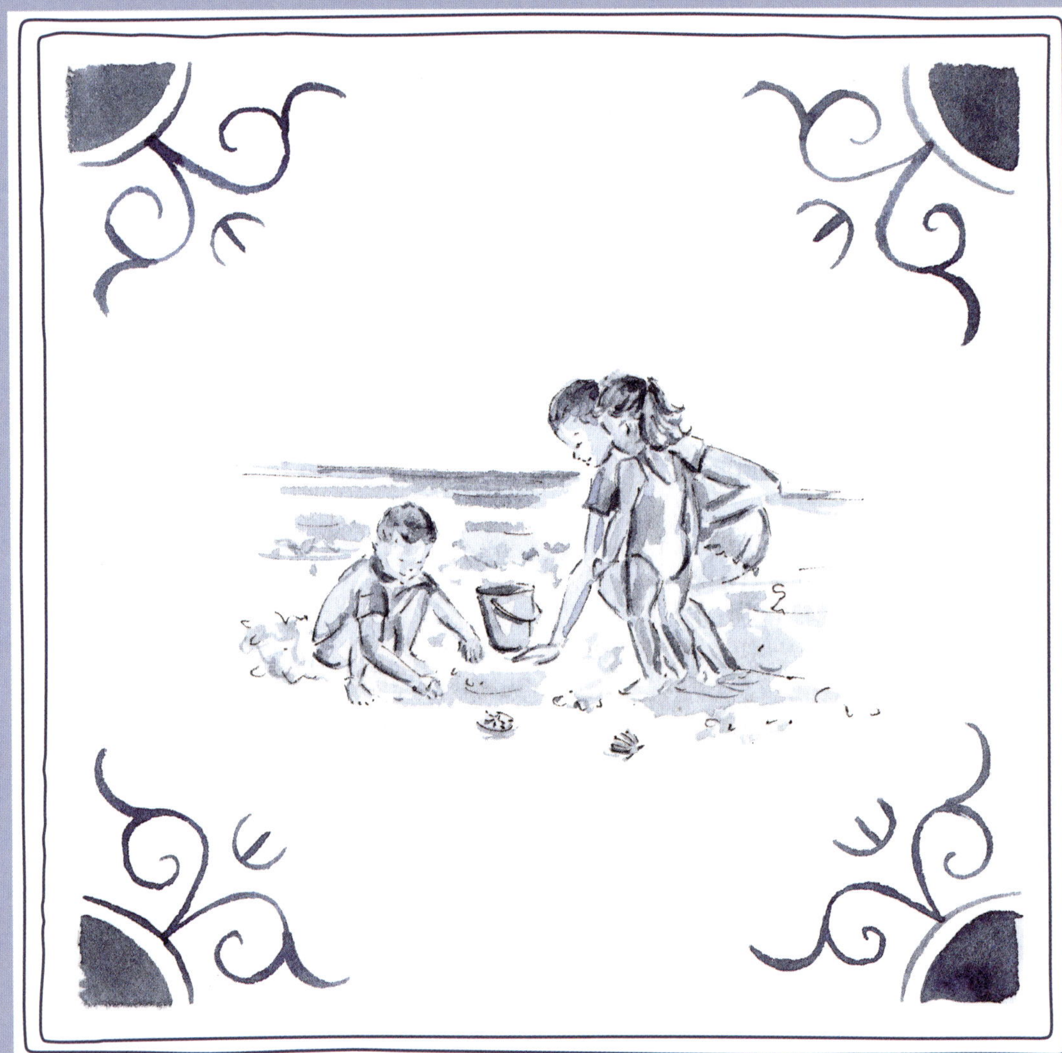

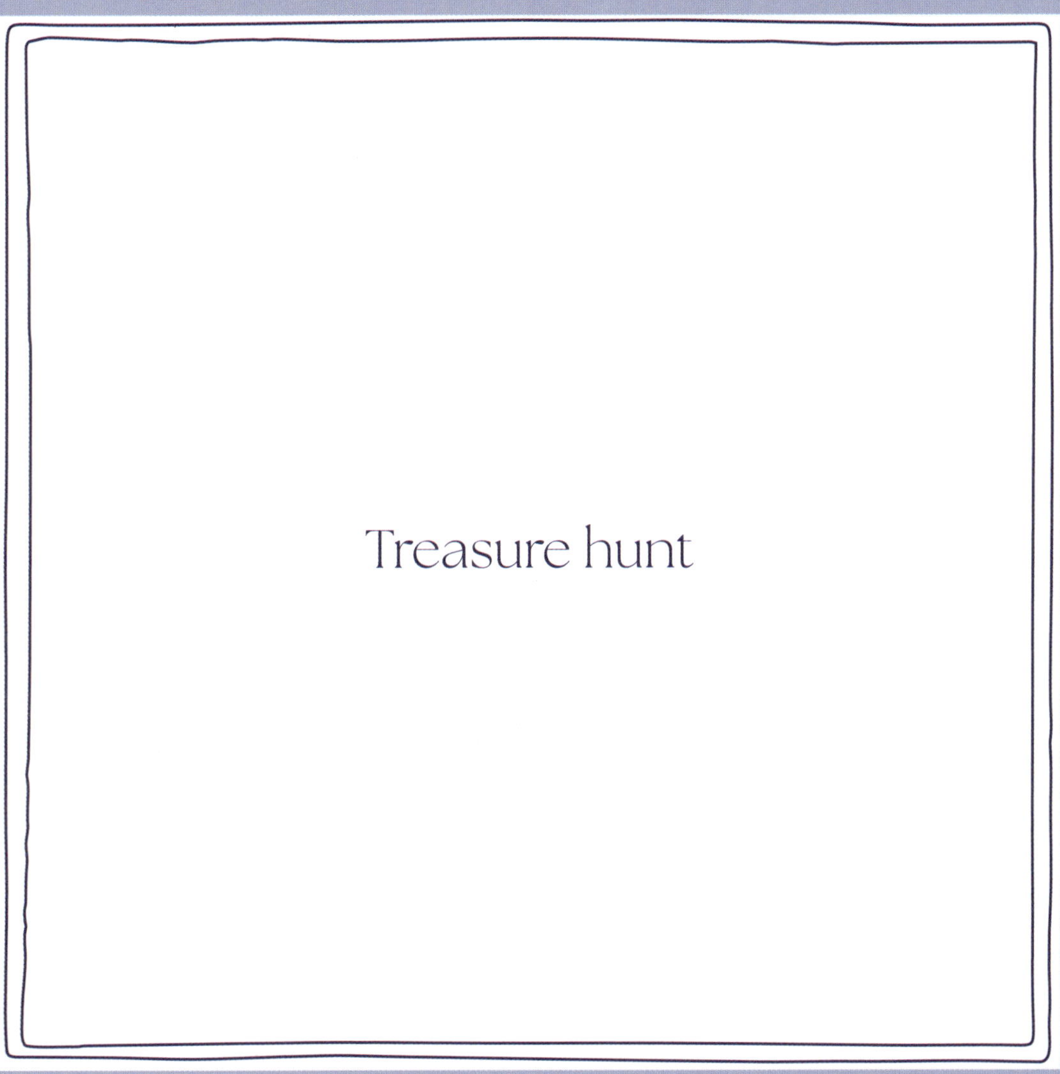

Treasure hunt

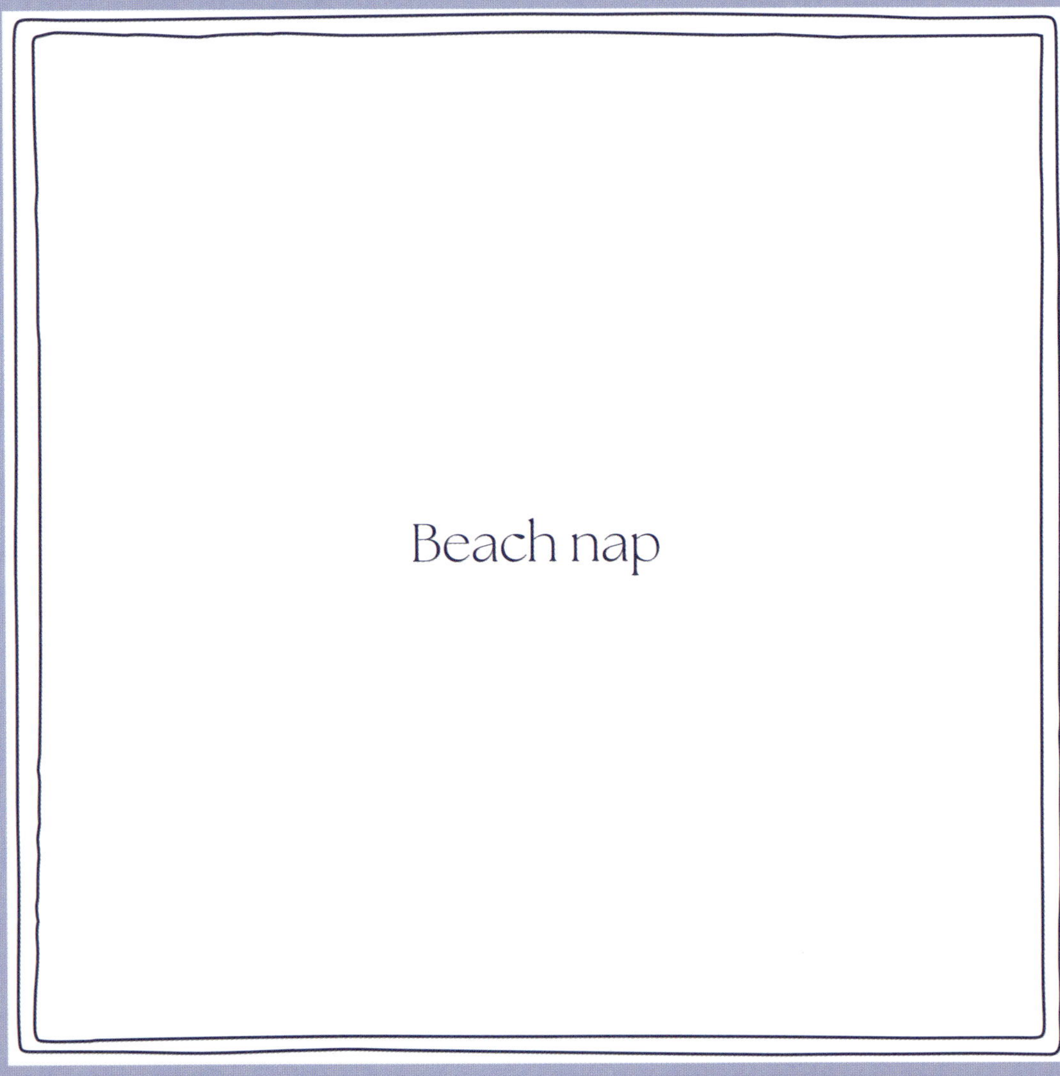
Beach nap

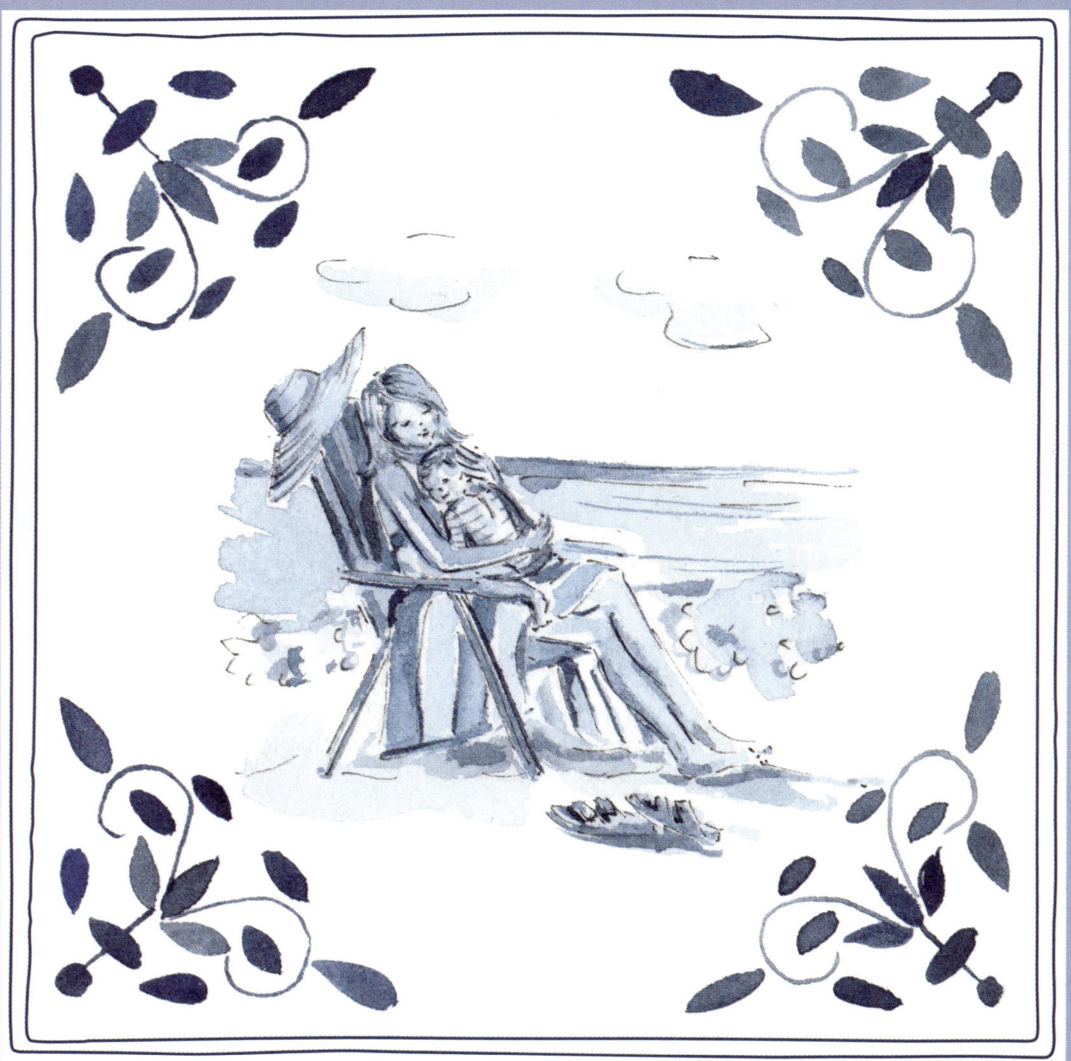

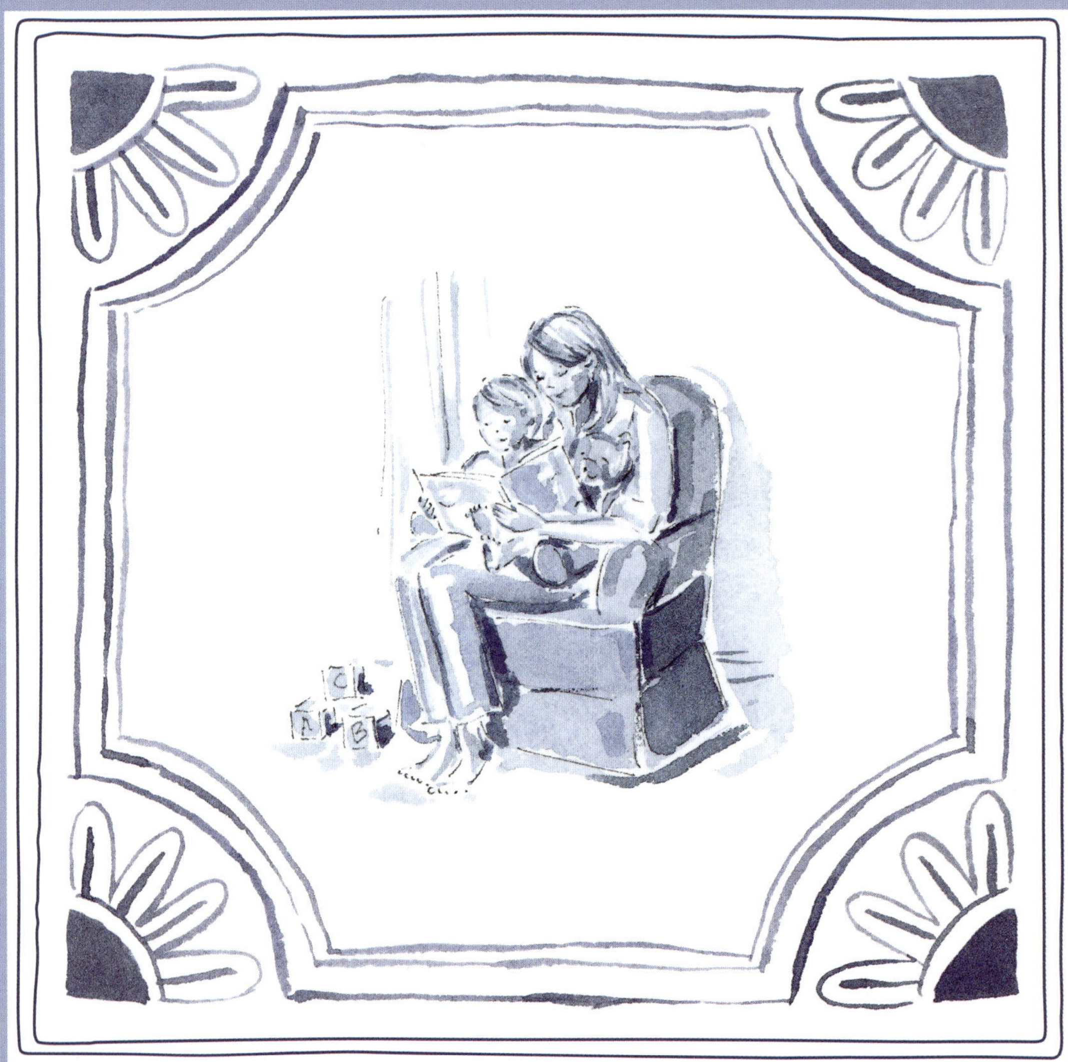

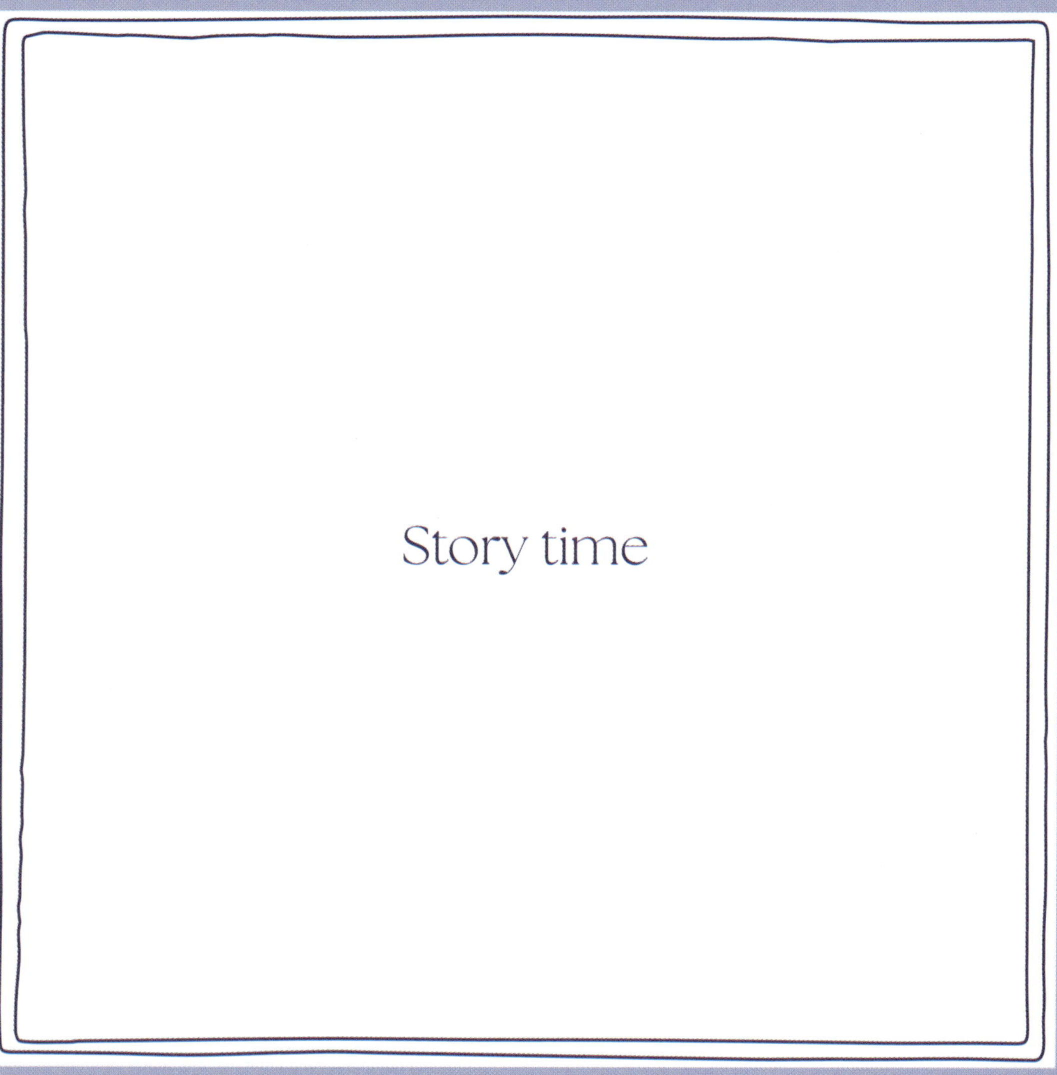

Story time

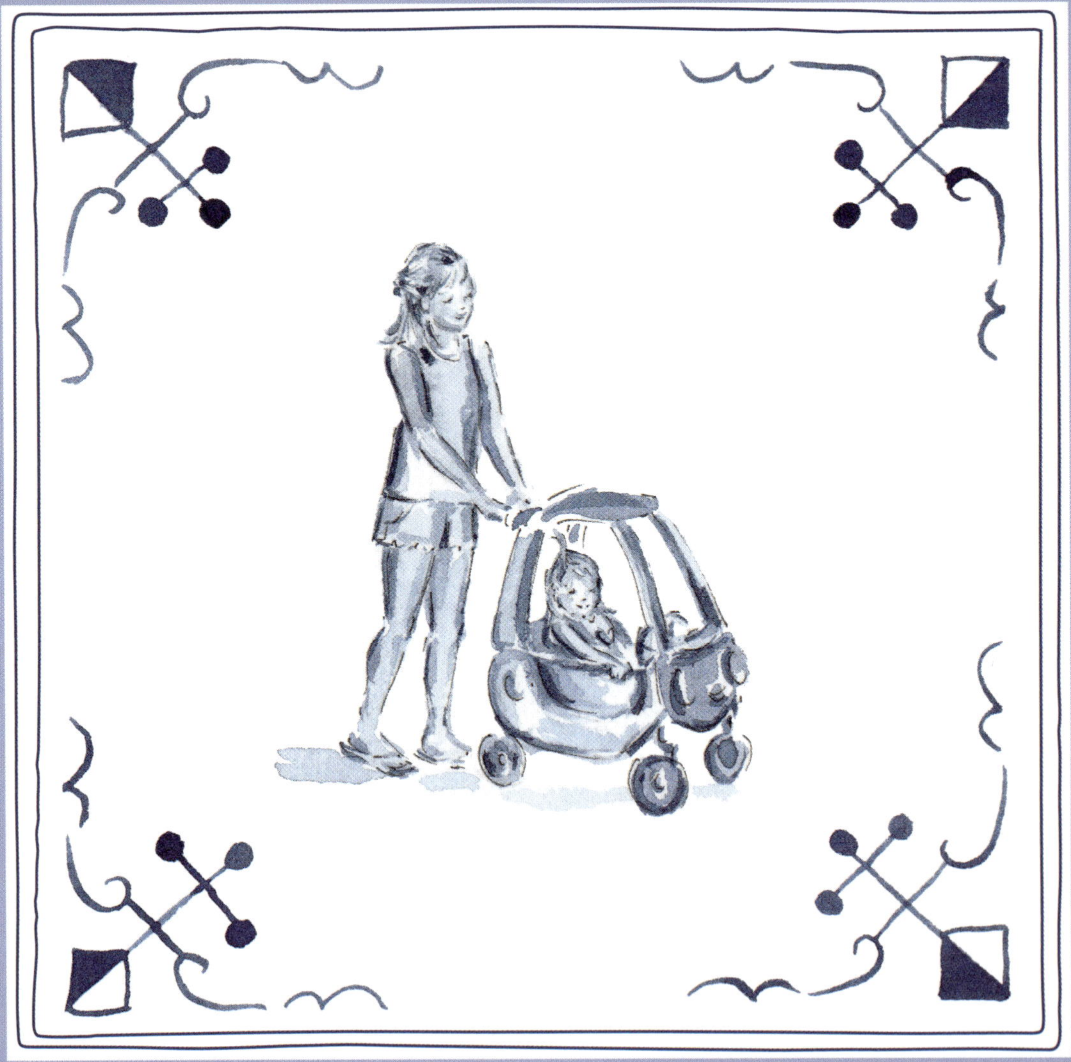

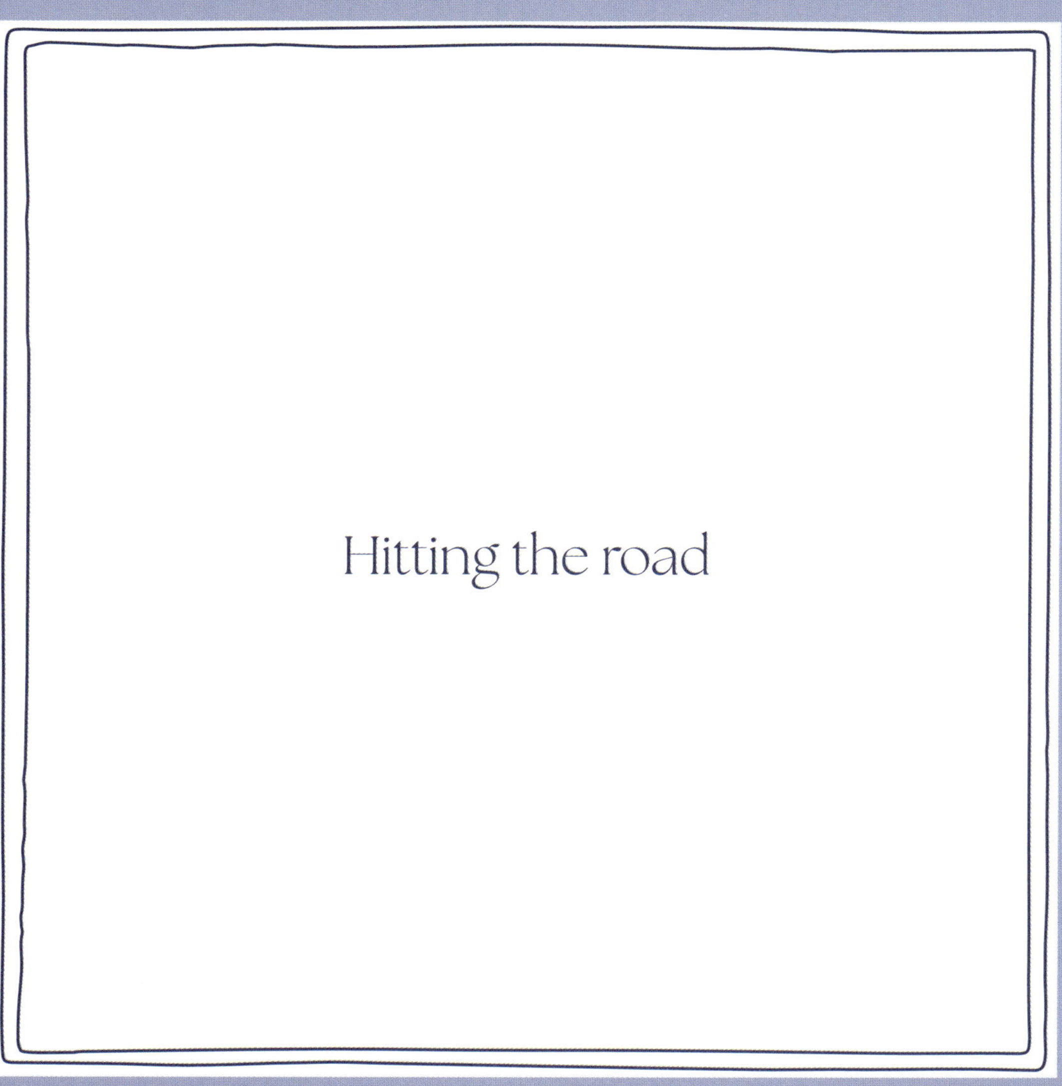

Hitting the road

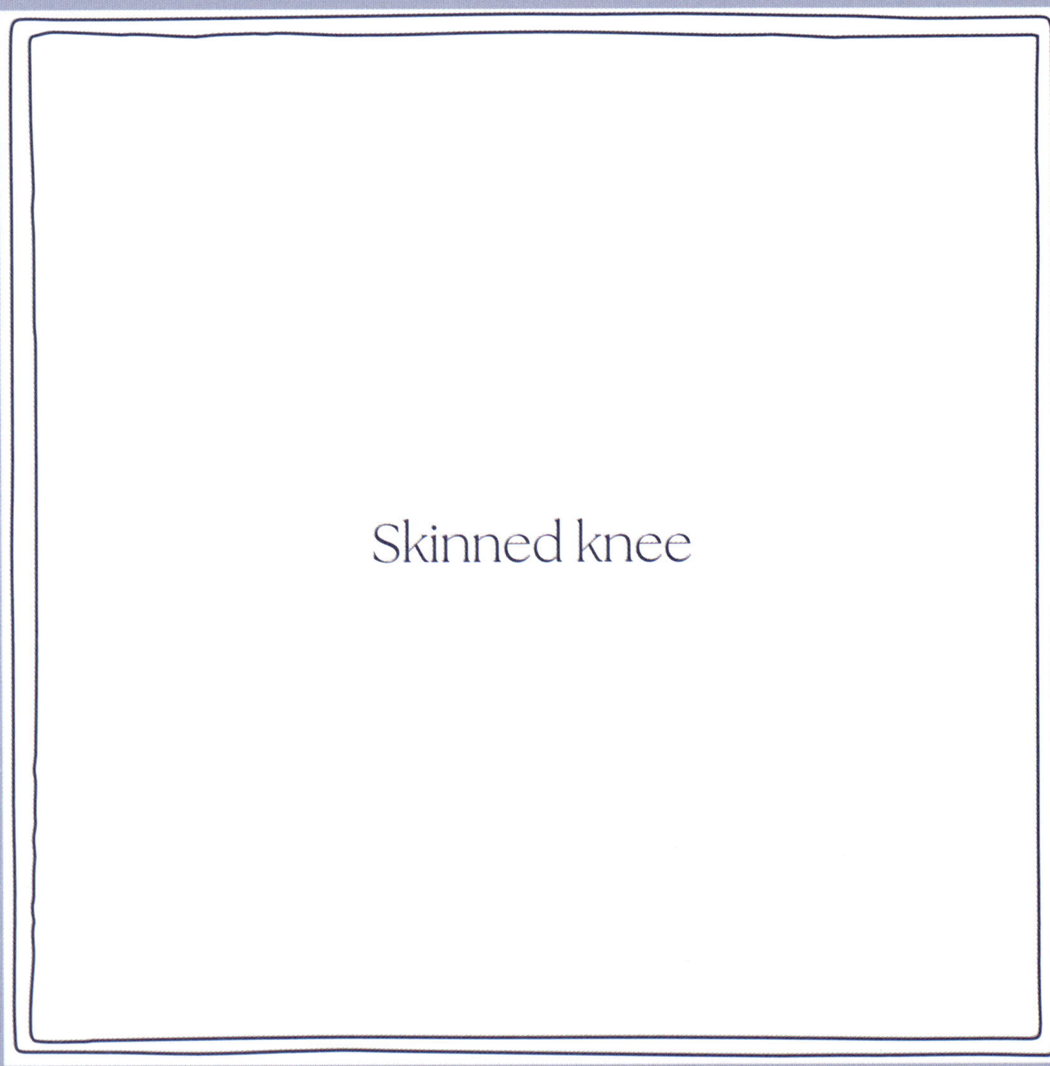
Skinned knee

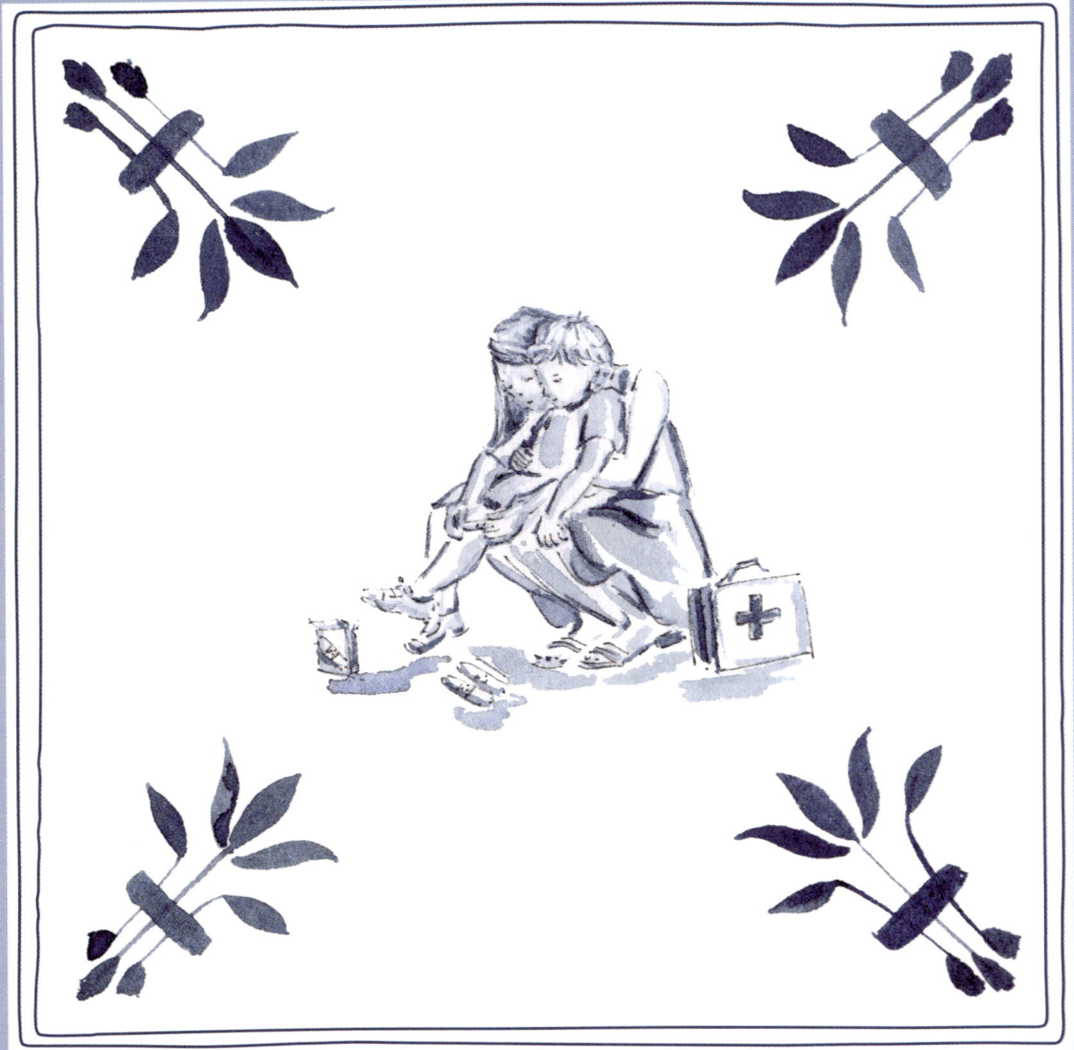

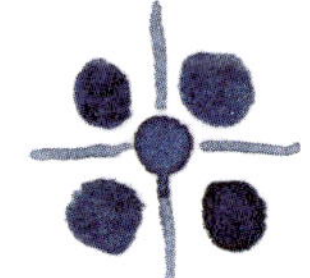
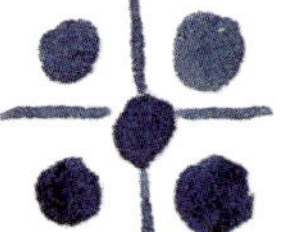
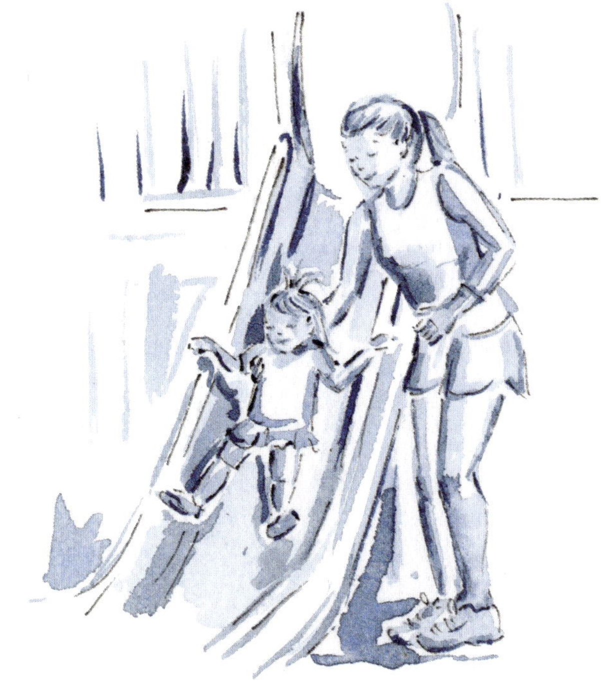
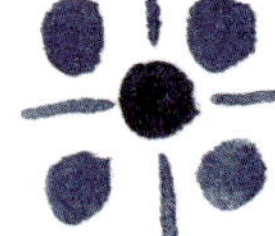
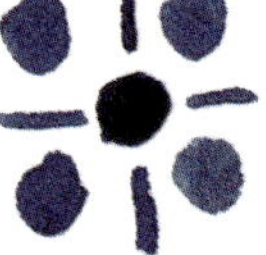

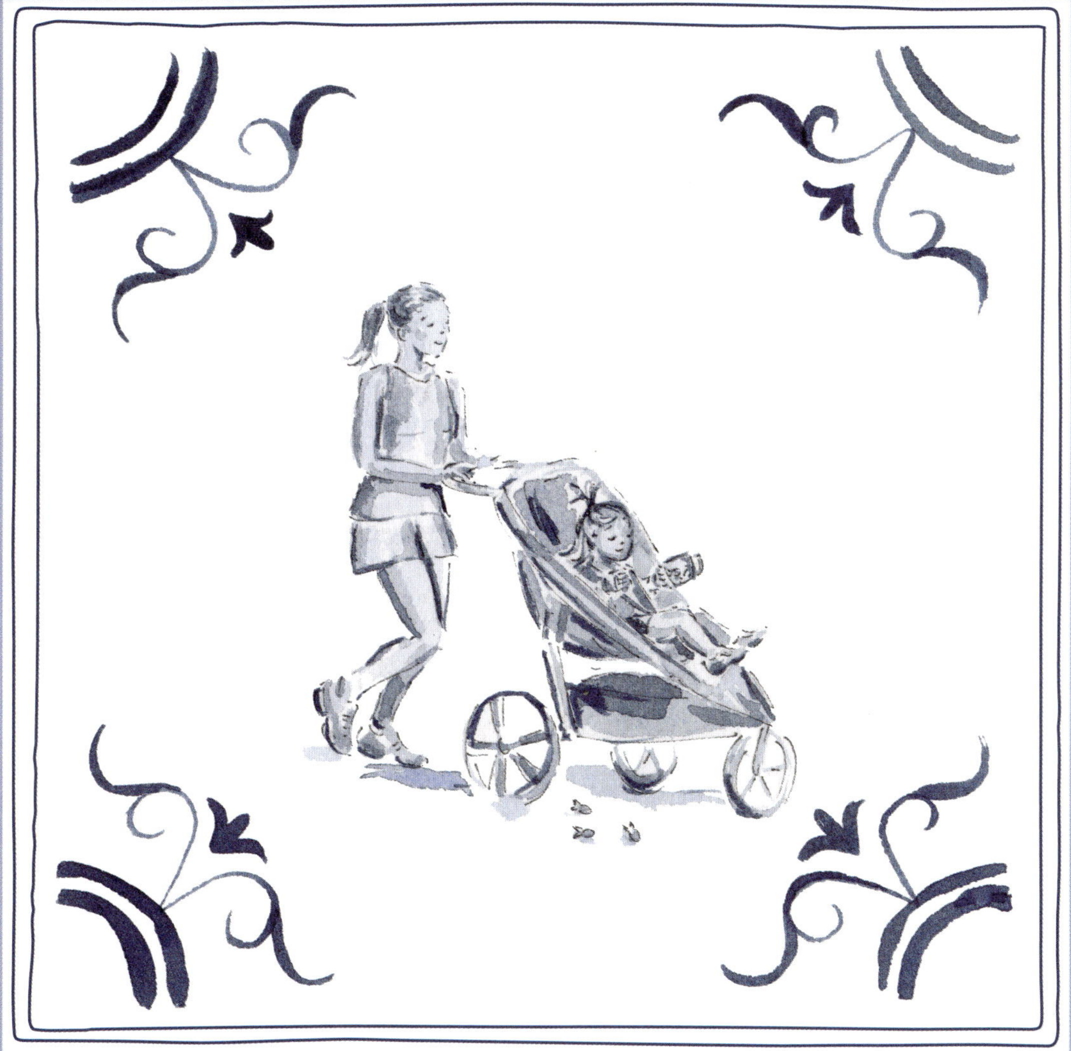

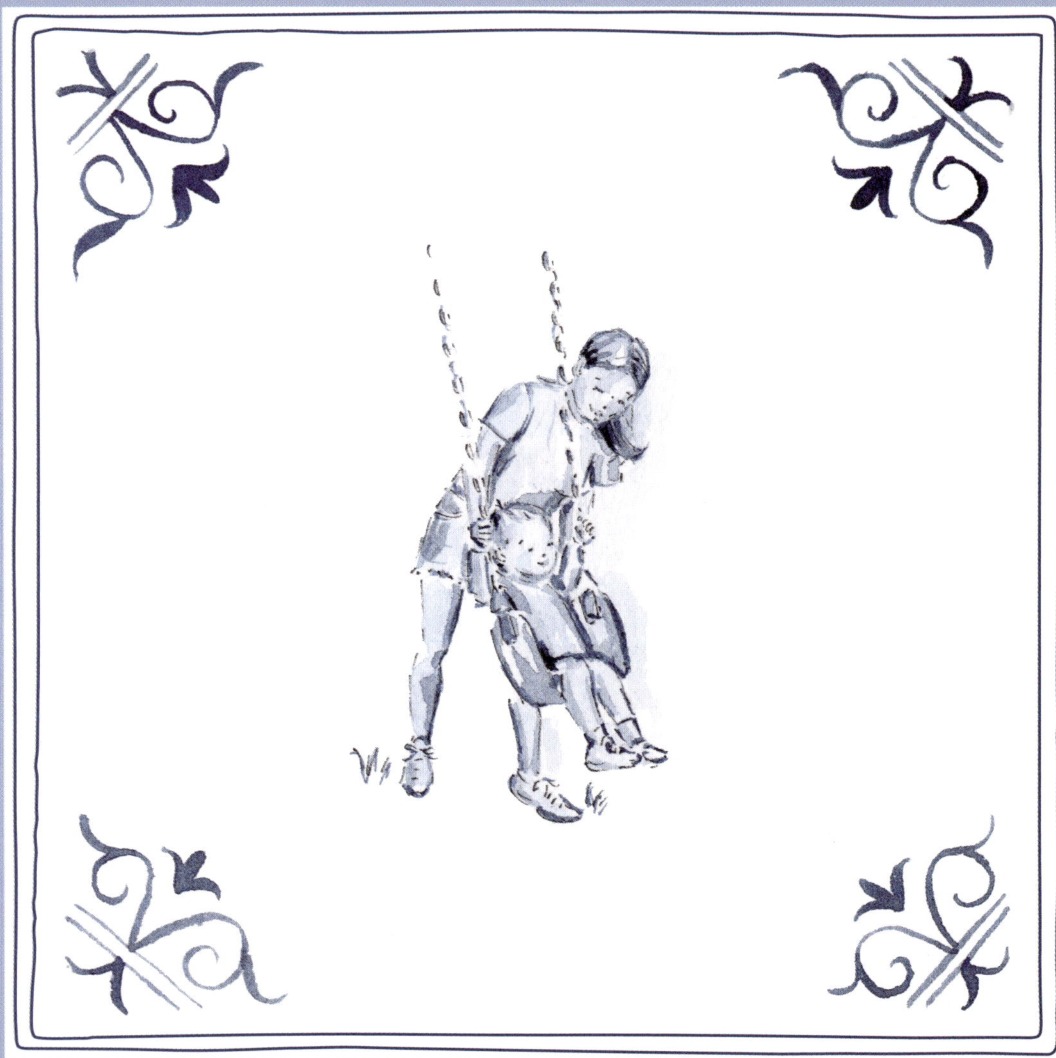

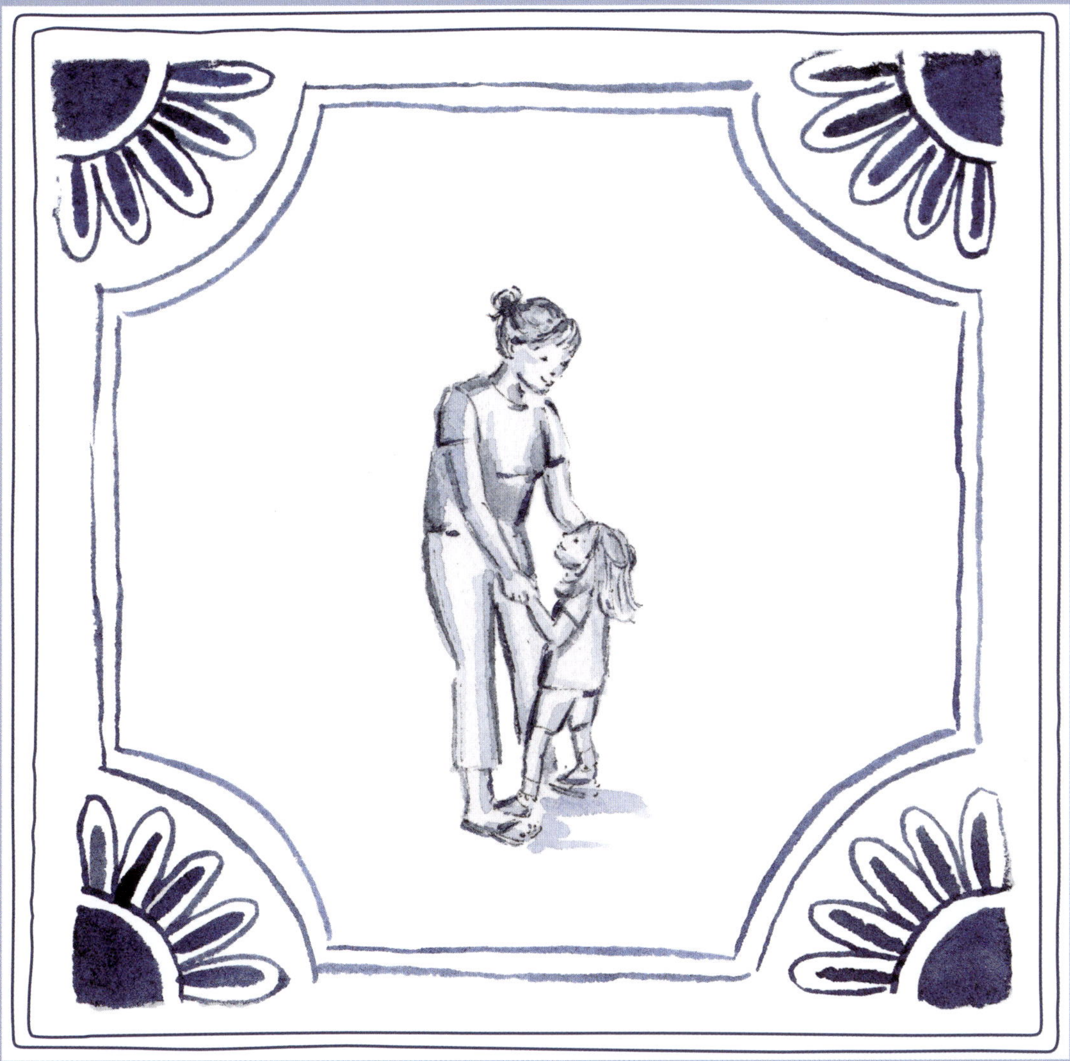

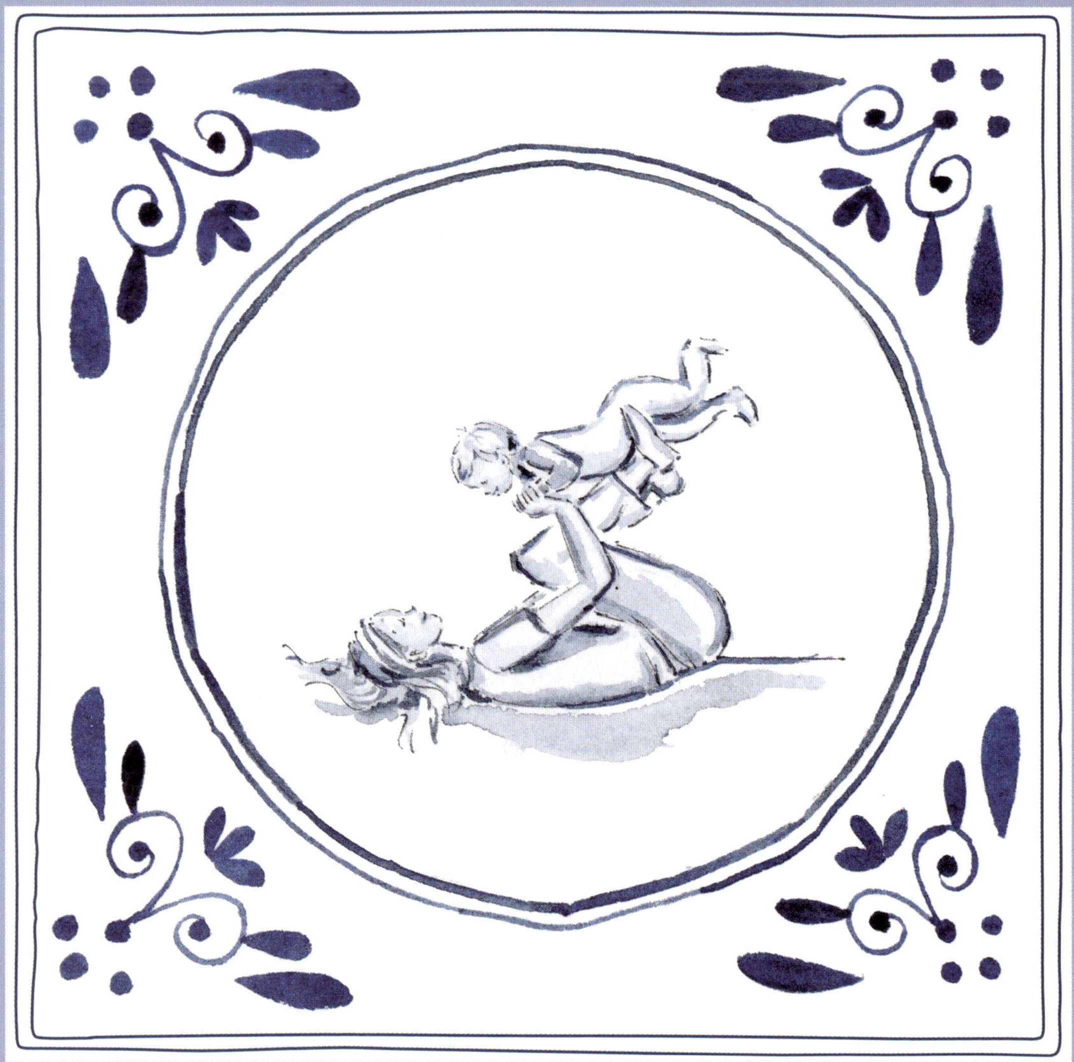

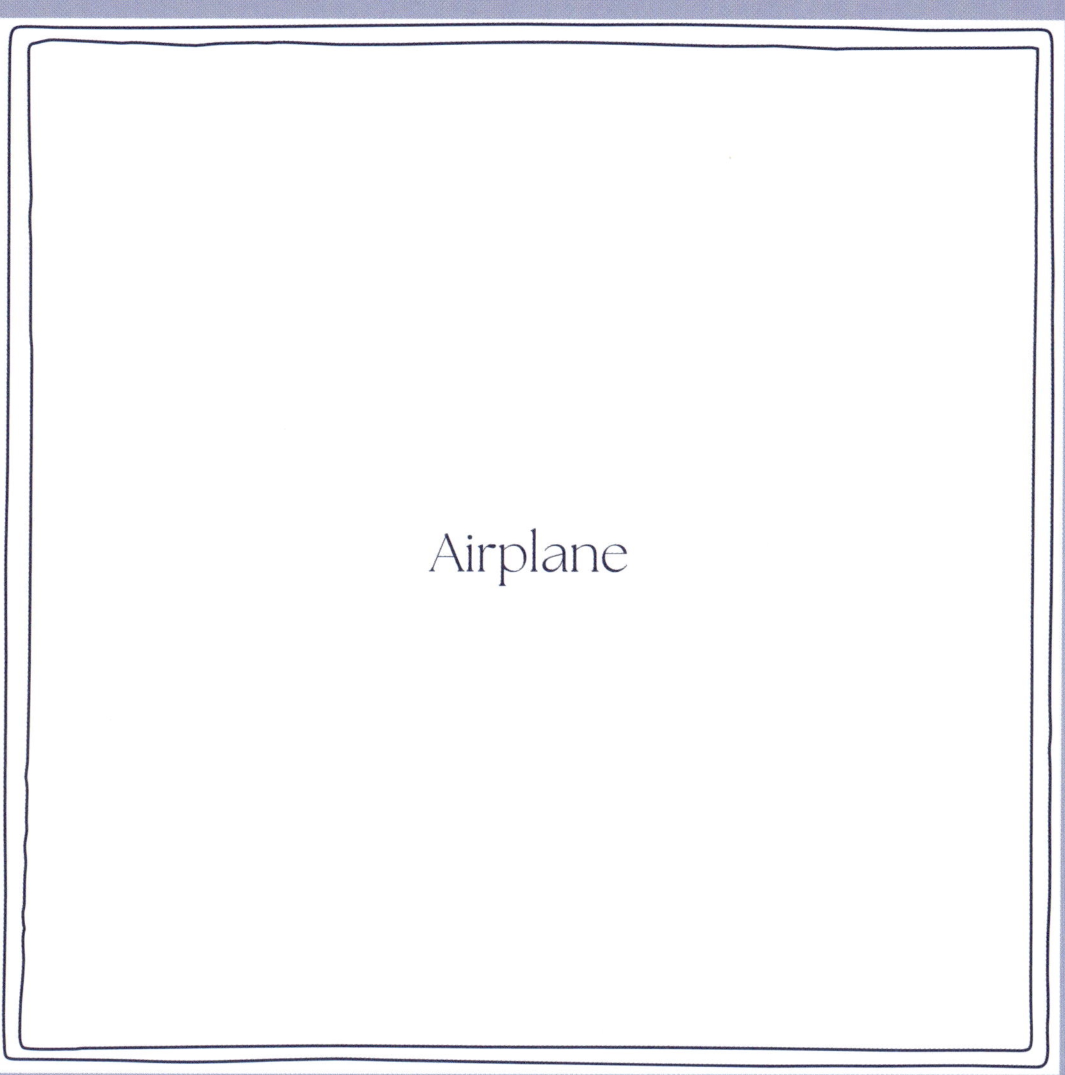
Airplane

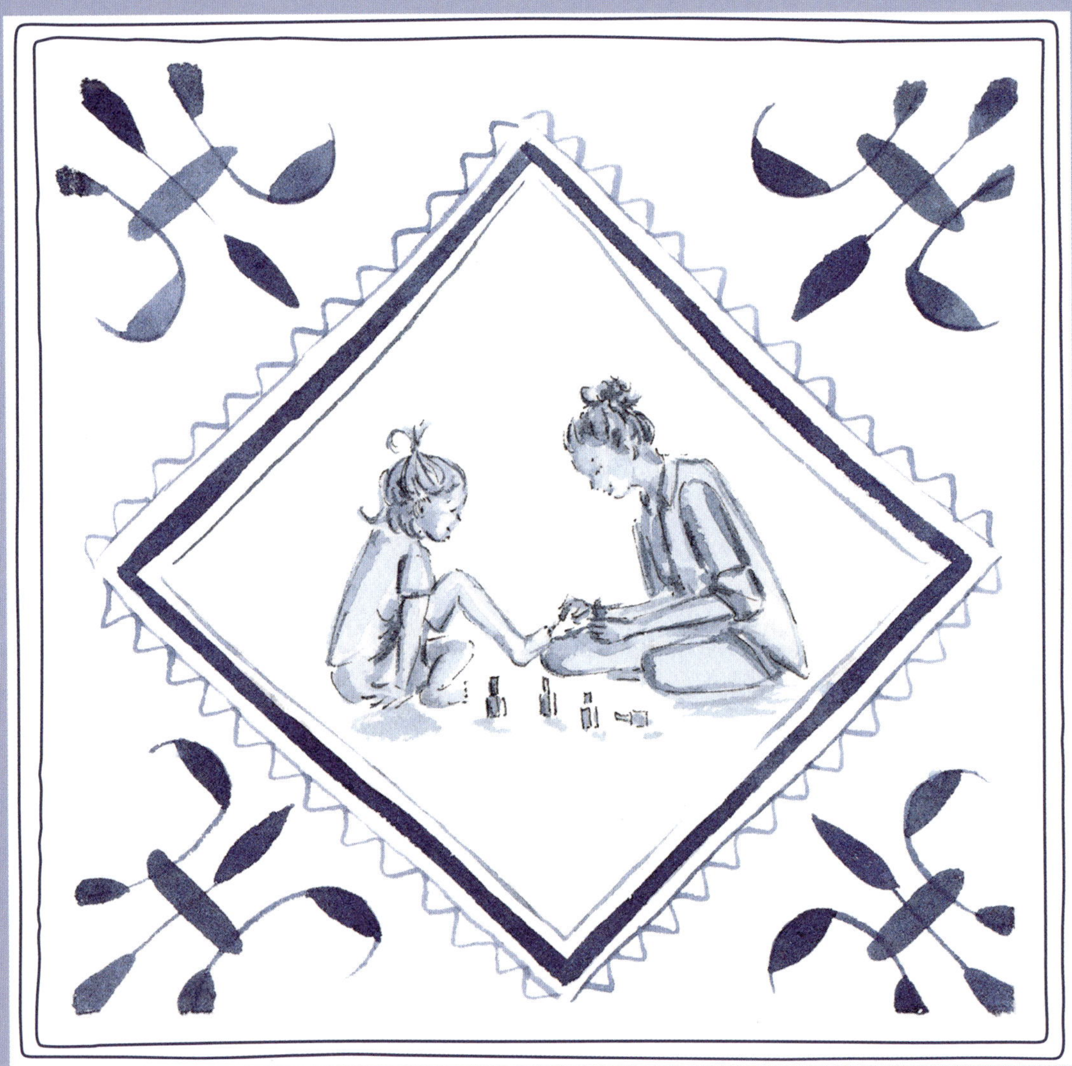

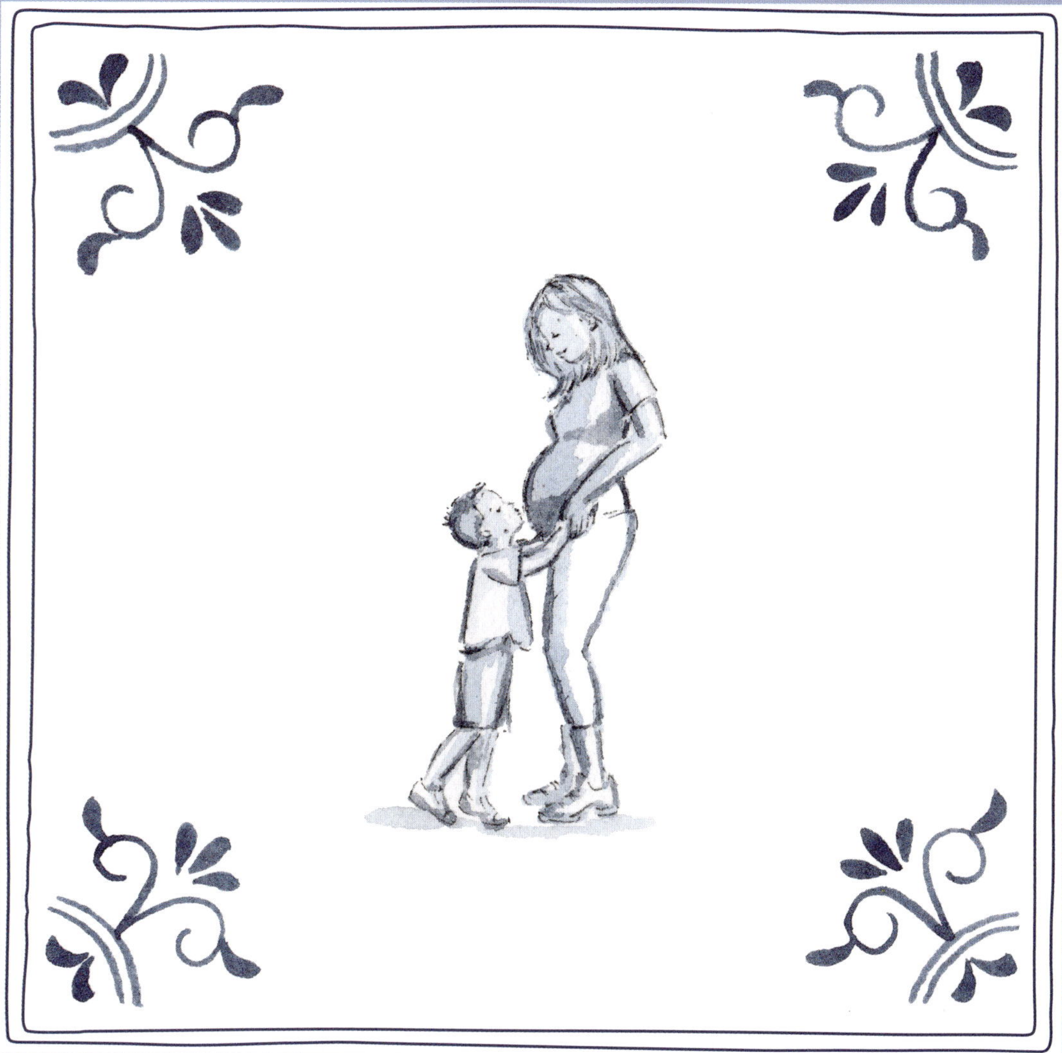

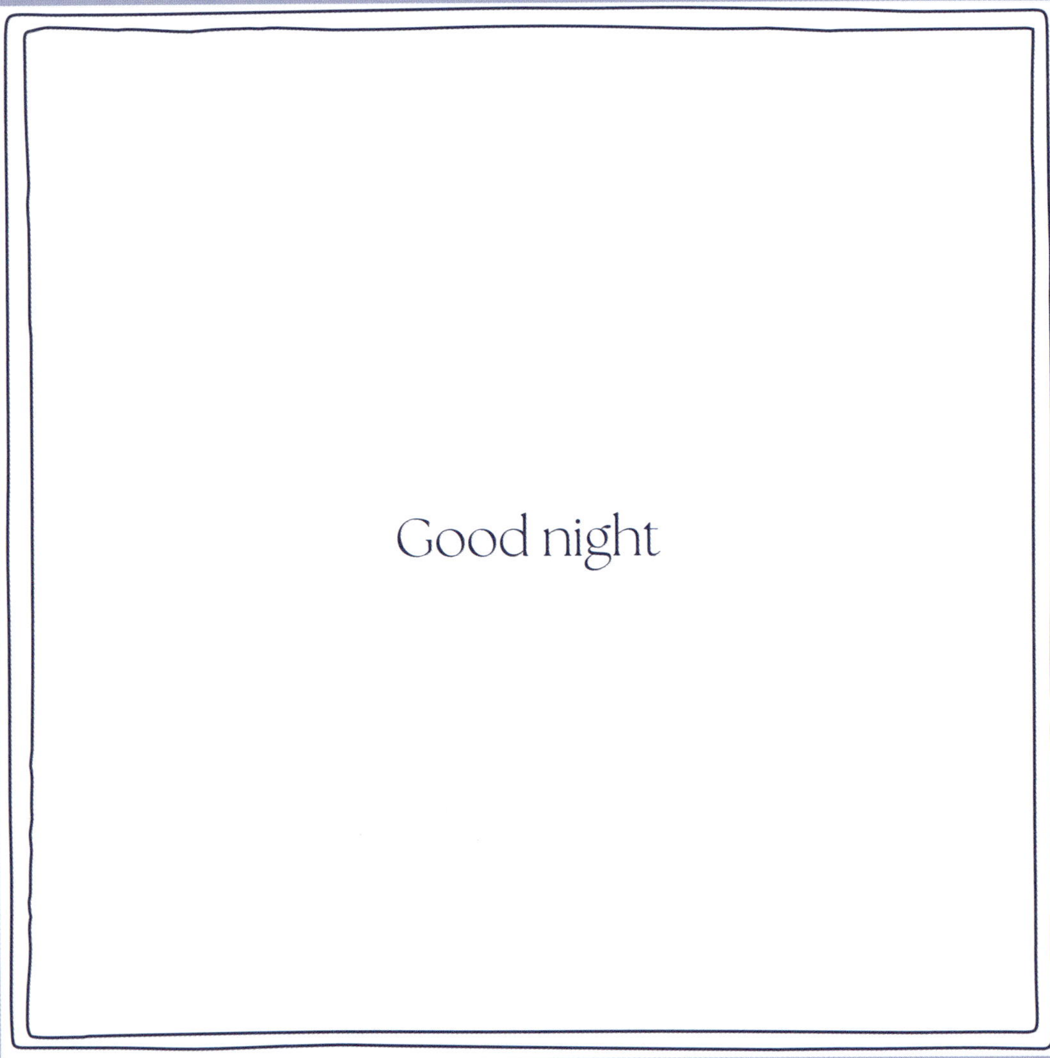

Good night

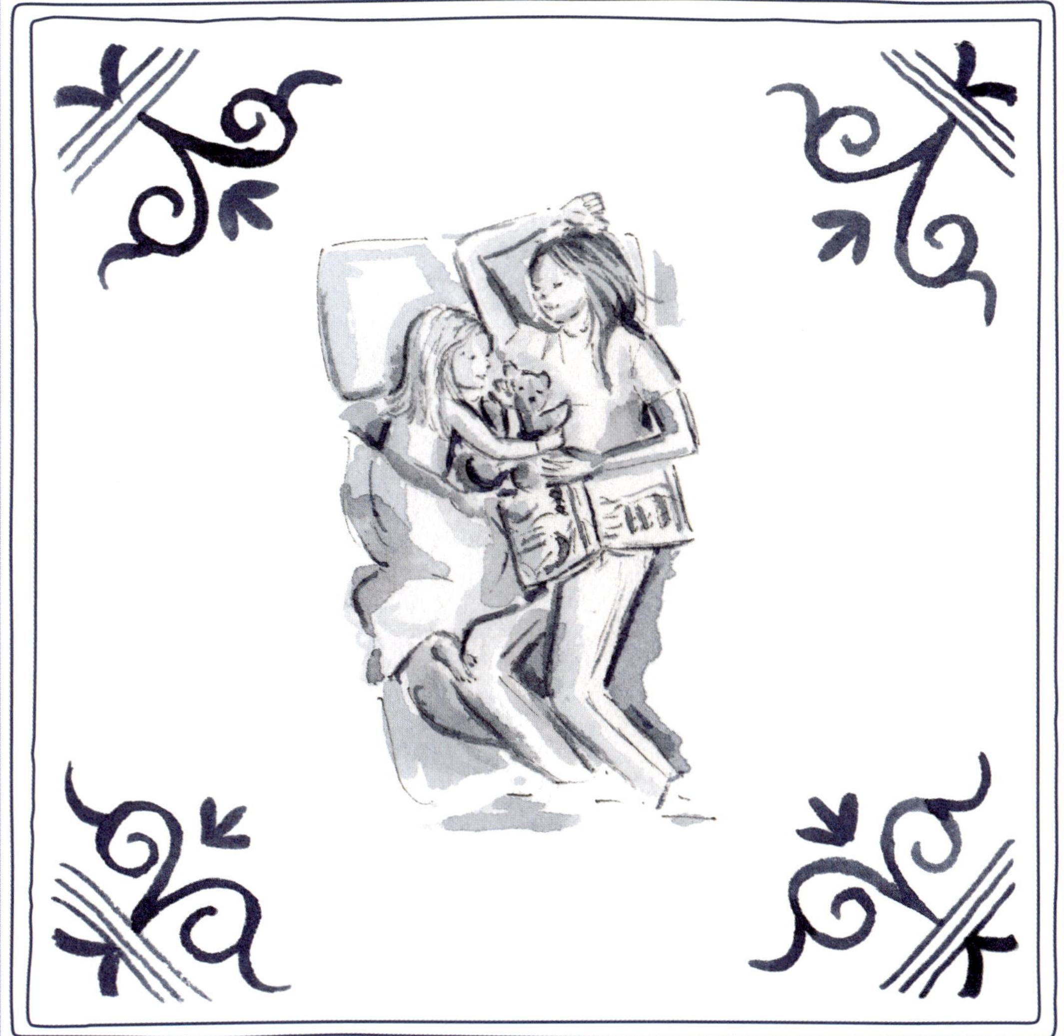

Acknowledgments

It is often said that it takes a village to raise a child, and the same is true for writing and illustrating a book.

To my agent, Leigh—thank you for believing that I could illustrate (and write!) a book before I let myself speak my dream to do so out loud! None of this would be possible without you.

To my editor, Soyolmaa—thank you for believing in this project from the beginning and for your gentle and thoughtful approach to editing and steering me in the right direction throughout this whole process. I could not have dreamed of a more perfect and caring editor.

To my husband, Dylan—my version of "modern motherhood" would not be possible without you. You are the best dad, and watching you take care of Bryn makes me a better mom.

To my parents—Mom and Dad, you have always made me believe that I could do anything I set my mind to. That is the greatest gift, and I can only hope that I'm half as good a parent to Bryn as you both have been to me.

To all four of Bryn's grandparents (Mom, Dad, Nancy, and John)—thank you for helping us raise and nurture our kind and curious little girl.

To "Nat," Ms. Marisol, Ms. Isabel, Ms. Lissette, and all the teachers and caretakers in Bryn's future—thank you for teaching and caring for Bryn and for making her feel so loved.

Finally, thank you to everyone (friends, family, old coworkers, sorority sisters, clients, customers . . .) who has supported this dream of mine in any way, shape, or form—I am endlessly grateful and wouldn't be writing this without your encouragement from day one. As I always like to say, the best is yet to come.

About the Author

Riley Sheehey is a watercolor and multimedia artist and textile designer. Before becoming an artist full-time in 2017, she taught elementary school art and developed a love for whimsical styles and playful details. Her artwork, which has been featured in *Southern Living*, *Veranda*, *Victoria*, and *The Cottage Journal*, reflects this childlike view of the world with fun color palettes and an attention to detail that evokes a viewer's curiosity. While her work and new ventures are constantly evolving, she continues to prioritize incorporating personal elements in her art that connect the viewer with her practice. She lives in Falls Church, Virginia, with her husband, daughter, and dog.

Editor: Soyolmaa Lkhagvadorj
Designers: Diane Shaw and Sophie Xu
Design Manager: Danielle Youngsmith
Managing Editor: Lisa Silverman
Production Manager: Katie Gaffney

Library of Congress Control Number: 2024941006

ISBN: 978-1-4197-7735-6
eISBN: 979-8-88707-435-1

Printed and bound in China
10 9 8 7 6 5 4 3 2

Abrams Image books are available at special discounts when purchased in quantity for premiums and promotions as well as fundraising or educational use. Special editions can also be created to specification. For details, contact specialsales@abramsbooks.com or the address below.

Abrams Image® is a registered trademark of Harry N. Abrams, Inc.

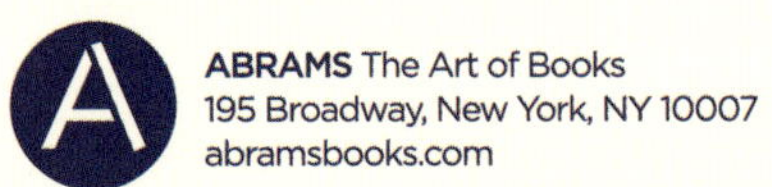